CLASS AND THE COLOR LINE

POLITICS, HISTORY, AND CULTURE

A series from the International Institute at the University of Michigan



Sponsored by the International Institute at the University of Michigan and published by Duke University Press, this series is centered around cultural and historical studies of power, politics, and the state—a field that cuts across the disciplines of history, sociology, anthropology, political science, and cultural studies. The focus on the relationship between state and culture refers both to a methodological approach—the study of politics and the state using culturalist methods—and a substantive one that treats signifying practices as an essential dimension of politics. The dialectic of politics, history, and culture figures prominently in all the books selected for the series.

# CLASS AND THE COLOR LINE

INTERRACIAL CLASS COALITION IN THE KNIGHTS OF LABOR AND THE POPULIST MOVEMENT

JOSEPH GERTEIS

Duke University Press Durham and London 2007

Printed in the United States of America on acid-free paper ∞
Designed by Heather Hensley
Typeset in Adobe Caslon Pro by Keystone Typesetting, Inc.
Library of Congress Cataloging-in-Publication Data appear on the last printed page of this book.

## CONTENTS

# ACKNOWLEDGMENTS

In this book, I examine the dynamics of organizing across racial lines in two social movements in the US South during the 1880s and 1890s. The Knights of Labor and the Populists were the largest and most influential movements of their day, and they challenged traditional divisions of race. My goal is to provide a better understanding of the sources and the limits of this moment of radical possibility. In particular, I examine the development of interests as a process within the movements' cultural narratives linking race and class, and as an active process of negotiation at the local level.

I advance three basic arguments in the following pages. First, the movements were both inclusive and exclusive at the same time. The Knights and the Populists included some and excluded others, and they changed over time. Despite a continuing historiographical debate over whether they were sincere or cynical in their organizing efforts, I maintain that the better question is, where did the movements draw the boundaries between an "us" to be organized and a "them" to be excluded, and why?

Second, I argue that the movements' republican emphasis on civic virtue offered a basis for cross-race organizing, but also provided constraints. Previous literature, especially on "whiteness," has documented how the republican idiom was primarily used as a weapon of exclusion by white labor movements at an earlier period. I find that it both opened doors for some (black workers, particularly in areas where black civic life and labor organizing was well established) and closed it for others (especially new immigrants).

Third, interests varied across local contexts, and they were continually renegotiated over time. The pattern of civic life in both the black and white communities was vital to the strength of the interracial project, as were the economic and political conditions that were beyond the control of movement members or potential converts. But it is not enough to pronounce the movements' interracial efforts as simply "successful" or "failed" in any given local area; the way both white and black fellow travelers saw the costs and benefits of coalition changed with experience.

In writing this book, my goal has been to avoid the cavalier attitude with which both sociologists and historians have sometimes marked the boundary between their respective fields. The traditional defense of the disciplinary boundary has never made much sense to me, in large part because the scholars I most admire have always had a foot in both worlds. I am a sociologist, and my training in this discipline shows through in my analytical focus and in my pursuit of systematic data. Some historians have found this focus too rigid and have objected to the fact that with a few exceptions I have generally suppressed any lengthy discussion of the complex historiographical debates surrounding the Knights of Labor and the Populists. At the same time, some sociologists have found even a little historiography to be too much, and others have wondered why we should care at all about "failed" nineteenth-century movements. There is probably no such thing as a perfect balance, and it is not possible to please everyone, yet in this book I hope that scholars from many fields will find something of value. It is my aim to stand with the large and growing group of scholars who rely on varied analytical methods, an appreciation for theory, and careful data collection. Many people and institutions have helped me to do this and to remind me why it matters.

In the process of writing this book I have racked up a lot of institutional debts. A dissertation improvement grant from the National Science Foundation funded my initial data collection. Support from the University of Minnesota in the form of a summer stipend allowed me to focus on beginning the revision of my dissertation into a book manuscript. My work would not have been possible without the libraries that I relied upon, most centrally the

Walter Royal Davis Library at the University of North Carolina, Perkins Library at Duke University, the Library of Congress, and the Walter Library at the University of Minnesota. My thanks are due in particular to the editors at Duke University Press, especially J. Reynolds Smith, and to George Steinmetz and Julia Adams, editors of the series Politics, History, and Culture. They all spent more time than they wanted with the manuscript. I owe a very large debt to the Social Science History Association for providing an interdisciplinary forum for this work, as well as for awarding to the manuscript the President's Book Award in 2005. Portions of chapters 1, 2, and 7 have appeared in *Social Science History* and in the *American Journal of Sociology,* and the publishers of those journals have kindly allowed me to draw from that work.

My personal debts are deeper and more varied than my institutional ones. Although the members of my dissertation committee are divided by geography, discipline, and institution, they helped me think through the initial research upon which this book is based. François Nielsen and Charles Kurzman provided me with an intellectual home in the Department of Sociology at the University of North Carolina during my otherwise isolated final year of graduate work. Larry J. Griffin and Leon Fink set very high standards for good interdisciplinary work in the area of historical social science and also provided very good examples of how it could be done. Although Mike Savage did not directly serve on the committee, he played a large role in my thinking about class and historical sociology generally. My deepest thanks are due to Peter Bearman and Craig Calhoun, who provided to me intellectual guidance before and after my dissertation. Peter deserves special recognition for his long and difficult labor as my advisor and committee chair, even when his commitments had to be carried out at long-distance phone rates. Likewise, Craig has continued to provide insightful advice on both practical and theoretical matters.

There are other personal debts that I owe as well. During my time in North Carolina, Steve Pfaff, Rich Frankel, Jeff Wenger, Art Alderson, Indermohan Virk, Jim Moody, and Jim Kirby all provided friendship, encouragement, advice, and debates about the things that really matter in life. I have been fortunate to land in a dynamic and exciting scholarly community at the University of Minnesota, and many of my Minnesota colleagues have commented upon various parts of this work as it developed. Ron Aminzade, Doug Hartmann, Robin Stryker, and Penny Edgell in particular helped me to think potential, despite the supposed "exceptionalism" of the American case. To others, their equally sudden collapse has provided proof of the claim that American class movements are always hampered by individualism, ideology, and internally divided interests. Of course, one of the most obvious and salient divides has been that of race, and here a similar question drives the debate: Should we see the movements as offering a viable platform for interracial class coalition, or should we instead see the failure of the movements as evidence of the folly of such grand dreams?

The disagreements in fact tap into much broader debates about class, race, and their interconnection. The fact that race and class have been closely bound together in American history is not in question. Class interests have structured the way racial boundaries have been defined and understood, while racial divisions have generally thwarted attempts to build viable class coalitions. From one point of view, racial animosity between working people can be understood as the result of resource competition. Because competition over scarce political or economic resources so often overlapped divisions between racial groups, racial animosity could obscure or trump class interests. An opposing argument points out, just as persuasively, that the durable economic and social divides between groups was the result of racism in the first place.[1] Whether racism maintains class divisions or class divisions maintain racism, the divide between black and white working people has seemed insurmountable. But as C. Vann Woodward (2000 [1955]) pointed out so powerfully, this era presented a moment of possibility when the Jim Crow–era racial order was not yet set in stone and alternatives were possible.

Certainly, these movements began to make some surprising claims about the importance of breaching the "color line" as the first wave of southern organizing got underway. In January 1880, an official based in the Mobile area wrote to the national leader of the Knights of Labor to report on his progress in recruiting. "We are making a strong effort to organize the colored element in this city and county," T. L. Eastburn explained. The next month, he wrote again to say that a new assembly of "coloured Creoles" had been established, and another black assembly was soon to follow.[2] Later the same year, a member named William Wright wrote that a black assembly wanted to reorganize in Warrior, Alabama, after its members had moved from another nearby mining town. Wright was the "Master Workman" of an all-white assembly, and he admitted that some of his own white members "object to working in the same A[ssembly] with negros. This is the reason we dont take them." All the same, he was keen to get permission for the black assembly. "I am ancious to have them in the order, for we can do better with them than without them," he said. "I told them I would meet with them, & help them all I could. If I am rong correct me & oblige."[3]

Wright and Eastburn held different positions in the movement, and the differences in the spelling and the tone of these letters make it clear that they probably came from very different backgrounds. But both saw the importance of bringing black workers into the movement. Both were also motivated by practical rather than moral concerns—Eastburn wanted to expand the regional membership and political clout of the Knights, while Wright wanted to avoid having black and white workers pitted against each other in the frequent labor disputes of the mining districts. Yet both came to the conclusion that it was in their own interest to breach the wall of tradition and mistrust that separated white and black working people. Some black members clearly felt the same way about the movement. "Our mottoe is go forward it is the Noblest order in existence for the Laboring man most especially the Colored in which I am a member of," wrote the secretary of a black Knights of Labor assembly in rural Arkansas. "I can see many changes in the owners of Land already and I am satisfied there is others who dig in the soil can see the same."[4]

Still, the Knights and the Populists engaged with race in ways that were complex, varied, and at times contradictory. The Knights opened their doors to black members and declared that racial divisions must be overcome if working people were to advance in the new era of Gilded Age capitalism. Significant numbers of black members were inducted across the South, but they were typically organized in segregated assemblies. The movement shunned new immigrants altogether and defended this practice in language that was often explicitly racist. The racial legacy of Populism is similarly murky. In its early form as the Farmer's Alliance, the movement was truly segregated, with two organizations formed to accommodate white and black members separately. But the separate organizations worked in a quiet coalition, collaborating on collective goals. During the later phase of the movement, the white leaders of the People's Party campaigned openly for black votes in the name of a broad coalition of "the people," yet they also rejected any idea of more fundamental equality.

When applied to these movements, the debate often centers on whether the Knights are best understood as racially inclusive or exclusive, and whether the Populists were cynical opportunists or idealistic egalitarians. Even if the movements were truly sincere in their attempts to breach the color line in the name of building a grand coalition of working people, perhaps their eventual collapse meant that they were merely exceptions to the general rule in America that racial divisions will trump any attempts at class unity. In fact, these competing interpretations—open or closed, callow or sincere—miss many of the important puzzles. For example, on racial matters it is relatively easy to portray the Knights of Labor leader Terence Powderly or the Populist hothead Tom Watson either as dewy-eyed idealists or as embittered cynics, depending on one's inclinations. Such caricatures, however, do not really capture the paradoxes of these leaders or their movements. Powderly was always willing to settle for separate and often unequal arrangements in terms of organizing, but he did so in the interest of forging a broader unity. Watson was always an outspoken racist on questions of "social equality," but he worked sincerely for "political equality."

The deeper point here is that any movement has to define its identity and interests through the deployment of social and symbolic boundaries. In doing so, it necessarily includes some and excludes others. The relevant question to pose about the movements is not whether boundaries were drawn but where they were drawn and why. At the end of the nineteenth century, racial identities were deep-seated; despite the frequent statements that the movements made to the contrary, they could not truly be color blind. Yet it was not inevitable that racial divisions would overwhelm collective class interest.

In this book I examine this moment of possibility—its sources as well as its limits. One of my central premises here is that race and class are not just objective structures but also cultural constructs. Because of this, scholars make a mistake when they assume what is in the interests of a given group. Instead, the emphasis should be on the process by which people try to make sense of their own interests. Rather than try to engage in abstract argument about the ultimate interests or intents of the movements with regard to race, my goal is to reconstruct the way that the movements made sense of their own interests and identities at two levels—in relation to established cultural frames of reference and in concrete local settings. Specifically, I investigate the way that race and class were connected within movement-level narratives, where the movement's racial boundaries took shape in relation to broad class languages; and in the course of practical action, where ongoing strategic considerations of interest were squared against local economic, political, and social conditions and local histories of interracial cooperation.

## RACE, CLASS, AND INTERRACIAL ORGANIZING

In attempting to build a broad class coalition, the Knights of Labor and the Populists necessarily confronted issues of race. What made them particularly important was the fact that these movements challenged the color line by engaging in interracial organizing. Some clarifying remarks may be useful here to head off potential confusion over the central terms that orient this study—class, race, and interracial organizing. What counts as a "class coalition"? Does the color line apply only to the division between white and black Americans, or do Chinese, Italians, Poles, and other immigrants count as racial "others"? Given all of the variations and compromises inherent in organizing, when can we consider a movement to be "interracial"?

I want be clear from the outset that I understand class to be a relational and historically variable concept rather than a natural one.[5] To engage with class is essentially to set up a boundary question. It involves the partitioning of social space into an "us" and a "them," defined in terms of economic positions and relations. I have stated that the Populists and the Knights of Labor were class-based movements, but measuring them against a rigidly modern, a priori definition of class creates some obvious difficulties. Their broad range of members—from farm hands and day laborers to planters and proprietors—has led some later observers to wonder whether these were really class movements at all. The movements were generally seen by those involved as working people's movements, not working-*class* movements as we might use the term today. That does not mean that class was not relevant, however. Indeed, the central claims of the movements were organized around a quite explicit definition of their members as "producers of wealth." One of the central questions posed in the book is how this particular class frame of reference shaped the movements' understanding of racial interests. Specifically, I am interested in how class conceptions provided motivation for a reevaluation of the racial divide in organizing, as well as some discursive and practical limits to that project.

Similarly, I consider race to be a socially constructed concept rather than a natural one. At its heart, this means that racial distinctions have a social reality independent of any natural biological underpinning. This idea is widely accepted but its implications are not always well understood. To claim that race is socially constructed is to say that the definitions that matter most are not those of the analyst, but rather those of the actors in a given setting who are themselves negotiating, constructing, and maintaining social boundaries (see Stoller 1997). The fluidity and the gamesmanship surrounding racial boundaries is part of the story, but in social life race is more commonly treated as an essential categorical attribute. This was certainly true of late-nineteenth-century America, where, for example, a person with predominantly "white" ancestors could be defined as "black" by convention and by law. For this reason, in this book I attempt to grasp racial boundaries in the way that the movements defined them. For example, the movements did not attempt to subvert the distinction between black and white (arbitrary as the boundary may have been in fact). Nor did they attempt to remove the boundary altogether, despite their sometimes grandiose claims that they were able to overcome the color line. What they did accomplish, at least partially, was a reinterpretation of what the racial boundaries meant within the context of the movements' goals—who was in and who was out; who was acceptable and who was to be rejected.

Finally, I use the term "interracial organizing" to describe the projects that these movements embarked upon in reaching across the color line in service of broader economic and political goals. This term, too, comes with some baggage. Some authors have distinguished between "interracial" movements and "biracial" ones, for example. Interracial movements are said to be those in which integration is fully achieved at both the organizational and personal levels. Biracial movements are those in which most interaction is segregated by race, so that black members associate only with black members and white with white. Yet this distinction can obscure as much as it clarifies, since movements like the Knights of Labor and the Populists do not fit easily into either category. One reason is that it dichotomizes what has really been a much more varied set of arrangements. The other reason is that until well into the twentieth century, even the most radical movements fell short of being truly "interracial"—in other words, if the dichotomy is understood in a strict way, one side of it was simply unattainable for any movement of the time.

I find it more useful to treat interracial organization as a matter of degree—some movements, and some local contexts, came much closer than others.

The Knights of Labor came closest to being a truly integrated movement. Most black and white members were organized into separate local assemblies (and in some cases in separate regional "district assemblies" too), so the Knights fell far short of an interracial ideal. Still, mixed-race assemblies did crop up, and a significant degree of coordination between black and white members occurred on practical issues. Populism is less easy to categorize. In its first manifestation as the Farmers' Alliance, it was farthest from the interracial ideal, since black members were organized in a completely separate group. Its later electoral vehicle, the People's Party, occupied an uneasy place in the middle. Party leaders, particularly Tom Watson, were far more frank about racial issues than were any leaders of the Knights of Labor. Watson in particular also risked his personal reputation and career in pursuit of his call for political equality. Most white Populists, including Watson himself, were at the same time outspoken racists on other issues.

Moreover, the movements did not occupy fixed positions. The degree of interracialism under the movements was wildly different across different locations and it varied within each movement over time. In addition, organizational "biracialism" was often in service of sustained "interracialism" in practice. One of the points that I will make is that the coalition between white and black working people worked best when it was built on relatively equal footing—where whites were conditioned to expect some independent black sources of power.

### MOVEMENT NARRATIVES AND LOCAL PRACTICES

The remainder of this book is organized in three major sections. The first is devoted to introducing the movements and the intellectual contexts in which they have been understood. Chapter 1 provides an introduction to the movements and the context of the sweeping social changes of the American Gilded Age in which they blossomed. Special attention here is on the emergence and expansion of the movements across the South and their initial confrontations with the color line. In this chapter I also establish the intellectual context within which the movements have been understood. In particular, I set up the later analysis by discussing the renewed scholarly appreciation for the radical potential of the republican class idiom that was at the heart of these movements. The sections that then follow consider the Knights of Labor and the Populists in turn.

What made attempts to mobilize across racial lines possible and what limited such efforts? The remaining chapters explore two different kinds of answers to this question. One answer has to do with the movement-level narratives linking class and race. Here, the cultural context of the movements is in the foreground, particularly the role of the republican class lens in how the movements made sense of their own identities and interests. The second answer foregrounds the more fragile and temporally defined processes by which interests were considered, and often renegotiated, in particular social contexts. Consequently, I weave back and forth between broader examinations of the narratives linking race and class at the movement level and local analyses of interracial organizing in the South.

Many scholars today focus on narratives—stories that individuals and collective actors tell in order to make sense of themselves, their actions, and their environments. Among these scholars, however, there are different reasons for doing so.[6] My interest is in using the movement-level narratives of the Knights of Labor and the Populists as a way to empirically grasp the role of the deeper cultural and historical patterns shaping the movements' own definitions of their interests and identities. That is, the narratives offer a window onto the cultural process through which the Populists and the Knights made sense of the tangled boundaries of race and class. Indeed, the movements each had stable but divergent narratives linking class and race—the movements simultaneously pursued strategies of racial inclusion and exclusion and defended both in the name of collective interest.

For the Knights, the puzzle is that the movement was willing to embrace black workers while it actively rejected Chinese and other new immigrants. In a nutshell, the logic was that the immigrants had to be rejected because they *were* a competitive threat in the labor market, but blacks should be organized or else they *would be* competitors. The Populists also harbored some deep anti-foreign sentiments of their own, but the real puzzle was a dual response to black workers that employed both competitive and cooperative logics. These contrary tendencies have long been apparent, but they have remained puzzling in large part due to the thin poles of the debate posed above. Rather than ignore competitive struggles or excuse racist sentiment, my goal is to ask how the threats were understood by the Knights and by the Populists and what they meant to them.

One of my central claims in this book is that these seemingly contradictory tendencies toward racial exclusion and inclusion were linked in the movement narratives by a consistent logic provided by the republican lens through which the movements viewed class. Republicanism, at least by the late nineteenth century, was not a logically consistent ideology but rather an idiom—a common language through which hopes, dreams, and discontent could be expressed. Its common acceptance was due in large part to its very deep roots in American life. In the words of Bruce Laurie, classic republicanism posed an "enduring tension between virtue and commerce, the self and the market" (1997: 49). Yet as Laurie notes, building on the work of Joyce Appleby, republicanism branched off into two separate traditions by the nineteenth century—the entrepreneurial "free labor" tradition and the radical republicanism adopted by the early labor movements.

The independence and self-sufficiency of the artisan and yeoman remained central ideals for the latter tradition, prompting a later generation of observers to see such republican claims as reformist, middle-class minded, and "backward looking" in orientation rather than as fully class-conscious. It is more adequate to view it as part of what has been termed a radicalism of tradition—familiar understandings and repertoires of protest turned to new ends, often with unforeseen results (see Calhoun 1982, 1983). Fundamental to this republican idiom was a broad definition of class identity that included all "producers" rather than a narrow band of laborers or tradesmen and an emphasis on civic virtue as a central resource at stake in labor struggles. Indeed, labor republicanism was concerned with citizenship, democratic participation, and social status as much as the later holy trinity of hours, wages, and benefits. Still, it provided a common and compelling basis for a moral critique of shifting economic, political, and social conditions that affected working people's lives. In a word, it became a way of seeing class.

In the process, moreover, it also became a way of making sense of racial boundaries. Several authors have noted the racial implications of the republican class idiom. For David Roediger, the republican lens was central to the way antebellum white workers saw both their racial and class positions. At the same time that the idiom provided a ready language for resisting new economic arrangements in which artisans became workers, it also resisted those below. As Roediger puts it, "Republicanism itself carried a strong suspicion of the powerless, not just of the powerful, and a fear that the top and the bottom of society would unite against the 'producing classes' in the middle" (1991: 44). In particular, unfree black labor became the central "other" against which white workers came to define themselves. Alexander Saxton (1971) has noted the way that the labor republican idiom also excluded Chinese immigrants at a later period.

Making the connection between labor republicanism and race is thus not new. This book contributes to the conversation in a number of ways, however. First, my discussion of the language of republicanism in movement narratives is built from a systematic empirical analysis, as I will outline below. This is important because it provides a way to answer some simple but fundamental questions that could otherwise be answered only anecdotally. For example, how exactly were the various racial "others" connected to the different claims about the movements' economic, political, and status interests? When the Knights and the Populists engaged in discussions of race, to what degree was the focus on black workers as opposed to other groups?

Second, the analytic focus in the discussion of movement narratives is on the dual nature of the boundaries that were drawn—they were not simply inclusive or exclusive but rather both at once. Moreover, both sides were linked by the republican idiom, albeit under economic and social conditions that had shifted greatly since the Civil War. The republican idiom allowed a broad conception of the "we" involved in wealth production. In the decades preceding the Civil War, black labor had been the central "other" against which this republican framework defined white labor. The acceptance of black workers as fellow "producers" and worthy citizens was bumpy and problematic in the post-Reconstruction era, yet the same republican class schema opened a place for it. Other groups were rejected, primarily on the grounds that they were not willing or able to subscribe to the ideals of civic virtue that the movements professed. The republican idiom thus provided not only a source but also important limitations to the extent of interracialism.

The construction of the racial boundaries for the movements was therefore shaped by the way class boundaries were understood in movement-level narratives. Such understandings do not, however, exist on an abstract plane divorced from the events and problems that arise in practical experience. Another set of conditions enabling and constraining the degree of interracialism can be seen at the level of practice. In any given local arena, the Knights and the Populists faced a great deal of uncertainty over their choices of method and strategies, over the choice to build or forego coalitions. While the economic or racial "interests" of the movements may seem clear to analysts after the fact, the people involved had to work out what to do amid a great deal of doubt. Movement leaders, members, and fellow travelers had to consider strategies (for example, whether or not to abandon long-established traditions and institutions by entering interracial coalitions) amid the fog of uncertain outcomes.

Chapter 2 addresses the movement narratives connecting race and class in the Knights of Labor, while chapter 5 does the same for the Farmers' Alliance and the People's Party. In each chapter, my goal is to delineate the narratives empirically and then explore their cultural logic. While my discussion of the movement narratives is presented in an accessible way, it relies on a careful method of data collection and a formal, if simple, analytical strategy.[7] Although a more complete account of my data sources and methods appears in the appendix, I will provide an overview here. The analysis rests on data from the central journals of the Knights of Labor, the Farmer's Alliance, and the People's Party, as well as supplemental sources such as the letters sent to Terence Powderly from southern working people. These sources are well known, although I treat them in a new way here. These data allow the different movement narratives to be defined based on two central elements—the racial "others" that were the central characters in the narratives, and the frames of interest that formed the plots.

The success of the interracial project within these movements varied by location and over time. These actors also had to square their decisions with the concrete lessons learned from past experience and with ways of thinking developed in relation to past circumstances in local settings.[8] The degree to which the movement narratives matched the conditions that local actors saw in front of them provided one important source of this variation. Part of the fit had to do with economic and political conditions that were beyond the control of movement members or potential converts. The pattern of civic life in both the black and the white communities was vital to the strength of the interracial project as well. In particular, the interracial project fared better when the black movement adherents held a degree of autonomy in terms of organizational, political, or community resources. Even in contexts where conditions were favorable for the movements, the ideas expressed by black and white working people about the wisdom of collaboration varied over time. The changing calculation of interest during the course of organizing is thus a central part of the story within each setting.

Chapters 3 and 4 present grounded case studies of the Knights of Labor in two local contexts. In these chapters, I consider the potential for interracial class alliance against the backdrop of the social, political, and economic organization of each community. My data sources and methods of analysis are more eclectic in these chapters. The local-level analyses rest on a variety of data sources, including county-level census records, careful block-by-block residential data drawn from city directories, local movement and community newspapers, and other movement documents, as well as a host of excellent secondary sources. Accordingly, these sections incorporate quantitative snapshots of political, economic, and population structures with a more standard analytical narrative that is sensitive to the temporal dimension of interracial organizing.

Chapters 3 and 4 present grounded case studies of the interracial project of the Knights of Labor in Richmond and in Atlanta, respectively. The comparison is important, since the two cities were quite comparable in some ways; for example, in the relative size of the black population—a simple measure that is often used as an indicator of competition between white and black working people. Yet the two cities had very different outcomes. As an old city of the upper South, Richmond had a significant black population before the Civil War, as well as an established black working class. It also developed a vibrant black community life and political tradition, which served as a basis for the adoption there of the Knights of Labor. Most important, it had both a strong and sustained interracial coalition under the Knights. In contrast, Atlanta was a newer and much less established city. Although Richmond is a relatively well-known case, Atlanta is not.

The Knights were well represented in Atlanta, but the black assemblies were short-lived and did not wield any significant power, despite the city's relatively large black population. I point to a number of explanations for this difference, including the different economic and political histories of the cities, but the most general issue was the level at which the black members in the two cities could maintain a degree of autonomy and self-direction. In Richmond, the relative autonomy of the black members—both within the organizational structure of the movement and in the broader associational life and neighborhood structure of the city—helped to sustain the interracial project there. In Atlanta, there was no such autonomy and in fact no significant history of self-organized black labor organizing. Consequently, the white members did not expect that black involvement in the movement would require any real compromises on their part, and the black members were not in a position to demand any.

Chapters 6 and 7 present case studies of the Farmers' Alliance and the Populist movements in Georgia and Virginia, respectively. Again, these contexts provide a good contrast with their differing social, economic, political, and historical conditions. The state-level analysis is more appropriate here, since the Alliance was built around state organizations and the political aspirations of the Populists were often organized around state offices. My primary focus in these chapters is on the involvement of the Alliance and the Populists in the political arena, where the discussions about race were closest to the surface.

In contrast with the Knights, Populism met with a great deal of success in Georgia but relatively little in Virginia. Georgia's dependence on cotton as a cash crop and its high tenancy rates allowed for more success on a statewide basis. In Virginia, diversified farming and low rate of tenancy limited the degree to which the message of the movements resonated with white farmers, and limited the degree to which white farmers defined common interests with blacks. The pocket of counties known as the "Southside" was the core of both Alliance and Populist strength in Virginia. Not only were these counties majority black, but they also were reliant on a single cash crop (tobacco) and had relatively high rates of tenant farming. Beyond these given structural limitations, in these chapters I show that the expressions of interest in interracial organizing changed over time with experience in the political process. Here again, the point is not to paint the movements as either altruistic or cynical. The enthusiasm for interracial alliances in Georgia and in Virginia's Southside was strategic, but it was genuine as well. The contingencies of the political process changed whether or not white Populists and black Republicans saw an interest in coalition. The historical precedents that indicated that such a coalition could work were extremely important early on, and yet very different conclusions were often read into the same precedents later, as early optimism was replaced by wariness and then cynicism.

CHAPTER 1

# REPUBLICAN RADICALISM

> Unless a halt, all along the line, is called, the sun of American liberty might just as well set now as to wait a few more years and then go down in blood. The drift of events all tends to[ward] a certain destruction of this republic, and if men who join the Alliance fail or refuse to learn the lessons that should there be taught, a few more years will wind up the whole concern on to a few billionaires, and they will own white and black trash alike.
> —*ALLIANCE FARMER* (CHIPLY, FLORIDA), REPRINTED IN THE *NATIONAL ECONOMIST*

In quoting a small Populist newspaper, one of many scattered throughout the South, the official journal of the Farmers' Alliance called attention to the urgency of the movement's mission. Although written in the fevered style typical of both the Populists and the Knights, the passage reprinted from the *Alliance Farmer* highlighted some central concerns about the direction of late-nineteenth-century life. For both farmers and industrial "mechanics," America's Gilded Age seemed to present a stark choice: organize or perish. The economic side of the argument was driven by the contrast between the harsh new economic realities and the long-established identities of those who saw themselves as free and independent citizen-workers.[1] This was nowhere clearer than in the tendency of the movements to refer to both wage labor and tenant farming, with all seriousness, as conditions of "slavery." The economic concerns were entangled with political and civic concerns as well. As the social status and independence of the working people of America became imperiled so did "American liberty" and thus the republic itself.

Finally, and significantly, the *Alliance Farmer* quote pointed out the connection between class and race. The political and economic dimensions of the class critique were stated in an established republican idiom that would have been familiar to working people a generation before. Yet this critique was tied to a new understanding of the need to organize across the color line. This was an uncomfortable conclusion for white adherents of the movements, particularly in the South, who desperately wished not to be reduced to the status of "black trash." Nevertheless, the class concerns had direct implications for the color line. In the post-Reconstruction South, working people both black and white could be "owned" in the same way.

The Populists and the Knights of Labor have been widely understood as pivotal movements. Labor scholars have pointed out that the development of these organizations marked a crucial point in the history of American class formation where the republican traditions of the nineteenth century became linked to the political challenges and labor protests of the twentieth. But they have also been seen as pivotal because of their approach to the color line. At this liminal moment, an old language of class could offer new orientations toward racial boundaries. Both in terms of class and race, the movements were notable for their inclusive boundaries that began to build broad coalitions across enduring divides of skill, ownership, and race.

In this chapter I provide an overview of the sweeping economic and social changes of the 1880s and 1890s. Against this setting I introduce the Knights of Labor and the Populist movements within the context of two significant theoretical and historiographical shifts—the first concerning the nature of class interests and identities, and the second concerning the connection between class and race. The first major part of this chapter concerns the movements and the way that they construed their interests through an established republican lens. Modern scholarly work has tended to see class as a historically and culturally constructed set of relationships and identities rather than as fixed entities with objectively given interests.[2] This shift has prompted a significant reconsideration of the radical potential of the republican class idiom of the Knights and the Populists. In particular, the "producerist" class identity of the movements allowed for a broad construction of the movements' class boundaries, encompassing skilled and unskilled workers, independent farmers and tenants, sharecroppers and farmhands. It also led to a fundamental and uniquely republican challenge to the economic, political, and social conditions of the era.

A parallel shift has occurred in the way recent scholarship has understood racial boundaries and their connection to class by focusing on racial formation as a dynamic process and the relational contexts—historical and cultural as well as economic—in which that connection is forged. While this new work has set the stage for a similar reconsideration of the radical potential of the movements, their racial legacy has remained a point of some confusion. In the second major section of this chapter I sketch the way the movements approached the "color line," and in so doing I set up the main focus of the book—the sources and limits of the interracial project. Organizing across the color line necessarily involved making sense of race in relation to class, and on both sides of the color line it involved asking questions: Are these folks with us or against us? Do our interests dictate that we compete or cooperate?

## TRANSFORMATION AND CONTENTION IN THE GILDED AGE

Americans of the Gilded Age witnessed massive changes in industrial and agrarian economies as well as the unparalleled organization of working people into mass movements. In manufacturing, skilled-trade industries began to give way to deskilled factory systems, while traditional fraternal trade organizations and artisan guilds shifted to full-fledged labor movements.[3] A similar process occurred in farming, as rising tenancy rates accompanied declining prices for agricultural products and agrarian movements began to publicly advocate major changes in economic and monetary policies. Moreover, the era saw the unification of these industrial and agrarian movements—culturally, rhetorically, and to a degree organizationally—into what its adherents saw as a great reform movement devoted to reclaiming a more equitable and respectable position for all "producers of wealth."

Although the immense changes in production during the era did not completely do away with older arrangements, they did alter the conditions of economic and social life to a degree that was obvious to working people. The emergence of class protest in the industrial Northeast is the most familiar part of the story, but the southern states were an equally important location of major economic and social transformation, and they also became a key site for the central protest movements of the 1880s and 1890s. Significantly, the South was also the context for the most direct renegotiation of race within the protest movements, as the *Alliance Farmer* quote above suggested.

Boosters and speculators touting the industry and entrepreneurial spirit of the "New South" were fueld by hope as much as fact (see Woodward 1951; Ayers 1992). Still, they had some impressive evidence with which to back up their claims. Following Reconstruction, the economic transformation of the South proceeded at a stunning pace. The South never came close to catching up with the rest of the country in terms of the absolute level of industrialization. Yet the transformation was proceeding much more quickly in the former Confederate states—for example, in the increase of over 200 percent in a single decade in the capital invested in manufacturing (see table 1).[4]

The expansion of railroads in the region spurred the emerging industrial economy and changed the social and physical landscape of the South as well.[5] Established cities saw the birth of new factories, cotton mills, and other capital-intensive industries that transformed traditional trade and employment relations. New cities developed alongside the expanding mining and railroad industries, and in so doing became hubs of commerce that drew migrants from the surrounding countryside and across the country. Enabled by new rail connections, rural industries created labor camps in the middle of sparsely populated areas, such as those made for logging and turpentine production in the pine woods of North Carolina. Like the urban factories, these rural industries were the subject of bitter complaints. Particularly salient concerns included the competition with convict labor gangs and the use of "scrip" payment good only at the company store. As one worker attested from such a camp in Mississippi: "I do beleave that we are treated worse than any human on earth, and to call our selfs free men we have to leave home to go to work before daylight & it is black dark when we get home again."[6]

The railroads also played an important part in the transformation of agrarian economies, in particular by facilitating the spread of cotton cash-crop farming to smaller farms and previously diverse agricultural regions. In the process, older economic institutions took on new forms in the decades after Reconstruction. Big trading merchants had long held a compound role as

TABLE 1 Changes in farm and manufacturing economies, 1880–1890

| | Southern states | | |
|---|---|---|---|
| | 1880 | 1890 | % change |
| Capital invested in manufacturing (in $) | 133,253,225 | 402,546,402 | 202.1 |
| Total wages paid in manufacturing (in $) | 37,116,085 | 129,876,666 | 250.0 |
| Value of manufactured products (in $) | 240,441,395 | 540,993,633 | 125.0 |
| Value of raw materials in manufacturing (in $) | 151,882,286 | 296,401,325 | 95.2 |
| Total number of farms | 1,252,248 | 1,524,948 | 21.8 |
| Average farm size (in acres) | 322,416 | 400,042 | 24.1 |
| Tenant farms (as percentage of all farms) | 38.4 | 41.1 | 7.0 |
| Value of farm products (in $) | 547,567,526 | 653,059,698 | 19.3 |
| Cost of fertilizer purchased (in $) | 13,219,648 | 20,282,395 | 53.4 |
| | Non-Southern states | | |
| | 1880 | 1890 | % change |
| Capital invested in manufacturing (in $) | 2,642,159,120 | 6,091,756,853 | 130.6 |
| Total wages paid in manufacturing (in $) | 904,209,839 | 2,137,652,884 | 136.4 |
| Value of manufactured products (in $) | 5,101,307,494 | 8,789,161,348 | 72.3 |
| Value of raw materials in manufacturing (in $) | 3,229,818,993 | 4,846,171,021 | 50.0 |
| Total number of farms | 2,712,958 | 3,024,903 | 11.5 |
| Average farm size (in acres) | 209,561 | 290,162 | 38.5 |
| Tenant farms (as percentage of all farms) | 19.9 | 21.9 | 10.1 |
| Value of farm products (in $) | 1,644,740,665 | 1,803,403,530 | 9.7 |
| Cost of fertilizer purchased (in $) | 15,322,161 | 18,157,508 | 18.5 |

Source: Calculated from "Historical, Demographic, Economic, and Social Data: The United States, 1790–1970." Ann Arbor, Mich.: Inter-University Consortium for Political and Social Research, 1984.

bank, agent, landlord, and financial agent for cotton producers. In the cash-poor and credit-starved environment of the postwar South, local merchants took on the roles that the large cotton "factors" once held. Local merchants would advance seed, fertilizer, and credit to tenants and other small farmers for the coming year.

Because farmers generally did not have the cash to purchase goods outright, the purchases were commonly made on credit, often at interest rates of 20 percent or higher. The arrangement was typically handled through the merchant's lien on the future crop. The sale of the resulting crop allowed some farmers to break even or in certain cases end up the year with a small profit. Many more went into debt and became ever more dependent upon the lien system to provide for their needs for the next year. Merchants controlled the terms of the trade, since they could collect the cotton at harvest when the price was low and then sell it when the terms suited them better. In the words of Harold Woodman, local merchants became "the most important economic power in the Southern countryside" (1990 [1968]: 296).[7] Larger planters could manage to avoid being subject to the whim of the merchants (some were in fact merchants themselves), but they too were squeezed by the difficulty of obtaining sufficient credit as well as by contracting prices when it came time to sell their crop.

A great deal of the discontent among small farmers was expressed as a fear of foreclosure and a loss of independence. Of most concern to southern farmers was the slow growth of tenancy arrangements, whereby tenants "rented" farms in exchange for cash, or much more commonly in exchange for a share of the expected future product. The spread of southern tenant farming does not seem large in the aggregate statistics, but here the figures have to be read carefully. By 1890, over 40 percent of all farms in the South already operated on the basis of some kind of tenant arrangement. Southern tenants also operated on a much more tenuous basis than their counterparts elsewhere. Tenant farms in the rest of the country were not appreciably different in size from owner-run farms—they most commonly ranged between 100 and 500 acres, according to census classifications. Southern tenants were scraping by on a much more meager scale, typically working between 20 and 50 acres. In other words, southern tenancy was a survival strategy, not an entrepreneurial enterprise.

In this context of fast-changing industrial and agrarian relations, the Knights and the Populists became the first large-scale movements of working people to organize across America, and the first to organize in the South in a serious way. Because of their size, their influence, and their ability (at least for a time) to bring working people together across significant lines of division, these movements captured the attention of the nation. The Noble and Holy Order of the Knights of Labor was founded in December 1869 when skilled garment cutters in Philadelphia decided to reorganize their mutual benefit society into a secret fraternal order. The membership grew little by little, but the Knights' rules of secrecy kept its growth limited both spatially and numerically. By 1874 there were more than eighty local assemblies of the Knights of Labor, all concentrated near Philadelphia (Ware 1959: 24–26, 30). The birth of the southern Populism was similarly local and unremarkable, beginning with the formation in 1877 of the "Knights of Reliance" in Lampasas County, Texas (Goodwyn 1976: 33–36). Soon afterward, the organization changed its name to the Farmers' Alliance and began to spread into neighboring counties. By 1880, there were twelve local chapters (later known as "sub-alliances") in three contiguous counties in north-central Texas.[8] The small organization began arrangements for expansion by putting a lecturer in the field and issuing charters to new sub-alliances. The 1886 meeting of the Texas Alliance reported 104 Texas counties organized (Dunning 1975 [1891]: 40–51; Schwartz 1976: 92–93). Both organizations soon began to expand beyond their initial locales, however, and within the space of a few years they had won massive memberships as well as the attention of the nation as a whole.

Spurred by a well-publicized and initially successful strike against the railroad baron Jay Gould, the Knights of Labor membership grew to over 100,000 members in 1885 and then to more than 700,000 the following year.[9] Throughout the country, new local assemblies were being organized faster than they could be chartered by the Knights' central office, and the demand for new organizers seemed insatiable. The Knights were not able to hold this peak membership for long, however. The 1886 boom brought the movement wide popular notice, but it was a mixed blessing. The prolonged struggles with Gould left the organization overextended financially and organizationally. The Knights' success also brought a new level of opposition from industry (Phelan 2000; Voss 1993). By 1890, the membership had declined to about 100,000. After this point, internal conflict and membership decline became harder to ignore. Membership records were not published after 1890, but it is clear that the strength of the organization was quickly dwindling.[10] Despite its boom-and-bust life cycle, the cultural and political impact of the Knights of Labor was enormous. Over its life, nearly 12,000 local assemblies of the organization were founded nationally.

The Knights of Labor was also the first national labor organization to organize extensively in the South—1,909 of the assemblies were located there. Indeed, the Knights' victory over Jay Gould in 1885 was "won in considerable part in the shops of Texas and Arkansas," according to C. Vann Woodward (1951: 230). The southern expansion of the movement followed the arc of the

Knight's fortunes nationally.[11] The first southern assemblies of the Knights of Labor were chartered in Alabama and Tennessee in 1878.[12] The Tennessee group, designated local assembly (LA) 857, was composed of coal miners and was likely organized by a member who had been initiated in Pennsylvania's mining country and later migrated South in search of work. Alabama's first assemblies were located in its cities, two in Mobile and one skilled assembly of printers in Montgomery. Fourteen new assemblies were organized in 1879—there were three each in Birmingham and Mobile, and most of the rest were in smaller Alabama mining communities such as Jefferson Mines, Newcastle, Pratt Mines, Warrior Station, and Helena. A more sustained organizing effort began in 1882 and soon spread across the South. In the peak year of 1886, there were 718 new local assemblies chartered throughout the region.

The explosion of interest in the Alliance also began after 1884, when the movement sent traveling lecturers into areas surrounding its base in Texas. This effort was compounded by a complex series of mergers and combinations with like-minded organizations that began to make the Alliance into a powerful force throughout the South. The first, between the Texas Alliance and the similar Louisiana Farmers' Alliance, gave the movement its first regional foothold. The new organization, dubbed the National Farmers' Alliance and Cooperative Union, was incorporated in 1887 with the Texan Charles W. Macune as president. Macune made arrangements to send "well-trained, careful organizers" into the southern states to increase membership, and by summer 1888 there were reportedly 350 organizers working for the Alliance in North Carolina, Alabama, Florida, Mississippi, Georgia, and Tennessee, as well as in Missouri and Kentucky (Dunning 1975 [1891]: 64–65, 77; Saloutos 1960: 77). The Alliance also sent representatives out to another rival organization known as the Agricultural Wheel. After some negotiating, a new amalgamation occurred in late 1889, at which point the official name of the organization changed again—first to the Farmers and Laborers' Union of America, and finally to the National Farmers' Alliance and Industrial Union.[13]

Eventually, the organization made a deep impression in every southern state. By July 1888, the Alliance announced that it had 9,629 sub-alliances organized in 419 counties, with a reported membership of about 360,000.[14] The next year, it claimed 12,000 sub-alliances and 700,000 members. Membership figures after this point are suspect, in part because the movement was beginning to shift into electoral politics (Saloutos 1960: 77).[15] The success of

Alliance candidates in the 1890 election led to a more sustained third party effort under the banner of the People's Party. Electoral Populism seriously challenged Democratic control in many places for the first time since the end of Reconstruction. In 1892, the fledgling party won the South Carolina gubernatorial race and narrowly lost in several other states, despite a bitterly fought campaign and massive vote fraud that persisted over the next several years.

### CLASS FORMATION AND REPUBLICAN RADICALISM

Thus far the story of the Knights and the Populists is a familiar one—widespread structural changes led to new levels and forms of social protest, and these movements were at the center of this contentious era. The movements did not simply react to the new conditions, however. New economic, political, and social realities were read through existing languages of class. In particular, the language and imagery of the republican tradition were crucial in shaping the cultural expressions of identity and interest in the movements by juxtaposing the independence of the artisan and yeoman with the dependence of wage workers and tenants.

Recent research has emphasized the formation of the social boundaries of class as the product of both longer-term historical patterning and shorter-term projects of maintenance, contestation, and transformation. Although the shift is often labeled a "cultural turn," it is better described as a constructivist or relational turn because the main thrust has not been to deny the importance of objective economic or political forces but rather to point out that class does not exist independently of the cultural and relational context of its making.[16] E. P. Thompson provided the classic statement of this position when he argued that class should not be seen as "a 'structure,' nor even as a 'category,' but as something that happens (and can be shown to have happened) in human relationships." Similarly, class consciousness should be understood as "the way in which these experiences are handled in cultural terms: embodied in traditions, value-systems, ideas, and institutional forms" (1966: 9–10).

In seeing class as a historically and culturally variable set of relations rather than an ontologically independent "thing," Thompson influenced a voluminous modern literature that has explored the cultural and historical "making" of class and its variable formations over time and in different contexts.[17] A key insight of this work has been that the resources and dispositions that shape class relations are never entirely about economic conditions alone but rather are also linked to conditions of civic, democratic, and even domestic life (Joyce 1991, 1994; see also Calhoun 1982). Political interests relating to class are similarly "historically and socially bounded," related not only to the material organization of social life but also to the already experienced history of such organization (Steinberg 1991: 266).[18]

This relational turn has enabled a change in the way scholars have understood the Knights and the Populists by shifting attention to the way that the members and leaders of the movements defined their own identities, their interests, and the boundaries of their movements. Particularly with regard to the Knights, earlier scholarship tended to dismiss the movements as middle-class, "reformist," and backward looking for not conforming to a purportedly true definition of class and class interest.[19] Selig Perlman (1928), for example, considered the Knights a utopian failure. In particular, he found the Knights wanting in comparison to what he saw as the American Federation of Labor's more pragmatic outlook.[20] For Perlman, the broad "producerist" class idiom of the Knights blunted the movement's radical potential and stood in the way of true class consciousness. Although Norman Ware's (1959) account is more charitable than that of Gerald Grob (1961), both treated the movement's leadership (in particular, Grand Master Workman Terence V. Powderly) as inept and more concerned with romantic ideals than with hard-headed responses to the practical problems of the day.

The classic work on Populism is generally kinder, although the movement's political manifestation as the People's Party received more notice than its organizational roots in the Farmers' Alliance. Still, Gene Clanton has pointed out that many early accounts treated Populism "as if it sprang from an historical vacuum," while by the 1950s it was often treated as an "unsavory, illiberal, retrogressive political interlude" (1991: xvi-xvii).[21]

A recent spate of work has reconnected with the radical potential of the movements by seeing them as legitimate responses to the genuine problems faced by working people of the 1880s and 1890s, and thereby providing a powerful voice for American farmers and laborers.[22] This work has also reassessed the leaders of the movements—Terence Powderly as well as Populist leaders like Charles Macune and William Lamb—as rational if humanly flawed men struggling to find the best solutions they could for the problems at hand.[23] In doing so, this work has reevaluated the importance of the movements as bridges between nineteenth-century forms of protest and later forms in the Progressive Era. Beyond this work on the movements' radical potential, recent scholarship has also reassessed the movements by connecting them to the historical and cultural contexts of their "making," particularly their common republican class framework and their "movement culture" of solidarity. The Knights and the Populists, not only despite their republican roots but also largely because of them, were important vehicles for the formation of class solidarity.

## REPUBLICANISM AND RADICAL REFORM

As a cultural language through which class was understood, nineteenth-century republicanism was a "backward-looking" tradition that nevertheless provided a platform for potentially radical social change.[24] The lament from the *Alliance Farmer* about the larger stakes of the labor struggle—nothing less than the decline of American liberty—was typical of the way these movements linked a critique of material and social conditions to the erosion of an ethic of civic equality that, in the eyes of many, imperiled the republic itself. The Knights and the Populists in fact proposed nothing less than a grand reorganization of the economy and the polity to reflect the interests of the producers. The broad appeal of the movements showed the resonance of this framework. "[I am] a strong sympathiser with the cause of both the Knights of Labor and Alliance," one adherent wrote from the Alliance birthplace in Lampasas, Texas. "I have never before seen the people so stirred up in politics & so united as the laboring class are. They are reading & thinking for themselves for the first time in life."[25]

As early as the 1830s, republicanism differentiated the working people from their employers, but also reaffirmed the traditional values of autonomy and pride in craft (Wilentz 1984: 96; Laurie 1997: 51–52; Schultz 1993). The traditional republican language of Jefferson provided the same function for the independent "yeoman."[26] The republican class framework found political expression in particular with the Jacksonian-era Democrats. According to Alexander Saxton, the party was so successful at fostering this "populist idyll" that "workingmen for generations to come would look back on Jacksonian America as a classless society in which the fraternity of citizen producers had directly controlled government power" (1990: 145).[27]

As a labor idiom, republican radicalism was not a tightly defined ideology but rather a looser cultural package that came with ironies and contradictions (see Sanders 1999: chapter 11). Paradoxically, labor republicanism became particularly salient, and the "producers" more cohesive, with the decline of the very conditions of production that formed the basis for the republican ideal. Despite the increasingly tenuous nature of artisan production, the importance of the idiom was that "the artisan remained, in politics, the 'noble mechanics,' graced with an assumed unity of purpose and interest" (Wilentz 1984: 75).[28] The idiom provided a platform for a radical critique of the encroachment of market forces that threatened to reduce the traditional independence of the farmers and artisans—for them, wage labor and tenancy marked a loss of control over their own productive capacities that amounted to nothing less than "slavery" (see Sanders 1999: 4; Montgomery 1967: 30).

Labor republicanism also provided a platform for civic claims by the farmers and artisans about the importance of a rich community life in maintaining freedom and equality.[29] Republican class demands were inseparable from arguments about the place of working people in the democratic community more generally.[30] In other words, this outlook placed a great deal of importance on the maintenance of a particular kind of resource that might be termed civic virtue—the capacity and inclination to uphold the conditions of the *collective* good within the democratic community (Schneirov 1998: 30–32). Supporting the public good meant more than simply fighting for better hours or working conditions, it also meant a broader and more democratic organization of economic and political life. This civic and moral side of class interest was prominent in the Knights' declaration of principles: "To secure to the workers the full enjoyment of the wealth they create; sufficient leisure in which to develop their intellectual, moral, and social faculties; all of the benefits, recreations and pleasures of association; in a word, to enable them to share in the gains and honors of advancing civilization."[31] The Populist appeal was based on the same kind of claim, as manifest in the Alliance motto "Equal rights to all and special favors to none" as well as in its economic and political aims.[32]

The popularity of fraternal orders in this era of "joiners" reflected the republican emphasis on civic virtue (Schlesinger 1944; see also Clemens 1997; Kaufman 1999). Such brotherhoods commonly fulfilled social as well as economic functions, mixing principles of self-betterment, charity, and mutual aid with elaborate ritual (Clawson 1989; Montgomery 1993: 80; Laurie 1997: 50).

By midcentury, the fraternal model had been adopted by urban tradesmen and farmers and it formed the basis for orders such as the Knights of St. Crispin and the Knights of Husbandry (better known as the Grange), which infused the fraternal functions with a distinct focus on the fellowship of the producers (Dawley 1976; Woods 1991). The fraternal ideal similarly became an important part of what Lawrence Goodwyn (1976) termed the "movement culture" of solidarity for Populists and for the Knights.[33] The fraternal tradition permeated a great deal of the culture of the movements, from the titles of the officers—"master workman," "worthy foreman"—to their elaborate systems of symbol and ritual.[34]

The importance of the rituals and symbolism declined as the movements grew, and eventually the secret nature of the organizations became a hindrance as well. The Knights in particular began to garner broader notice and influence as the organization moved away from the pageantry and secrecy that marked its beginnings.[35] Terence Powderly himself had little use for the elaborate rituals, and he played a central role in retiring the secrecy rules of the Knights (see Phelan 1999: 22, 30–32, 35–37). Yet the republican emphasis on solidarity remained important in shaping the way that the grand aims of the movements were expressed. This kind of solidarity could be seen in the many kinds of self-help efforts of the movements, but it could also be put to radical use, as the Alliance's continuing efforts at political education showed. Through its famous "Alliance Schoolrooms" and the lessons printed in its central paper, the *National Economist,* the Alliance attempted to teach history, arithmetic, and economics as a way to encourage an analysis and critique of current conditions (Mitchell 1987). The Knights and the Populists thus provided a bridge between the small, local fraternal model of nineteenth-century organizing and the large-scale national labor movements of the twentieth century.[36]

The Alliance's Leonidas L. Polk described the Knights and Populists as "millions of American freemen—united by a common interest, confronted by common dangers." Particularly among the dangers was what Polk described as "centralized capital, allied to irresponsible corporate power." As for the political aims of the movements, "the great absorbing question . . . is not whether the Democratic or the Republican party, with their evident subserviency to the will of corporate and money power, shall be in the ascendancy; but the question is, whether under our republican form of government the citizen or the dollar shall be the sovereign" (National Farmers' Alliance and

Industrial Union [1891: 4–5, 10]).[37] The republican culture brought more to the movements than their rituals and fraternal form; more deeply, it shaped the way they defined their class identities, their interests, and the boundaries of the movement itself.[38]

The "producerist" definition of class was one of the most central legacies. Rather than championing a narrow band of workers or tradesmen, this inclusive understanding of the movement's boundaries rested on a distinction between "productive" and "unproductive" labor rather than ownership of the means of production. The boundaries of the term "producer" were fuzzy, but the concept included industrial "mechanics" as well as farmers and even some independent professionals and small merchants. The membership policies of the Knights and of the Alliance reflected this understanding. The Knights were composed mostly of wage workers, but as Leon Fink has pointed out, "only those associated with idleness (bankers, speculators), corruption (lawyers, liquor dealers, gamblers), or social parasitism (all of the above) were categorically excluded from membership in the Order" (1985: 9).[39] The membership policies of the Alliance similarly brought together agrarian producers of very different means, including tenants and farm laborers but also small farm owners and a few large planters.

If this inclusive conception of the class boundary around the "producers" blurred the line between wage workers or tenant farmers on the one side and owners on the other, it also blurred the line between the skilled and the unskilled, and thus provided the basis for a broad coalition that later, more narrowly organized trade unions or farmers' movements could not.[40] Recent work on the Knights of Labor has pointed out that it was among the first of the labor organizations to effectively bridge the skill divide, though not always smoothly (Voss 1988, 1993; Conell and Voss 1990).[41] As such, the movements provided the basis for a broad alliance of working people as a whole.

The producerist class distinction allowed for a powerful critique of the economic, political, and social trends experienced by working people of the Gilded Age, and it was placed squarely within the popular understanding of the nature of the republic itself. The banks, speculators, political "rings," and monopolists were a problem for the reform movements not simply because they were "capitalists" but because they used their power to control the liberty and popular will of the people. More broadly, the problem facing the farmers and industrial laborers was not capital itself but the particular social organization of capital that produced a competitive system in which different actors were forced to work against the best interests of each other. According to the movements, prices and wages set in a competitive market only served to give employers incentive to exploit workers, and speculators and financiers a way to exploit farmers. The movements argued that capital should not be abolished but instead made to benefit everyone.[42] In the pithy formulation of the Knights, "labor creates all wealth" and all wealth "belongs to those who create it."[43]

For the Knights of Labor, practical action occurred on two fronts—political action and workplace demands backed by threats of boycotts or strikes. From a pragmatic point of view, Powderly and others believed that strikes did more harm than good since large companies could wait out a work stoppage much more easily than could workers. In place of strikes, the Knights often backed boycotts of certain manufacturers' goods. Equally important, though far less fully developed, were the movement's cooperative efforts. In Powderly's words, replacing the competitive wage system with a cooperative one "will eventually make every man his own master,—every man his own employer" and "will give the laborer a fair proportion of the products of his toil."[44] By the mid-1880s the Knights had largely abandoned their efforts at building cooperative enterprises, but the larger goal of a more fully democratic economy continued to shape the goals of the movement.[45]

For its part, the Alliance pushed the cooperative ideal to the center of its own organizing efforts in order to address the twin problems of obtaining necessary goods for farmers at lower prices and marketing the resulting crop at higher prices.[46] The initial Alliance efforts came in the form of trade agreements between the Alliance and individual merchants to supply goods at a guaranteed price. More direct and ambitious were the Alliance cooperative stores. Members bought shares of the cooperatives, which then purchased supplies in large quantities and sold to the members at near-wholesale prices.[47]

More ambitious yet was the Alliance Exchange, which combined both purchasing and marketing functions into one organizational mechanism. Exchanges sprang up first in Texas and then in Georgia, Alabama, and Florida. In theory the Exchange worked as a protective buffer between farmers and the market. In effect, the Alliancemen mortgaged themselves to the Exchange instead of to the local merchants, thus bypassing the middlemen and saving members a great deal of money (Dunning 1975 [1891]: 357–62; Schwartz 1976:

217–19; Saloutos 1960: 91–93). The success of the plans varied from place to place, but in many cases during their period of existence they provided improvements to the condition of southern farmers. One careful analysis has found that the Exchange reduced prices for the goods that farmers needed by 40 percent in Texas and as much as 60 percent in some areas of North Carolina. Most importantly, the various Alliance enterprises had a measurable impact in reducing land mortgages and crop liens (Schwartz 1976: 211–13, 218).[48]

A significant part of the practical orientation of the Alliance was the demand for monetary reform. The Alliance argued that the only way to raise prices for farm products was to increase the total amount of money available by abandoning the gold standard in favor of a silver or a "bi-metallic" system, and thus reducing the power of the national banks to control the monetary supply (Peffer 1975 [1891]: 262).[49] The call for an increased money supply was imported directly from the Greenback-Labor movement of the 1870s, to which the Alliance often referred.[50] The more radical and controversial sub-treasury plan was a sweeping proposal to make the monetary system work for "producers" and to circumvent vagaries of the market. The proposal was for warehouses to be built under the auspices of the Treasury Department. These "sub-treasuries" would take in cotton, tobacco, or grain crops from farmers in the surrounding area and then store them. The farmer would then receive a low-interest cash loan for the value of the crop in treasury notes printed for this purpose. In essence, then, the plan proposed to add farm products to gold (or silver) as a unit of value on which American currency would rest (Tracy 1975 [1891]: 336–37).[51] The Alliance suggested that farmhands and other wage workers might benefit alongside the farmers. "Working people would earn money just as they do now," claimed one Alliance advocate. But the Alliance scheme would "force [the farmers'] money into productive industry instead of into mortgages, as now, thus creating new and permanent demand for labor; it will increase the value of products of labor, and that will be good cause for demanding advance in wages" (Peffer 1975 [1891]: 268).

The emphasis on civic virtue and democratic self-governance also pushed both the Knights and the Alliance toward direct involvement in politics, although not without bitter internal debates. Many within the movements (Powderly and the Alliance leader Charles W. Macune among them) argued against electoral involvement on the grounds that it could prove corrupting, as well as divisive to members. Yet some movement goals, like the common demand for reform in monetary policy or labor policy, could only be realized in the political arena. Here too republican movements provided a political voice to working people that set the stage for the later, state-oriented political agenda of the progressive age—what Elisabeth Clemens has termed the "people's lobby."[52]

Personal political involvements were never frowned upon; indeed, for several years Terence Powderly was himself simultaneously Grand Master Workman of the Knights of Labor and the mayor of Scranton, Pennsylvania. Other Knights were entering the political arena, too. In 1880, the *Journal of United Labor* noted with approval that one member from Alabama had been elected to the state legislature and would insure that "any bill . . . that bears unjustly on the interests of labor will receive at least one negative vote."[53] Several years later another newly elected southern Knight reported his willingness to take on the labor question in politics. As he stated, "I found two other Knights in the Tennessee legislature besides myself, and we managed to get a bill through the lower house to abolish scrip and other forms of robbing poor people."[54]

Instead of discouraging political activism, the Knights urged workers to break from their traditional Democratic or Republican identifications and support whomever would back the movement's goals. In time, the Knights of Labor became a political force in its own right by maintaining a national lobbying effort to advocate for labor-friendly legislation and by placing a great deal of effort into the political education of its members. Eventually the Knights launched direct third-party challenges under the banner of the "Workingmen's Party," which elected candidates to local and state offices throughout the country (see Fink 1985). By 1889, the Knights were also becoming more directly involved in Populism. "The labor question of to-day is a political question," declared the Knights' Ralph Beaumont. "The next move that must be made by the working people of this country is that they vote their oppressors out of existence."[55]

The Farmers' Alliance initially faced the same ambivalence about direct political involvement, and many Alliancemen hoped to apply moral and political pressure in a way that would influence policy decisions without making the Alliance itself into a partisan organization. While the movement wanted to have political influence, most white Alliancemen were lifelong Democrats unwilling to break with the party. Several of the movement's leaders, including for a time its president, Leonidas L. Polk, were convinced that partisan political action would destroy the organization. The political question that divided the Alliance also divided later scholarship. At times, it has been claimed that the People's Party emerged from the Farmers' Alliance movement much as a caterpillar emerges from its cocoon—that is, transformed from its early, ungainly state into the mature form it was meant to become (see Goodwyn 1976). Others have described the same transformation as something more akin to a parasitic invasion—while the third party movement was initially contained within the Alliance, the new organism destroyed the old one to fuel its own growth (Schwartz 1976). The reality, however, is more complex than either image might suggest. The Alliance and the People's Party might best be thought of as two parallel paths that crossed periodically. By a certain point, the paths overlapped to such a degree that they were functionally one and the same.

At first, the Alliance began to make inroads into electoral politics even while claiming to be strictly independent of any party. The movement's tentative solution was to acknowledge that direct political involvement was necessary, but that it would remain nonpartisan. The "Alliance yardstick," rather than party affiliation, was declared the measure of the candidates for office. In practice, measuring up by the Alliance yardstick meant stating allegiance to the movement's platform of demands.[56] Some candidates refused to stand wholeheartedly by the platform, yet still managed to gather support from the Alliance movement. Both "Pitchfork" Ben Tillman of South Carolina and James Hogg of Texas were elected governor with Alliance support in 1890, despite their rejection of the sub-treasury plan. Elsewhere, candidates for the 1890 state and congressional elections proudly declared that they measured up. In the Georgia and Tennessee governor races, state Alliance leaders were elected with Democrat Party support. Alliance-backed representatives gained the balance of power in the state legislatures of Georgia and North Carolina and made substantial gains in Alabama and Florida as well. Scattered victories for Alliance candidates were recorded in Texas, Tennessee, and Virginia.[57] The Alliance legislatures proved to be relatively ineffective, however, due to the inexperience of the representatives and the fact that many of the Alliance demands could not be met at the state level. Although the Alliance sent a number of representatives to Congress, they did not have the numerical strength to sway national policy. It was also true that on many issues, including racial tolerance, the Alliance legislators and the regular Democrats were not far apart.[58]

After 1890, the Alliance moved into a more explicit union with the third party movement. At this point, the Alliance itself was at its peak, but the political question was splitting both the rank and file and the leadership. The most public dispute was between L. L. Polk, the Alliance president, and C. W. Macune, the past president and the editor of the *National Economist.* Polk had eventually become convinced that independent political involvement was the only path open for the Alliance, but Macune continued to support nonpartisan action. The issue came to a head at the Alliance's 1890 convention in Ocala, Florida. Macune brokered a compromise to hold off any final decision on the matter until the next annual meeting, but the intervening year saw the collapse of the Alliance's business concerns and the rapid loss of membership in many states.

At the 1892 convention of reform organizations in St. Louis, the Alliance and the diminished Knights of Labor as well as a host of others decided in effect to make the labor struggle and the third party effort one and the same. After this point, the Alliance continued to exist in name, but it was functionally and organizationally inseparable from the People's Party. The first major campaign of the People's Party as a fully independent third party was in 1892. Any hopes that the Populists may have had for the presidential race suffered a serious setback when L. L. Polk, the assumed nominee, died unexpectedly before the convention. The southern Populists fared better in the state and local races, despite a significant degree of fraud committed by local Democratic machines.[59]

As a result of the bitter losses and the widespread challenges of fraud, the Populists began to pursue "fusion" arrangements with established parties in 1894. Initially, these arrangements took the form of agreements between the Populists and the Republican Party to support each other in political races rather than divide the non-Democratic vote between two full tickets. The results were mixed, and the Georgia Populists were narrowly defeated in the midst of massive fraud. In other states the Populists moved from disarray in 1892 to victory in 1894, including Virginia and North Carolina. In Alabama, Reuben Kolb lost his second race for governor, but fusion arrangements sent two Populists and two Republicans to Congress and won several seats in the legislature.[60]

Arrangements became more complex in 1896, when Populists began to pursue fusion with the Democrats, largely on the basis of monetary policy (McMath 1993: 196). The question of fusion with the Democrats was touchy;

many Populists appreciated the concessions that the Democrats were making on the question of monetary reform, but others remembered the fraud and violence of the Democrats in 1892 and 1894 and thought of the personal cost that they had borne in abandoning the "old party."

Those favoring fusion with the Democrats were given a boost by the Democratic nomination of the pro-silver William Jennings Bryan as their presidential contender (McMath 1993: 200–1).[61] Despite heated debate on the floor of the Populist convention of 1896, the Democrat was named as the Populist presidential candidate, with the Georgia Populist Tom Watson as his running mate—despite the fact that Bryan had a different running mate on the Democratic ticket. The situation became more absurd when Bryan proceeded to ignore the People's Party nomination. Bryan won most of the South but lost the election. He never publicly accepted Watson as a running mate, and Watson's name did not even appear on the ballot in some places. At the local level, Populists in some states proceeded with fusion arrangements with Republicans, in which they managed to make a good showing in the legislative elections in North Carolina and to run close races in Alabama, Texas, and Georgia. But the 1896 elections marked the end for any hopes of an institutionalized and independent third party, as well as any hopes for a viable interracial coalition.

### CONNECTING CLASS AND THE COLOR LINE

The relational approach to class has allowed for a reinterpretation of the importance of the movements as central vehicles for class mobilization during the last decades of the nineteenth century. Newer work has rediscovered the radical potential of the movements, particularly in the way that their republican class language underpinned far-reaching economic and political agendas that spoke for a broad coalition of "workingmen." A parallel transformation has been occurring in new work connecting race and class. This too has been shifting the ways that researchers have understood the relational nature of racial boundaries and the constructed nature of racial interests within given cultural contexts. There has yet to be a commensurate reconsideration of the radical potential of the Populists and the Knights of Labor in connecting class and the color line, however.

The classic and still influential work in the social sciences has treated both race and class as fixed categories, and has construed their connection as a matter of objective, a priori interests. This traditional framework has emphasized the role of competition between white and black working people over scarce economic, social, or political resources as the core structural root of enduring racial animosity and as the central barrier to a broader class unity.[62] Economic competition has historically been the clearest form. Different versions of the competition argument have emerged but all point to the same conclusion. Edna Bonacich argued that because racial and ethnic cleavages have historically overlapped price differences in the labor market, class-based disputes between higher-priced (native white) labor and cheaper (black or immigrant) labor has been manifest as racial conflict and exclusion. In Susan Olzak's (1992: 28) version, it was competition from "niche overlap" in labor markets that instead drove ethnic and racial antagonism.[63] Competition over political resources such as voting blocs has similarly kept white and black working people apart.[64]

This model has been dominant in analyses of nineteenth-century race relations because it explains the broader trends so well. Racial divisions *did*, in general, undermine broader attempts at class unity. Everywhere, employers used the threat of cheap labor as a way to undercut the power of the white labor movement, and the labor response was severe. Competitive struggles between white and Chinese labor ultimately took legal expression with the Chinese Exclusion Act of 1882.[65] In the South, white workers were primarily concerned with black competition. A common response was the attempt to create castelike closure around certain jobs (Bonacich 1975, 1976). More violent methods of exclusion were also employed: Olzak (1992: 107) has demonstrated a correlation between the strength of white labor unions and violent attacks on black Americans. By the same token, E. M. Beck and Stuart Tolnay (1990) have shown that hard times for southern farmers, indicated by declining prices for cotton, were correlated with increases in lynching rates. In the well-known account by William Julius Wilson, these political, economic, and physical forms of exclusion tracked together. "As the economy of the South gradually drifted toward industrial capitalism in the last quarter of the nineteenth century, the white working classes there were finally able to exert some influence on the form and content of racial stratification," he wrote. "White working-class efforts to eliminate black competition generated an elaborate system of Jim Crow segregation that was reinforced by an ideology of biological racism" (1980: 60–61).

This competition model has provided an important basis for understanding the conditions under which racial animosity generally occurs, and it provides a tempting purchase from which to understand the responses of the Knights and the Populists. Both movements faced the issue of competition and the deep-seated animosities that went along with it. For the Knights of Labor, competition was sometimes a result of manipulation by owners, as with one member from Fort Worth who complained that a company broke a strike by getting "colored men to take the longshoremens places at 40 and 60 cents per hour. The [white] men then offered to take there places back at the company terms. But the company replied that they had pledged themselves to give the colored men the work as long as they proved satisfactory."[66] The same claim about unfair competition was made with equal vitriol against Chinese and other new immigrants. Similarly, comments in the Populist papers after 1892 often complained about black voters who were too willing to be bought or manipulated by the Democratic Party. Although the Populist movement varied enormously in its openness toward blacks, potential black support for the Populists threatened to loosen Democratic control of southern politics.[67]

Treating class and race as natural categories with fixed interests is a useful and legitimate simplification that is often necessary for establishing and testing the theory across different contexts and at different times. Yet competition is not a given, and the dominance of the competition model can in fact stand in the way of an adequate appreciation of the possibilities and paradoxes inherent in the different kinds of answers that emerge.[68] Fortunately, a newer paradigm connecting class and race has begun to examine the formation, maintenance, and transformation of the interests and identities more directly.

This shift has provided an important alternative to the more rigid competition theories by pointing to the variability as well as the relational and cultural contexts in which these questions are worked out. Even the language used in this new work has taken its cues from the recent shift in class studies, as with Michael Omi and Howard Winant's coining of the term "racial formation" to describe the "sociohistorical process by which racial categories are created, inhabited, transformed and destroyed" (1994: 55).[69] Barbara Fields's rethinking of the notion of race in American history stands as one important guidepost in this new work by pointing to the variability as well as the relational and cultural context of such racial formations. While race should be seen as an "ideological medium through which people posed and apprehended basic questions of power and dominance, sovereignty and citizenship, justice and right," changes in the southern social structure after Reconstruction meant that the established narratives took on new meanings (1982: 162). Alexander Saxton (1971: 59), another pioneer in this work, pointed out for example that while the hostility of white workers toward Chinese immigrants on the West Coast was framed as an issue of competition, it resonated within the republican class framework that asserted that the basis of the competition was simultaneously economic and civic in nature.[70] Saxton also pointed out that variations across locale and industry resulted in very different patterns of interaction. In mining, the Chinese were kept out of skilled work but found a relatively stable niche in support industries, such as washing and cooking. On the railroads, despite a similar level of job segregation into unskilled manual labor, relations were far more hostile.

In the context of the South, the mining districts of central Alabama proved to be one locale that was relatively hospitable to interracial unionism in the post-Reconstruction era. Daniel Letwin's (1998) examination of the Birmingham area shows significant cooperation across the color line from the Greenback-Labor political uprising of the late 1870s through the Knights of Labor in the 1880s and the United Mine Workers of the Populist era and after. Letwin suggested that this was at least in part due to the fact that the area's industry, and most of its population, was new; without existing occupational divisions of status and skill, white acceptance of black workers in the workplace and the labor movement never had to confront longstanding racial custom.[71] At the same time, collective organizing around class continually confronted limits in the enduring social divisions surrounding race. While the class logic of "stomach equality" proved to be an acceptable position for white United Mine Workers to embrace, social equality remained a divisive idea (Roediger 1994; Kelly 2001). The experience of organizing across the color line was thus complex even in relatively favorable circumstances (see Kelly 2001; McKiven 1995).

Interestingly, it is in studies of the formation of "whiteness" as a racial category that the relational and historical construction of racial boundaries has been most obvious. This may be because the category "white" was quite variable over the course of the nineteenth century, while "black" remained relatively rigid. Successive waves of immigration shaped American understandings of who counted as "white." Before the middle of the century, for example, it was common for Americans to refer to "Anglo-Saxons" and "Celts" as entirely different "races." By the end of the century, "white" had generally become a broad enough term for both groups, but it was still not clear that

Poles, Italians, and others belonged (Jacobson 1998; Ignatiev 1995; Stoller 1997). In short, like the boundaries of the "working class," racial boundaries have held substantial power even as they have been historically variable. Moreover, the cultural frameworks of whiteness have been connected to those of class (Roediger 1991).[72]

In addition to its attention to the dynamic nature of the race/class connection, this work has also paved the way toward a more adequate reconsideration of the movements in its greater attention to the level of meaning. Rather than laud movements and their leaders as saviors or condemn them as failures in their approach to the color line, this work has attempted to understand the basis of race/class distinctions from the point of view of the people involved in making them.[73]

For the more critical and relational scholarship, David Roediger's *The Wages of Whiteness* has been particularly influential in making the point that white working-class identities in America have been in large part supported by racial identification. The terms "*white* and *worker* . . . became meaningfully paired only in the *nineteenth* century" (1991: 20) as whites moved into employment relations based on wage labor. The rise of white wage labor in the middle decades of the nineteenth century meant freedom and independence in the sense that it marked the demise of earlier forms of white indenture, and thus the partial realization of the republican dream of a nation of politically, legally, and economically independent citizens. "Freedom" in this sense took its meaning in relation to the position of black slaves. At the same time, it corresponded with the demise of the independent white artisan and yeoman, previously recognized as the paragons of the republican vision.[74] As a boundary marked by both race and class, "whiteness" was thus both unifying and exclusive. The exclusions, too, were simultaneously marked by class and race. Neil Foley (1997) has pointed out that in the early decades of the twentieth century Mexican immigrants in Texas came to be seen as distinctively nonwhite based on their economic position as much as on their ethnicity, and indeed white tenant farmers and sharecroppers themselves became "ambiguously white."

## RACE AND THE REPUBLICAN MOVEMENTS

By the end of Reconstruction, the "race question" had entered a crucial liminal period. While race relations remained contentious, concrete social relations—residential patterns, labor hierarchies, and social standing—were far from settled. The meaning of racial boundaries was being renegotiated, particularly in the South. As Woodward notes, it was "a time of experiment, testing, and uncertainty . . . alternatives were still open and real choices had to be made" (2002 [1955]: 33). These choices faced the Knights and the Populists in basic ways. They were posed as questions about racial interests ("Who stands with us and who stands against us?") and about the racial boundaries of the movements ("Who is in and who is out?"). These questions had no simple answers; instead they had to be worked out within the broader movement narratives and the ongoing daily practice of organizing. In seeking a coalition across the color line, the Knights and the Populists opened the door for a potentially transformative reconfiguration of the joint boundaries of race and class. This radical potential carried its own paradoxes and limitations, however. The legacy of the movements with regard to race has remained something of a puzzle. Coming to a better understanding of the way the movements confronted the joint boundaries of class and race is the central concern of this book; here, the movements' confrontation with the color line is sketched broadly in order to introduce the more detailed analyses that follow.

If the republican tradition shaped the way that the movements understood class, it was no less important for its connection to race. In the early part of the nineteenth century, republican identity was wide ranging but not universal. The very condition of inclusion for the producer ethic—independence—also marked an important exclusion. The growing dominance of wage labor over indentured servitude for whites and the elimination of property restrictions on white male voting rights were particularly important factors in the emergence of republicanism as a way of understanding class and politics. These changes gave white working men a direct stake in the democratic community. This republican freedom took its meaning in relation to the position of black slaves. In Saxton's words, racial exclusion "defined the boundaries of republicanism" (1990: 127).

By the last decades of the century, the distribution of citizenship and civic freedom had changed considerably. The racial boundaries of exclusion and inclusion in the established republican language of class shifted in turn. As Woodward notes, although the status of black Americans in civil society was precarious, they "voted in large numbers, held numerous elective and appointive offices, and appealed to the courts with hope for redress of grievances" (2002 [1955]: 33)."[75] The emergence by blacks into the public sphere also involved adopting the cultural symbols of American patriotism and the republican language of independence.[76] In this new context, the republican understanding of class boundaries opened the possibility for a broader coalition that included both black and white "producers" alike.

These changes did not render black labor unproblematic for the largely white movements. Instead, the relationship between black and white laborers became an open problem to be dealt with. This moment was fragile, however, and it had its own limits and contradictions. The Knights and the Populists both struggled with the degree to which black working people should be included, and their answers were sometimes also in tension with other kinds of exclusion. This has led to some significant confusion over the racial legacies of the movements and their leaders. The central problem that has to be addressed is that the movements were not simply exclusive or inclusive. Rather, they were both at once.

The tension is especially notable in the Knights of Labor. On the one hand, the Knights repeatedly maintained their commitment to organizing workers regardless of race or color. The Knights maintained a degree of interracial unity in practical matters that surprised its contemporaries and later observers alike. At times, the organization made a public show of that fact with interracial picnics, marches, and celebrations. At other times, these actions were less public, as when white Knights in Alabama's mining districts began quietly organizing black workers in an effort to undermine the ability of employers to pit the two groups against one another.[77] On the other hand, the movement often fell short of its own stated goals. While membership in some locations in the South was nearly half black, the harmony suggested in the movement's grandest claims often gave way to local tensions. The Knights explicitly excluded Chinese workers from membership and were openly hostile in their reaction to Polish, Hungarian, and Italian immigrants. Earlier immigrants, themselves at first seen as threatening, had by the 1880s amassed not only political power but also a degree of respectability as citizens and producers. The new immigrants, by contrast, were widely considered "something less than men" in the republican sense (Laurie 1997: 193, 197).[78]

The diffusion of the Knights of Labor assemblies across the South marked the beginning of an era of southern labor radicalism that was somewhat different from the emphasis of the national organization. According to Philip Foner, "race prejudice, built up assiduously for over a century by the ruling class, suffered serious setbacks at the hands of the fellowship of labor" (1955:

69). Others have painted a more pessimistic picture, seeing the Knights' racial policies as something of a failed compromise between northern reformers and the more racist views of the southern white members (McLauren 1978). What all observers have agreed upon is that race became an inescapable issue for the movement as it began organizing in the South.

In the two decades before the turn of the century, the South as a region remained roughly 30 percent black, or about ten times the average for the rest of the country.[79] Many southern counties held large black majorities, particularly in cotton-producing regions. While immigration came to be a major issue for the labor movement in the Northeast and the West, southern organizing had to confront long-standing racial attitudes and traditions that were reinforced by the localism of the southern workforce. The degree of interracial organizing was highly variable from place to place; dependent not just on the relative size of the black population but also on population shifts and the political and social legacies of different locations. Louisiana, for example, showed a relatively high level of interracial labor militancy, which was manifest in several integrated local assemblies and in interracial support for black strikes in New Orleans and in surrounding plantations. A few other locales, such as Richmond, had a very high level of both black and white membership but were organized along the lines of "separate but equal." In many other locales, there was at best mixed support for interracial organizing.

Unfortunately, it is impossible to know with certainty how many black members or even black assemblies were in existence at this time. Of the southern assemblies, 116 are known to have been exclusively black and an additional 19 were mixed race. Due to underreporting, especially after 1887, many black Knights of Labor assemblies are not designated as such in the official records, and so these figures almost certainly underestimate black involvement in the movement (Garlock and Builder 1973a; Garlock 1982). In 1886, the Knights' general secretary estimated that there were 60,000 black members, and the following year the New York *Sun* reported that there were over 400 black local assemblies, and that "they are growing at a rate out of proportion to the increase of white members" (Foner 1955: 67). In practice, however, Powderly and other leaders of the Knights were reluctant to put real pressure on white members, and there were serious misgivings on the part of both blacks and whites about the stability of such a coalition (Foner 1955: 67; 1974: 52–58). While no explicit discrimination could be placed in the bylaws of the local assemblies, most commonly white and black members were organized separately.

The Populists had a similarly complex response to the "color line." Here, too, the legacy of Populism has remained an open question. Unlike the Knights, the Farmers' Alliance did not directly organize black workers. Instead, it worked in conjunction with a parallel but weaker organization known as the "Colored Farmers' Alliance." Nevertheless, the Alliance saw itself as working for the benefit of all farmers, and the term "Alliance movement" was often used to encompass both organizations. Moreover, the strict organizational separation broke down as the Alliance dissolved into the People's Party. White Populists, often avowed racists, claimed to be working with black Republicans only as a matter of common economic and political interest. This in itself was an astonishing affront to southern traditions, and despite the partial nature of the overture it opened the possibility for the emergence of a potentially transformative coalition.

Existing studies have generally accepted the idea that the Alliance movement held some promise for black tenants, sharecroppers, and farm laborers. Some authors have been more skeptical of the sincerity of the white Alliance's commitment to the interracial project, however.[80] The development of the Alliance's approach to race was complex, reflecting the development of the organization itself.

From the beginning, the Alliance maintained that the class interests of black and white farmers were alike. "Since the negroes have been organized in the Farmers' Alliance," wrote the national secretary-treasurer of the white organization, "they have made considerable progress in the study of economic questions, and, judging from the utterances of their leaders, they are willing and anxious to sever all past party affiliations, and join hands with the white farmers of the South and West in any movement looking to a betterment of their condition" (Turner 1975 [1891]: 277–78). At the same time, the white Alliance never seriously attempted a more meaningful incorporation of black Alliancemen. The early history of the movement shows, however, that an integrated movement organization was not an entirely foregone conclusion.

There was no mention of race in the first National Alliance constitution, which was developed in 1887 upon the merger of the Texas and Louisiana Alliances. In many ways, the document espoused a very inclusive vision. Echoing the Knights, the stated purpose of the Alliance was to "demand equal rights to all and special favors to none." The only explicit membership qualification was that members had to be at least twenty-five years old. In practice, however, the constitution restricted the membership to whites by requiring new state Alliances to hold to the membership requirements of either the Texas or the Louisiana organization, both of which had racially restricted membership (Dunning 1975 [1891]: 58–61).[81] By 1889, the constitution still focused on a broad range of farmers, but the exclusive racial boundary of the movement was made plain. The wording of the new membership clause was as follows: "No person shall be admitted a member unless he has been a citizen of the State in which he resides for six months past, and not then unless he be a farmer, farm-laborer, country mechanic, country school teacher, country physician, country minister of the Gospel, and editors of strictly agricultural journals, of good moral character; believes in the Supreme Being; of industrious habits, and is a white person over the age of sixteen years."[82]

The racial boundary had to be negotiated again when the Alliance absorbed the Agricultural Wheel. The Wheel was not an all-white organization, rather its constitution simply stated that white and black members had to be organized in separate locals (Dunning 1975 [1891]: 209). The black membership of the Wheel was likely small, but black chapters in Tennessee and Alabama remained in operation even after the parent organization merged with the Alliance (Holmes 1975: 188). In the new Alliance constitution, the white-only clause was moved to the top of the list of restrictions. Yet alongside this more explicit exclusion was a seemingly contradictory new clause: "*Provided,* that each State and Territory shall have the right to prescribe the eligibility of applicants for membership, in reference to color, within the limits of the same. *Provided further,* that none but white men shall be elected as delegates to the Supreme Council" (Dunning 1975 [1891]: 171). To the extent that the self-contradicting membership statement meant anything, it indicated that the state-level Alliance chapters were free to make their own arrangements regarding the racial policies of membership when the Alliance absorbed the members of the Wheel. But any black members of the State Alliances would be barred from membership in the national organization, and therefore would be ineligible for election by the states to seats in the national offices.

For its part, the Colored Alliance was also formed as a secret society following the fraternal and ritualistic model of the Knights of Labor and directly paralleling the model of the white Alliance. Relatively little documentary evidence from the Colored Alliance exists, and the organization has generally been relegated to a curious footnote in the history of the white Alliance. The organization was started in late 1886 in Houston County, Texas. The handful of local chapters met together in a Baptist church to plan the growth of the movement. "After some discussion and earnest prayer, it was unanimously agreed that union and organization had become necessary to the earthly salvation of the colored race," remarked the white superintendent of the organization, R. M. Humphrey (1975 [1891]: 288). As a former Baptist minister among other things, Humphrey was the public face of the organization. The Colored Farmers' Alliance remained substantially run by blacks, however—its initial leadership was all black and the organization maintained black officers throughout its history. The exceptions were the superintendent himself and the other white lecturers who did liaison work between the Colored Farmers' Alliance and the white Alliance (Humphrey 1975 [1891]).[83]

An official charter was granted through the state of Texas for the "Alliance of Colored Farmers" in February 1887, and the organization began to spread through the rest of Texas and then through the South as a whole. A weekly paper, the *National Alliance,* was founded in 1889 and ran for several years.[84] By 1891 there were charters for state Alliances in nearly every southern state (Humphrey 1975 [1891]: 290). As with the white Alliance, the total membership of the Colored Alliance is impossible to gauge accurately. The official pronouncements stated that there were 1.2 million members.[85] In all likelihood, this was a wildly inflated number, but the quick growth of the organization clearly reflected a latent interest among black farmers.[86] By 1889, the *National Economist* reported that there were "two or three Alliance organizations among the colored people. They are said to be very similar in laws and usage to the Alliance organized among the whites."[87] One of the "Alliances" may have actually been the remaining black chapters of the Wheel.[88] The other organization (also called the Colored Farmers' Alliance) claimed a membership of 250,000 and merged with Humphrey's Colored Farmers' Alliance in 1890.[89]

The extent of the Colored Alliance's ties with the white Alliance, as well as its success in its own right, has been generally underestimated. In fact, by 1889 the formal relations between the white and black Alliances were close enough that they could not be considered completely separate entities. In that year and the next, the twin Alliances held their annual meetings in the same cities and at the same time, and each sent representatives to the other's meetings (Humphrey 1975 [1891]: 291).[90] The 1890 meetings of the Arkansas state Alliances met concurrently in the state capitol building, with the whites occupying the house chamber and the blacks in the senate.[91]

Humphrey's own history of the movement reports that the Colored Alliance founded some of its own cooperative trading stores with "varying success" (Humphrey 1975 [1891]).[92] The most radical and direct action by the Colored Alliance was, however, also one of the most unfortunate. Humphrey issued a circular from the Colored Alliance stating that on September 12, 1891, black cotton pickers across the South would strike in order to obtain the wage of one dollar per one hundred pounds of cotton—about twice the prevailing wage. The strike was a disaster for the Colored Alliance. Several days before it was set to begin, southern newspapers got word of the plans and widely denounced them. Most farm workers ignored the strike call altogether, and many who did go on strike were immediately fired. A related strike a week later in Arkansas was brutally repressed. Thirteen strikers there were accused of killing a police inspector. Nine suspects were arrested and lynched before they got to trial, while another escaped but was later shot.[93]

The year 1891 should have marked a further joining of the white and black Alliances within a broad confederation of reform movements. A circular in February 1891 announced that "all duly authorized delegations from the National Farmers' Alliance and Industrial Union, the National Colored Farmers' Alliance and Co-Operative Union, and the Knights of Labor and the National Citizens Alliance did meet in the city of Washington, D.C., and agree to enter into an organization to be known as the 'Confederation of Industrial Organizations'" which would "co-operate in securing the reforms in legislation now being demanded by the necessities of the producers of this country."[94] The prominent placement of the Colored Alliance was striking, and a relatively large number of seats were reserved for the black delegates.[95] Unfortunately, the disastrous cotton pickers' strike decimated the colored Alliance organization before the meeting took place. It is not clear that the decisions of that meeting would have been to the liking of the Colored Alliance delegates had they been there in force; the meeting cemented the decision of the reform movement, and especially the Alliance, to back the emerging People's Party.

Whatever tensions existed between the Colored Farmers' Alliance and the southern Alliance on matters of policy were only strained by the move of the white organization into independent political action.[96] The white Alliance was split over the issue, but so was the Colored Farmers' Alliance. Reminding the black delegates that as farmers they had common interests with the white Alliance, Humphrey argued that black Alliancemen should give "earnest attention to this all-absorbing question, and if by spirit of mutual compromise and conciliation you may be able to secure such pledges from the great labor organizations now represented in this city as will warrant reciprocal and hearty co-operation, doubtless great good will result to both the white and colored races."[97]

The Colored Alliance of Georgia had issued a proclamation several months earlier declaring their intent to stay out of politics.[98] Coalition with the People's Party might easily sap the remaining strength of the Republicans, and thus the remnants of black electoral power. Yet for many black Alliancemen the decision was not so clear, particularly because the Democratic machinery had become so dominant since the end of Reconstruction, and widespread efforts to contain black electoral power had badly decayed the Republican Party in many places. In several states People's Party clubs sprang up from the ashes of the Colored Farmers' Alliance. The degree to which practical coalitions between black and white voters were forged varied from state to state, for reasons that had as much to do with the history of party alignment and the resulting political identities as with narrowly conceived economic and political interests. By one well-known account, interracial support for the third party was most viable in Georgia, Alabama, and Texas, while the coalition was less promising in Virginia, North Carolina, Louisiana, and Tennessee, and even worse elsewhere (Gaither 1977).

## CONCLUSION

Material interests as well as political and status interests have structured the formation of race relations in the United States in clear ways. As a result, entrenched divisions and hostilities have stood in the way of interracial movements and broader social transformations. Yet interests can be understood in different ways, and at certain moments cooperation has seemed a more expeditious path. In this chapter I have provided a sketch of the movements and their approach to class and race boundaries within the context of two significant theoretical debates—one about how to conceptualize class and the other about how to understand the connection between class and race.

While the Knights of Labor spoke mostly for the "mechanics" and the Populists for the "hayseeds," both spoke the same basic language and emerged from the same republican traditions. Over and above the tenuous interorganizational ties that bound them directly to one another, the movements were made possible by the fact that industrial laborers, artisans, and independent farmers and tenants all came to see themselves as a class of "producers" with common interests. They found in the movements a new manifestation of an old language that made sense of their frustrations. This language offered not only a broad understanding of class but also provided a way for working people to articulate both the economic and civic stakes involved in the social upheaval of the Gilded Age.

Instead of seeing the movements as romantic failures or as backward-looking exceptions to a more hard-headed industrial or trade consciousness, newer work on the movements has not viewed the republican tradition of the movements simply as a hindrance but rather as a radicalism of tradition—a language that placed radical demands for social change into a traditional language that resonated with popular, if "backward-looking," conceptions of work, community, and democracy. In this case, the radicalism of tradition opened up a space for the consideration of sweeping change, from electoral reform to replacing the basis of the national currency and even replacing a competitive economy with a cooperative system of production. In terms of politics, the economy, and social status, republicanism shaped the resources that the movements thought to be at stake in their struggle. In particular, it was independence and not only accumulation that the movements were after.

The theoretical shift has also allowed a reconsideration of the radical possibilities for a renegotiation of interests surrounding race within the movements. One of the most important possibilities opened by the movements was the one that was initially least expected by their founders and least desired by many of their members—that is, a uniting of "producers" not only across the skill divide but across the color line as well. In attempting to organize across the color line—albeit in a partial and sometimes ambivalent way—the movements provide an important exception to the general trend of the racial exclusion and hostility of the class movements of the late nineteenth century and early twentieth. But this republican cultural frame also imposed limits to the interracial project. Both the Knights and the Populists justified forms of racial and ethnic exclusion even as they touted their inclusive vision. The Knights remained hostile to many new immigrants while the Populists rejected many

CHAPTER 2

# RACE, CLASS, AND REPUBLICAN VIRTUE IN THE KNIGHTS OF LABOR

The (outside) coloring of a candidate shall not disbar him from admission; rather let the coloring of his mind and heart be the test.—TERENCE V. POWDERLY

The historical record is unclear about how the racial legacy of the Knights should be understood. As Melton Alonzo McLaurin noted in his account of the southern Knights, "much depends on whether the viewer sees the bottle as half-full or half-empty" (1978: 147). On the one hand, the Knights went further than any other labor organization before it in organizing white and black workers together in a fraternal, democratic movement. The Knights of Labor maintained that working people could advance only by uniting across the "color line." The movement variously claimed moral and strategic reasons for engaging in interracial organizing. Strategically, the movement argued that black workers could either be organized as fellow Knights or be faced as competitors in the labor market. In moral terms, the Knights of Labor argued that as "producers of wealth," black working people deserved a place in the labor movement. Terence

Powderly's early decision on membership policy made plain that moral worth, not skin color, should be the criteria for membership in the Knights. Subsequent claims from the movement's leaders and members alike suggest that white Knights, despite frequent misgivings about their black "brothers," accepted this logic.

On the other hand, the organization seemed to contradict its own position by simultaneously advocating racial closure. Even as it claimed that it did not recognize the color line, it explicitly barred Chinese immigrants from becoming members and singled them out for ugly racial caricatures. Less often noted is the fact that the other new immigrants, particularly the Hungarians, Italians, and Poles, were vilified by the movement in a very similar way.[1] While the latter groups might now be treated under the rubric of "ethnicity" rather than "race," the Knights of Labor saw the new eastern and southern European immigrants as racially different.[2] The movement also provided both strategic and moral reasons for advocating racial closure. In moral terms, the new immigrants were thought to be unworthy because they were dirty, ignorant, and lazy—qualities that at the time were widely ascribed to blacks. Strategically, while the movement argued that it should organize black workers because they otherwise would be competitors, the hostile reaction to the new immigrants was justified on the grounds that they *were* competitors.

What allowed for the unprecedented level of interracial openness for the Knights of Labor, and where were its limits? Some of the answers to this question concern the resources and the practical experience of organizing in local settings—issues that are central in the chapters following. In this chapter, however, I look to the movement narratives of the Knights of Labor in order to address a different set of resources and constraints—those tied to the culture of the movement. In addition, I examine the way that class and race boundaries were jointly drawn in the movement-level narratives of the Knights of Labor. Specifically, the question I address is how the movement's underlying "language" of class shaped the way that it understood the problem of race, and why the claims about black workers and new immigrants developed so differently.

Securing a handle on the meaning of this connection is not easy, because it necessitates moving past the convenient explanations of the Knights themselves as well as the explanations of later observers. The connection becomes visible in the broader structure of the movement narratives' social narratives.[3]

The narratives provide an empirical window onto otherwise latent boundary distinctions and the way these shaped the movement's understanding of its interests. My focus is not on the stories of individual Knights but on the pattern linking the Knights' consideration of different groups to their claims about interest.[4] While every movement produces discourse to make sense of itself and its interests, not all of this discourse comes together into a coherent narrative form. Narratives include at least two defining elements. First, narratives involve a cast of characters who are either acting or being acted upon. Second, narratives incorporate basic plots that connect events together through direct or indirect causal accounts (Somers 1992; Bruner 1990).[5] Meaningful narratives can be said to exist when regularly occurring plots connect to key characters in a stable way.

In the first part of this chapter I outline the structure of the Knights of Labor's narratives connecting race and class. Here, the important characters are the racial "others" that the movement confronted. The plots are provided in the concrete frames of interest that linked race and class positions.[6] How did the white Knights decide which racial "others" were with them and which were against them? For the Knights, three distinct narratives connected class and race interests. The first two involved black workers and new immigrants, respectively. The third narrative concerned the changing social position of the white workers themselves and relied heavily on the comparison of "wage slavery" to chattel slavery. It was at its core a story about the social position of white workers. The apparent contradiction between the Knights' responses to Southern blacks and new immigrants was largely unacknowledged—they were simply part of different stories. Despite their differences, the stories were culturally of a piece. Each reflected the movement's republican understanding of class, which identified civic virtue as a central resource at stake in class struggle.

The following sections explore each of these narratives in turn, paying close attention to the level of meaning. My goal in these sections is to explain the cultural logic of the collective narratives. The last section of this chapter provides a bridge to the locally grounded chapters that follow by exploring how the movement-level narratives mapped onto local discussions of race among Southern members. In this section, my analysis shifts to examine letters from the South to the Knights' leader Terence Powderly. While the local understandings followed the movement-level narratives in broad terms, they also indicated a more ambivalent stand on racial issues that reflected the practical problems of interracial organizing.

### THE ORGANIZATIONAL UNDERSTANDING OF RACE

As George Steinmetz (1992: 490) has pointed out, movement-level narratives, such as those produced by the Knights, are emergent properties. Although they are empirically observable when individual-level stories are aggregated, they are not wholly present in the consciousness of individual actors. While it is relatively easy to identify individual-level narratives, it is more difficult to do the same for movement-level narratives. I employ a simple yet systematic method for doing so.

The official Knights of Labor newspaper, the *Journal of United Labor*, serves as the main source for my analysis of the movement narratives. The *Journal* was the most important site for the articulation of the movement's collective goals and identity, and it served an important integrative function in an otherwise far-flung organization. Apart from the annual General Assembly of the Knights, which only a few regional representatives could attend, the *Journal* was the only open means of communication for the organization at large. The paper published articles on the principles of the movement, biographies of its leaders, and reports on local labor conditions and organizing activity. The paper also solicited letters and editorials by members from across the country.[7] Subscription to the paper was voluntary, but strongly encouraged. In areas where the one dollar annual price was too much for individual members to bear, local assemblies were encouraged to sustain a shared subscription.

My analysis is based on the items that referenced both race and class in the *Journal of United Labor* from the paper's beginning in 1880 through the end of 1890.[8] While virtually every item in the paper was related to the class identities, interests, or positions of the Knights as "laborers," "producers," or "workingmen," a subset of these items also touched on the subject of race. Some included specific racial or ethnic labels ("white," "colored," "Chinaman," "Poles"), while others included discussion of racial statuses, such as a comparison of the social position of workers to that of chattel slaves before emancipation. The discussions of race came from leaders, organizers, and regular members, reflecting the relatively democratic nature of the discourse in the *Journal* generally.[9] I outline the structure of the narratives using two key elements of the Knights' own discussions. The first is the central actor in the

TABLE 2 Racial/ethnic "others"

| Group | Number | % |
|---|---|---|
| Black | 103 | 33.4 |
| Immigrant | 117 | 38.0 |
| Chinese, Chinaman, etc. | 42 | |
| Hungarian(s), etc. | 18 | |
| Italian(s), etc. | 17 | |
| Pole(s), etc. | 8 | |
| Other ethnic/national | 32 | |
| General | 79 | 25.6 |
| White | 9 | 2.9 |
| Total | 308 | 100.0 |

Note: Because some communications named more than one "other," the total exceeds the N of communications.

narratives—the racial and ethnic "others" to which the Knights' discussions referred. The second element is the frame of interest that tied race and class together in the Knights of Labor communications. These frames provided the "plots" for the movement-level narratives that are discussed below.

The terms used by the Knights to designate racial and ethnic boundaries reflected the social situation in which they were organizing.[10] Roughly a third of the mentions of racial "others" referred to black Americans. The particular terms that the Knights used accorded with the polite customs of the day—"colored" was most common, followed by "negro" and "black." The second category referred to foreign ethnic or national groups, primarily new immigrants. Chinese (also "Chinamen" and "coolie") were by far the most often mentioned, but Hungarians, Italians, and Poles were each the subject of a considerable number of comments in the *Journal.* Various other ethnic and national groups came up—including Irish, Swedes, "Hindoos," and Arabs—but none more than a few times. The remaining categories listed in table 2 require some explanation. The third category referred to racial difference in general terms, without naming a specific group. Instead, the communications mentioned the problem of "race" abstractly, or made a more specific reference to chattel slavery. There was also a minor category in which "white" was the relevant racial other, a product of items from black correspondents.

Whether these groups were seen as potential collaborators or as competitors had to do with the frames of interest that linked race and class in move-

TABLE 3 Frames of interest in movement discourse

| Interest frame | Number | % |
|---|---|---|
| Interracial organizing | 71 | 27.3 |
| Positive evaluations | 35 | |
| Neutral evaluations | 20 | |
| Mixed/negative evaluations | 16 | |
| Material/political interests | 78 | 30.0 |
| Competing interests | 69 | |
| Similar interests | 9 | |
| Slavery and social position | 75 | 28.8 |
| Wage slaves like chattel slaves | 59 | |
| White slaves like chattel slaves | 16 | |
| Other | 36 | 13.8 |
| Total | 260 | 100.0 |

ment discourse.[11] A number of cultural frames linked class and race interests for the Knights; each had its own minor variations. The first frame concerned interracial organizing. Most of the items either had positive evaluations of the prospects for such organizing, or else reported neutrally on the progress of the interracial project in various local contexts. A smaller number had mixed (or in one case, negative) evaluations. What is interesting is that this frame *presumed* common class interest and focused instead on its practical application. This was true even within the mixed evaluations, where authors were generally in favor of such organizing but reported the opposition of others.[12] By contrast, the second frame actively questioned whether the movement shared material or political interests with the racial others it confronted. The vast majority of the communications here focused on competing interests between groups, although a few statements took a different position by claiming that that group interests might be complimentary. The third major frame was of a different order: it was concerned with understanding the current social position of working people generally by categorizing workers as "wage slaves" or "white slaves."[13]

The important issue is how these characters and plots coalesced into meaningful narratives for the movement. In other words, how were the boundaries drawn? While there was by no means a mechanical connection between the two elements, there was a significant association between them (see table 4).[14] In fact, three central narratives emerge in the connection.[15] The first narrative connected black workers to the "interracial organizing" frame. The second

TABLE 4 Movement narratives of race and class

| Frame | Black | Immigrant | General | White | Total |
|---|---|---|---|---|---|
| Interracial organizing | **46 (44.7%)** | 2 (1.7%) | 16 (20.2%) | 8 (88.9%) | 72 (23.4%) |
| Material/political interests | 19 (18.5%) | **92 (78.6%)** | 4 (5.1%) | 1 (11.1%) | 116 (37.7%) |
| Slavery and social position | 20 (19.4%) | 8 (6.8%) | **52 (65.8%)** | 0 (0.0%) | 80 (26.0%) |
| Other | 18 (17.5%) | 15 (12.8%) | 7 (8.9%) | 0 (0.0%) | 40 (13.0%) |
| Total | 103 (100.0%) | 117 (100.0%) | 79 (100.0%) | 9 (100.0%) | 308 (100.0%) |

Note: Lambda = .427, approx. sig.: .000; Uncertainty coefficient = .275, approx. sig.: .000.

linked the immigrants to a discussion of material and political interests. The third was different, in that it reflected a way of talking about "race" without naming a particular group. Here, general references to race were tied to the "slavery and social position" frame. This narrative was important because it became a site for the construction of "whiteness" within the movement.[16]

Before tackling the interpretive work that is central to the next section, it is necessary to address the issue of temporality in the narratives. The first narrative was most prominent during the peak years for the movement, 1885–1887, when southern organizing was progressing at its fastest pace and the Knights for the first time gained a national reputation for organizing black workers. In relative terms, the second narrative was most prevalent in 1880–1884—before and immediately following the Chinese Exclusion Act. It is worth noting, however, that it remained prominent in the later years as well. The third narrative, like the first, was most prominent in the early period, although it was relatively well represented throughout.

More interesting than the short-term shifts is the fact that each of these narratives was tied to a longer history. The way they were appropriated by the Knights was linked to the changing distribution of the republican notion of "civic virtue." The historian David Montgomery has made the claim that at its emergence in the early part of the nineteenth century, republicanism "framed nascent awareness of class conflict in the vocabulary of patriotism, race, and rights" (1993: 6). Two major developments were important in the emergence of labor republicanism, according to Montgomery: the growing dominance of wage labor over indentured servitude for whites, and the elimination of property restrictions on white male voting rights. These changes gave white workingmen a direct stake in the democratic community.

TABLE 5 Temporal changes in narratives

| Narrative | 1880–84 | 1885–87 | 1888–90 |
|---|---|---|---|
| 1. Interracial organizing + black | 3 (15.8%) | 19 (38.0%) | 24 (19.8%) |
| 2. Material/political interests + immigrant | 10 (52.6%) | 21 (42.0%) | 61 (50.4%) |
| 3. Slavery/social position + general | 6 (31.6%) | 10 (20.0%) | 36 (29.8%) |
| Total | 19 (100.0%) | 50 (100.0%) | 121 (100.0%) |

Note: Totals reflect number of communications in narratives.

A central element of the republican ideals and the producerist class idiom was the idea of civic virtue, or the ability of groups to collectively engage in civil society. To a movement steeped in republican ideals, the degree of political and social autonomy of different groups was the yardstick by which they were measured. Groups that were far from the republican ideals of virtuous self-reliance, organization, and autonomy were likely to be rejected as potential members. They were seen as undesirable in the sense that they did not share the goals of the movement, but also in the sense that they were thought to be morally beneath those goals. They were also seen as unorganizable. Due to servile status, social atomization, or discrimination, certain groups were not embedded into the organizational fabric of civic life. Groups with little or no embeddedness in civic organizations posed a structural problem to labor movements generally. As a practical matter, such groups would likely prove hard to organize, since they could not be drawn in through existing institutions and since they may have little to gain from joining the movement. More fundamentally, the movement was unlikely to identify members of such groups as fellow travelers, given that they did not seem to share the same cultural values.

The vocabulary of patriotism and rights was thus defined against those who did not possess such civic virtue. In the early part of the century, this meant blacks. As David Roediger has argued "That blacks were largely non-citizens will surprise few, but it is important to emphasize the extent to which they were seen as *anticitizens*" (1991: 57, emphasis in original). By the late nineteenth century, a similar class language could grant a very different view of blacks than the one Roediger described. Southern blacks were formally free, but in urban areas especially many were also engaging in the same type of political and civic associations that the labor movement had so valued. This created tensions, as it meant that black workers became potential threats to the tenuous social status and political muscle held by white workers. But it was harder to maintain that they were unorganizable or undesirable in explicitly class terms. In short, the color line did not suddenly became less salient for the southern working class but it appeared more permeable. Other groups, however, were culturally written out of the movement in almost exactly the same terms that blacks were in the 1830s. Chinese and other new immigrant workers were not participants in the system of civic and political associations in their communities. Older immigrant groups, such as the Irish had by the 1880s amassed not only political power but also a degree of respectability as republican producers. The new immigrants, having neither, were widely considered "something less than men" in the republican sense (Laurie 1997: 197). In the eyes of native-born Knights, imbued with republican rhetoric, this lack of participation in the democratic community was a sign of their degraded state. Their lack of civic and political organization was also a practical sign that they did not share the movement's goals, even if they were in the same class position.[17]

### INTERRACIAL ORGANIZATION AND BLACK WORKERS

An 1881 editorial in the *Journal of United Labor* provided a bright view of the possibility for labor solidarity: "[The Knights organization] goes forth as the pioneer in labor reform, to persuade the toiler, the artisan, and the skilled mechanic . . . male and female, of whatever shade or color, to banish forever the spirit of selfishness from their minds and sweep it out of their Assemblies, . . . to feel that our brother's weal is our weal, and our brother's woe is our woe."[18] This sunny outlook hid the many practical difficulties that were to face the movement in the course of interracial organizing at the local level. It also elided the fact that the movement's claim to color blindness did not extend to all groups. Yet it did accurately convey the way that the first movement-level narrative presumed common class interest when it came to black workers.

When this statement was written, the movement had not yet begun to organize black workers in earnest. While the generally optimistic character of this first narrative was present during the early period of the movement's national growth, it might have died out after the organization began to confront the practical problems that came with interracial organizing. Instead, however, it became more firmly entrenched after 1885, when the movement did in fact organize substantial numbers of black workers, particularly in the South. The problems that were experienced at the local level, many of them reflected in the letters and notices sent to the *Journal*, did not stifle the movement's claim that black workers were also "producers" and thus to exclude them would be both practically and morally wrong. As one Southern Knight put it, "The problem down here is not a race or a color problem, but it is here as elsewhere, How shall the wealth producers secure the results of their industry?"[19] At least within the logic of this narrative, the only way to secure results was to organize black and white workers together.

The Knights of Labor leadership generally took a more progressive and moralistic position on racial matters than did southern members (see McLauren 1978). It would be a mistake, however, to draw this distinction between movement elites and rank-and-file white members too cleanly. It is significant in this regard that the majority of the statements on interracial organizing in the South come from letters—many from southern members—rather than from editorials. Many of these communications were in the form of value-neutral statements that related the practical ups and downs of the organizational effort without questioning the underlying class logic of doing so. "Our Assembly is young, and the members green, and the worst of all is we are uneducated," wrote one member from Summertown, Georgia. "The best of all is the majority of our members are willing to do anything they can for the Order. We are receiving applications at each meeting. Our Assembly is composed of both sexes and both races."[20] Other communications provided mixed evaluations of interracial organizing. In these, the authors were generally in favor of the project but reported internal problems surrounding its application.

Most central to this narrative were the communications that provided positive evaluations of the effort, often despite significant external opposition. Several letters reported that local elites were determined to undermine interracial class alliance. One white member wrote from South Carolina to say that the Knights there were told they could not meet in the Masonic Hall if blacks were invited. "That is their excuse," wrote the member, "but I know better. I see through their little game—they want to break up the Knights of Labor here, but we intend to have the Knights of Labor in spite of all opposition, for we know our noble Order is right."[21] At times, the response from white elites was more vehement. The strongest response came from planters and large landlords in rural counties:

> We protest against the high-handed treatment which the high-toned "gentleman" farmers of South Carolina are meting out to their colored farm laborers, who have had the audacity to organize into labor unions. For the past two weeks wild dispatches have been sent to the newspapers about an imagined threatened outbreak of negroes in certain counties in that state . . . All this fright would have been amusing in old slave times; to-day it is ridiculous. Nevertheless, the white men of one of the "disturbed" neighborhoods met on Wednesday, organized and began work. All were heavily armed, reports the correspondent, and they did their work quickly, quietly and well. They compelled the labor secretaries to show their lists of members, who were summarily brought before an "original court" . . . the laborers were thoroughly frightened, made to promise to steer clear of labor organizations in the future, and then sent home.[22]

In contrast to the letters and notices, editorial statements tended to discuss more abstractly the importance of organizing black workers. One early editorial established the general tone. "We should be false to every principle of our Order should we exclude from membership any man who gains his living by honest toil, on account of his color or creed," it stated. "Our platform is broad enough to take in all." This moral claim was connected to a strategic one—black workers must be organized or else they would be faced in the labor market as competitors. The same editorial continued:

> In every portion of our broad land, whenever a strike is resorted to . . . what is the first thing done by the employer? Does he not seek far and near for those who will take the place of the men on strike, without inquiring their nationality, color, or creed? Certainly he does. The only question asked is, "Will he work for less wages?" and if he will, he can go to work at your job and you can go tramping. Why, then, should workingmen allow a foolish prejudice against color to keep out of our organization anyone who might be used as a tool to aid the employer in grinding down wages? In the coal regions of Illinois, Kansas, Indiana, Ohio, and West Virginia, during the strikes last winter, colored men were put into the mines to take the place of the strikers, and we ask any white miner who objects to the admission of colored men into our Order, this question: If you are forced to strike against a reduction of wages, will your employer stop to inquire the color or nationality of any man who will take your place at the reduction offered?[23]

In this narrative, the problem of black labor was thus a problem of organizing. If black and white workers could come together within the movement, they could attain common class goals. This construction, as opposed to the obvious alternative of social closure and exclusion, rested upon the understanding of black workers as a morally and politically redeemable people:

> What are we to do with a race in our midst numbering 7,000,000?—a race becoming a competitor with the white race in all the affairs of life? They cannot, by reason of citizenship, be set aside—ostracized. They cannot, by reason of rapidly advancing mental development, be shut out from the competition of scholarship and of literature in its various forms . . . The Knights have a strong following in the colored people. They are good Knights, and so far have occasioned no trouble to the Order. We extend them our hearty recognition.[24]

There are a number of things that are remarkable about this formulation. The first is that it shows quite clearly that the narrative was not free from paternalism or even racism. Most white Knights thought that black members needed benevolent guidance—an assumption that caused a great deal of tension in the course of organizing at the local level. Second, the statement shows that the question of competition, when it arose, was linked to a discussion about organizing rather than to a discussion of opposing class interests. Third, and most important, the statement links inclusion to civic resources, expressed through a language of citizenship. This statement was more explicit in this regard than most, but the idea was implicit throughout.

The issue of citizenship brings up the longer historical context of this narrative. Civic virtue was identified as a key resource in labor discourse at least from the early nineteenth century. As Roediger (1991: 46) has noted, however, the claims by white workers to this resource cut two ways at once. On the one hand, it differentiated the producers from those above them who sought to reduce their power. On the other hand, it differentiated them from those below who were unable to claim such civic autonomy. Before the Civil War, black slaves were the clearest case of those below. By the late nineteeth century, the Knights of Labor had a very different perspective. What changed was not the republican class language that identified civic virtue as an important resource for the Knights, but rather the social position of black workers and, consequently, their command of this key resource. Southern blacks were formally free, but especially in the urban areas many were also engaging in the same type of political and civic associations that the labor movement valued (see Rachleff 1989; Rabinowitz 1978).

A capacity for civic virtue meant at a basic level an appreciation for the value of collective organization in order to pursue what Tocqueville had called "self-interest rightly understood," as well as a capacity to maintain such organization. Understandably, a central concern within the Knights' narrative was the capacity of black workers to maintain Knights assemblies. "Our colored brethren have a poor existence so far, but they are 'turning a new leaf' and manifesting more interest, and their meetings are better attended than heretofore; and it is to be hoped that they will yet build up a prosperous and useful Assembly. Our Master Workman and other members from our Assembly frequently visit them and encourage and help them along," stated one letter from Hot Springs, Arkansas.[25] A later report from Little Rock provided an even more positive assessment: "There are a dozen or more of these Assemblies, numbering, perhaps, a thousand men, making wonderful advancement, intellectually and morally. No one appreciates the order more than they; none have received closer attention or more wholesome instructions."[26] A traveling lecturer compared the republican enthusiasm of black members favorably with those of whites: "I delivered three lectures while in Monroe [Louisiana] —one public and one private to the white Local. The night I lectured to the colored local was rainy and disagreeable; but withal the audience was good, showing that the colored people are interested in the labor movement."[27]

It is also striking that the white narrative was mirrored by black members and movement supporters. A black member wrote from LA 9378 in Bartow, Georgia, to say that generally positive feelings existed between black and white members in his largely agricultural part of the state. As to the republican worthiness of black workers, he added "a few have, by strict economy, saved sufficient to purchase homes of from half and acre to one hundred acres in extent; and I think if my race (the colored) is given fair opportunities and living wages, they will prove themselves worthy members of the Order and society at large."[28] A black supporter wrote from Philadelphia to praise the Knights for organizing black workers when other labor organizations failed to do so. "The Southern negro must be made a self-respecting and respected man through labor organizations," he said. "If the Knights of Labor will assume this task, I think they will do a work that no other body has attempted to do, and will forever deserve to be called the saviors and up-builders not only of a race, but of the whole country, and will receive the unstinted praise of unborn millions."[29]

### COMPETITION, MORALITY, AND THE NEW IMMIGRANTS

The difference between the first and second narratives was neatly packaged in a short notice in the *Journal of United Labor* that read, simply, "in Savannah, GA., colored laborers refuse to work with Italians."[30] Labor competition over material resources was a common issue in Knights' communications, and it was a theme at the heart of this statement. Yet this statement makes clear that for the white Knights the competition came not from the black workers they primarily encountered in the South but rather the recent immigrants on the East and West coasts. While the first narrative suggested that organization was the way to overcome divisions, this was predicated on an understanding of black workers as able to share the civic goals of the Knights of Labor along with its organizational means. Yet the Knights wrote other groups out of the labor movement in almost exactly the same terms. As the second narrative shows, not everyone was thought to possess civic virtue. Instead of the civic potential ascribed to black workers, this narrative was driven by a supposed lack of civic virtue among new immigrants.

The Knights' reaction to the "immigration question" was both intense and long lived. In editorials, letters, and speeches, the Knights vehemently objected to "pauper labor." As the only ethnic group expressly excluded from membership in the Knights, the Chinese were singled out for the ugliest depiction in this narrative. But Hungarians, Poles, and Italians were similarly portrayed as ignorant, dirty, and reduced by poverty to a nearly subhuman level.

Chinese labor was particularly singled out as morally degraded, mentally limited, and physically grotesque. "China is the reservoir for cheap labor in the world," W. W. Stone and the California congressman William W. Morrow wrote in their article on Chinese Immigration in *The Labor Movement: The Problem of To-Day*. "Walled in by laws, customs and religion, her people have crowded against each other until her civilization has become stunted, her people pygmies, and women slaves" (1887: 429). Not all immigrant groups were vilified in this way. Immigrants from northern Europe, coming to northeastern cities that had already absorbed many of their countrymen in earlier waves of immigration, were not classified with the Chinese and southern

Europeans—who were described as able to withstand physical conditions of diet and housing that would not sustain American workingmen.

On the surface, these racialized descriptions were motivated by a simple economic analysis of competition. Chinese and southern European immigrants were commonly brought to the United States under labor contracts that undercut the established price of labor. As competition increased, wages and conditions worsened for white workers. At times the argument was presented in quite dispassionate, rational discussions: "We are faced to face with an ominous fact which we must not ignore, we can't evade it. If you allow in this country the competition of one class of laborers who are willing to live at a very low rate—upon a very low plane—then the tendency of that kind of competition will be to bring all other labor to that same plane. That is why we object to Chinese emigration. We have no hostility toward the Chinaman, but we recognize this: If the white labor in the market has got to compete on an even basis, on even terms with Chinese labor here, then the cost of living to the Chinaman will rule the wages of white men in the end."[31]

When describing the conditions under which Chinese and southern European immigrants lived, however, the language took a more pointedly hostile turn. Terence Powderly issued a series of editorials in 1888 in the *Journal of United Labor* detailing the filthy and crowded living conditions and diet of Hungarian and Italian workers. As one editorial put it, "The laborers of American and foreign birth who were neither Chinese nor Hungarian have declaimed long and loud against being compelled to compete with men who would grow fat on a diet of wind pudding, and sleep the sleep of the just in quarters that would be uncomfortable as a pig-sty."[32] The subtext was that while Chinese and other immigrants were used to conditions of extreme poverty and moral decay, this was the level to which all workers would be reduced if pauper immigration continued.

Described by one article as "worms" and "parasites," Chinese workers were likened to a disease that was rotting the otherwise healthy body of labor. Competition between the Chinese and the "American workmen" could serve to "enslave those [Americans] who are deluded with the belief that they are free citizens who have rights that the laws of the land and the powers of the government will protect."[33] According to another item, "the polluting tide is pouring in on our shores unchecked . . . No American can offer to work for wages so low that the Chinese will not bid lower."[34]

In response, a committed reaction to the new immigrants emerged. In California, "anti-Coolie" clubs and sporadic attacks on Chinese workers sometimes coalesced into broader riots as the anti-Chinese movement served as a vehicle for the development of political and class solidarity among white workers (see Saxton 1971). Yet economic competition was not the only problem, or even the most important one. After all, the Knights argued in the first narrative that one way to stop such competition was to organize all workers together. In this second narrative, the new immigrants were competitors not only because they were poor but also because they were not thought to be in command of civic virtue. The corporate metaphor built into the articles cited above was important in its economic implications as well as in its social and political implications about the worth of free laborers as members of the community and polity. If labor were a central part of the body of the republic, then the new immigrants were not just a threat to the white laborers but to the republic itself.

Part of this objection had to do with objective civic and political resources. The new immigrants were "imported," sometimes under binding contracts. This meant that their position was more like that of convict laborers or slaves than free people.[35] Additionally, the fact that they were not citizens meant that they could not take part in the democratic process. One letter to the *Journal*, remarking on immigration in a Pennsylvania mining community, heaped abuse on "Polanders," and then made a remarkable argument: "Let us have compulsory citizenship, and if they don't want to become citizens let them stay away[,] we don't want them; if they do well and good we will then welcome them."[36]

More broadly, the Knights argued in this narrative that the new immigrants were incapable of possessing civic virtue, since they did not share a republican understanding of the social worth of free laborers as members of the workplace, community, or polity. If forced to compete with them, native white workers would ultimately lose control of civic virtue as well. The following statement gives a glimpse of why the issue of Chinese labor loomed so large for the Knights, and did so out of line with their numerical strength: "Four hundred millions of Asiatic slaves confront us, and are now pouring in upon us, and though only 100,000 are here at present, yet, in many occupations, they have totally driven out our people, and in all branches are rapidly encroaching on our laborers and mechanics . . . How can we compete with a people who live like this, who support no churches, schools, academies, hospitals, deaf, dumb, blind, or orphan asylums, charitable institutions of any kind; who encourage the study neither of science, art, or literature; who take no magazines or newspapers; who never learn but one language, and whose soul is the almighty dollar."[37]

At issue in these statements was the possession of civic virtue as much as the control of economic resources. Indeed, the two were bound together in the Knights' narrative. The Knights feared that desperate conditions, requiring the pursuit of the "almighty dollar" over all other goals, would lead to the kind of cretinism and civic detachment that they not only ascribed to the Chinese and others (those who "take no magazines or newspapers" and support no "charitable institutions of any kind") but also feared for themselves. In Terence Powderly's eyes, "While we import ignorance under contract by the hundred thousand those who would, in this land, free our soil from the burden of landlordism and monopoly will have their hands full competing with cheap men; with men who are indifferent to their surroundings and are content to slave for $1 a day; content to live as dogs."[38] In the Knights' understanding, a certain standard of living was necessary for intellectual development as well as democratic participation. Laborers could not be engaged and participating citizens without a certain amount of leisure time to educate themselves about issues and participate in dialogue about them. As one speaker stated the problem, "Were the standard of living among American citizens reduced to the same level [as that of Italian immigrants], their intelligence would inevitably fall below that which makes the continuance of republican institutions possible."[39]

This second Knights of Labor narrative generally focused on republican institutions in the workplace and polity, but it also had to do with civic virtue in the community more generally, including the institution of the family. While native-born men desired to make enough money to keep a family, Chinese workers were said to have no respect for the Christian institution of marriage.[40] Hungarian workers by contrast destabilized the rightful balance of the home by bringing their wives into the workplace to help in the dangerous, hot, and dirty work of coal mining.[41] The immigrants were in this way "robbing their fellow-man of his just heritage—the right to live in a decent manner, and to raise his children to become useful citizens of this republic.[42]

It was exactly on this basis of civic virtue that the Knights thus drew a strong distinction between the Chinese and southern European laborers—coming from "pauper" backgrounds and unschooled in democracy and the republican understanding of labor's rightful place—and the northern European immigrants with whom they identified: "The vast majority of the Germans, English and Irish readily fall into our ways, become good citizens, and take as much interest in our labor organizations and in upholding wages as the best of those who are to the manner born . . . But the case is very different with that class of which the Italians seem to be good specimens. Such immigration is a horse of an entirely different color."[43] Or as Terence Powderly defensively stated the case in an editorial:

> An interested reader of the Journal writes to inquire if I am not prejudiced against the poor Hungarians and Italians. If what I have written on the subject of enforced and falsely stimulated immigration has in any way given rise to the impression that I am actuated by prejudice or race hatred I am extremely sorry, for nothing was further from my thoughts. If in bringing this question up for discussion I have had to single out a certain race or class, it is simply because I found them existing in a manner not consistent with American manners, customs, or manhood . . . If I had found the same number of Irish, Welsh, English, or Germans huddled together I would have written exactly the same . . . The word ignorance which I use may give some hypocrite or demagogue an opportunity to say that I am assailing the intelligence of the Hungarians, Italians, and others . . . I use the word in the sense that they are ignorant of our customs, our laws, our methods, and our language.[44]

Thus, the Knights' discussion of the new immigrants as racial others was articulated in terms of class competition. Yet, as the Knights declared again and again, the way to overcome the growing disparity of wealth and social worth in America was the "organization of all laborers into one great solidarity" without regard to race or nationality (McNeill 1887: 485). Ultimately, the reason the Knights saw themselves in economic conflict with Chinese and other immigrants rather than in common cause with them, lay in the civic conditions that made them seem to be "anticitizens" to the movement. The first narrative was directly tied to a longer history of labor discourse, within which black workers shifted from being seen as "anticitizens" to being seen as a redeemable people. This was based on a qualitative shift with regard to what I have termed the capacity for civic virtue. Despite the differences between the first and second narrative, what is clear is that both were tied to the same history. The fact that the Knights described the immigrants in ways historically reserved for blacks was no accident. For the Knights, the immigrants had become the new anticitizens.

### SLAVERY AND THE SOCIAL POSITION OF FREE LABOR

The third narrative was organized around the concept of slavery. In comparison with the other key narratives, the third one was not connected to any specific racial "other." Instead, this narrative was important for what it said about the white Knights' understanding of their own social position in relation to the historically racialized class system in America. Primarily, the third narrative was built on two terms, "wage slavery" and "white slavery," both of which emerged in the antebellum period as white workers, increasingly tied to wage labor, began to fear economic and social leveling with blacks (Roediger 1991). Discussions of "wage slavery" in the labor movement developed in tandem with the emergence of "free" wage labor as the dominant form of work relation in both England and America. Robert Steinfeld (1991, 2001) has pointed out that "free" labor was never entirely separate from "unfree" labor, such as indentured servitude. A host of legal and financial mechanisms kept workers tied to their employers. By the nineteenth century, property ownership was no longer necessary to define a person as "free," and wage workers, if they owned nothing else, formally owned at least their own productive capacity. Nevertheless, the defining characteristic of nineteenth-century labor was a somewhat contradictory combination of legal and political autonomy with economic domination, such that wage workers "were simultaneously independent and governed, publicly self-governing and privately subject to the rule of those who owned productive assets" (Steinfeld 1991, 186–87).

The terms "wage slave" and "white slave" survived into the Knights of Labor narrative of the 1880s, but their meaning was somewhat changed. Before the Civil War, the terms were important because they said a great deal about the construction of whites' identities as citizen-workers. This was no less true in the 1880s, but the terms implied something different for whites in a slaveholding republic than they did after the abolition of chattel slavery. This narrative therefore took shape in rather defensive terms. It was led by a fear of falling into servile status and grindingly poor material conditions—in other words, the reduction of historically "white" status to that of historically "black" status—rather than a positive identification of the common plight of working people of all colors. Yet, paradoxically, it was through this narrative that the Knights came to express their goals most universally.

Although there were many degrees of "unfreedom," chattel slavery as the most extreme form became an important trope for white wage workers to discuss their own changing conditions.[45] After the abolition of chattel slavery, white workers retained the term "slavery." While it was still clear that white wage workers were not going to literally become chattel slaves, it was no longer clear that they still held a protected civic status by virtue of their race. This change had two effects, both visible in the Knights of Labor narrative. It made the use of the terms "wage slave" and "white slave" more equivalent than they had been, and it also made them more racially open. "White slavery" was really no longer different from other forms, and wage slavery could be the same for all.

"Wage slavery" referred to the economic and social organization of labor. For the Knights of Labor, the objection to wage slavery was simultaneously economic and status-based. Economically, the term referred to the material conditions in which workers found themselves subject to exploitation—the "coercion" of the profits of labor away from the producer. The Knights lamented that formally free workers became like chattel slaves in terms of their social position, since they did not have a say in setting their hours, wages, or work pace. Within this narrative, it was economic and social "coercion" and not formal legal freedom that defined the condition of slavery: "The coercion of a man or holding of the labor of his hands, or the services of his faculties to the benefit of another without the freedom or power to compel an exact equivalent, is and always will be slavery, without regard to color, race, location or position . . . Whatever differences may exist between this and the holding of slaves in the South is in a degree only, and not in kind, as neither the wage slave or the chattel slave were in position to arrange the terms of competence for labor performed."[46]

Both black slaves and wage workers were thus bound in the same way. Not only were profits and terms of work out of their hands, but also the satisfaction deriving from work performed well. According to this narrative, the deliverance from wage slavery would have to come from the organization of all workers. "It was through unionism of our armies that our country has been free, and through unionism that the slaves of the South are free," one Knight wrote. "So, therefore, if the freedom of the nation and also the freedom of the colored people can be obtained through unionism, why can't the freedom of the labor[ing] people be obtained also?"[47]

Many of the communications conceded that being owned as property was in fact different from being legally free, and that this difference was important. But several argued that in certain ways formal freedom could be worse, since the slave owners had an economic incentive to provide for the maintenance of their slaves in a way that factory owners did not. Obviously, this argument rested on a romanticized view of the life of Southern slaves, if not of factory workers. Such claims, however, made a strong case about the ways in which even "free" labor systems rested on fundamental asymmetries of power. Under neither system were owners morally obligated to the producers of wealth, but at least under slavery owners had a financial incentive to provide workers with the bare essentials of life: "America is cursed by a worse system of slavery to day than the Southern States were thirty years ago. Then the slave had a life policy that insured him food, clothing, shelter, and medical aid as long as he lived; but, to-day, what has the wage slave to depend upon when sickness overtakes him? What has he to depend upon when his head is silvered by age, after a life of toil? The alms-house and a pauper's grave."[48]

Thus "free" labor could be in many ways the better deal for employers. Nor was this a problem for whites alone, as one editorial made clear: "It costs less to hire black men now than it did to support them and pay interest on their purchase money before the war . . . The fear of want and anxiety for his children is a sharper goad to force the negro wage slave to work than ever was the driver's lash."[49] For these reasons, several Knights attacked well-to-do humanitarians who supported the cause of abolition but resisted the labor cause. Better to condemn the wage system as a whole, according to the Knights.

While statements of this sort came from the North and the South, such comparisons underscore that this was a narrative maintained by whites. This fact was especially obvious in the statements that dealt with "white slavery." At least one recent discussion has suggested that there was an important difference between the connotation of "wage slavery" and "white slavery" as they first emerged in the first half of the nineteenth century (Roediger 1991). In the Knights' rhetoric, mentions of "white slavery" operated rhetorically along the same lines as the discussions of "wage slavery," but tended to be more exclusive of status. One item referenced the historical conditions of white bound laborers in the colonial period: "This class of servants often groaned beneath a worse than Egyptian bondage, as their masters, knowing that their servitude would last but a few years, treated them with a rigor more severe than they extended to their negro slaves."[50]

But even within the more defensive boundaries of the narrative, a comparison was made between the position of free white workers and that of black chattel slaves just over twenty years earlier. The conclusion was that there were common *class* interests shared by all working people. As Powderly put it, "He who speaks to-day for the slave speaks for men of skins as light as mine and yours as well as that of my brother who stands against the wall yonder. To-day there is no slave in this country who is known by his color. In this wage battle, in this question of industrial emancipation, we all stand as equals."[51]

Here it should be clear that this narrative was tied to civic virtue in a somewhat different way. The first two narratives were driven by the Knights' assessment of the capacity of different racial "others" for civic virtue—black Americans in the first narrative and immigrants in the second. This narrative was focused not on racial "others" but rather on the "we," as the term "white slave" implies. It was in this narrative that the movement most clearly confronted the joint racial and class position of white workers. As Orlando Patterson (1982) has shown, being owned by another is not the only, or even the most important, defining element of slavery. More critical is the loss of autonomy and social honor that the position entails. Slavery meant social—and therefore civic—death.

### INTERRACIAL CONTACT AND CLASS INTEREST

While the discussion outlined above helps to establish the ways that race was understood within the organizational rhetoric of the Knights, it may miss the much more variable ways in which racial understandings actually played out in the South. To examine the way that racial interests were constructed on the ground, in this section I make use of an analysis of letters sent to Terence Powderly from various southern states. These "backstage" communications were not meant for publication but rather asked advice, issued reports, and complained about working conditions, fellow members, and unjust treatment. Such letters help to paint a more complete picture of the construction of interest in the actual process of day-to-day organizing.[52]

There are two temporal elements worth mentioning here about the discussion of race in the letters sent to Powderly. The first is that race was always one element of local concern, but by no means was it the only concern. In fact, the frequency with which race was discussed declined over the course of the 1880s. In the early period of southern organizing, just over 17 percent of the letters mentioned race explicitly. As the organization became more firmly entrenched and as the volume of the letters ballooned, the frequency declined even while actual experience with cross-race organizing was more widespread. During the peak years of the movement, the figure dropped to about 13 percent, and it dropped again to about half that in later years.

The second temporal change is in the content of the interests in interracial organizing expressed in the letters. Because the letters were primarily about practical matters, they did not engage all of the different racial narratives identified above. However, these "backstage" communications show more conflict over the organization of black workers than do the communications in the *Journal of United Labor.* The mentions of race may be categorized in terms of the normative value of the interest in cross-race organizing that they express. The proportion of positive statements fell in each of the successive periods, while the neutral and mixed categories increased markedly in the second period, and the proportion of negative statement increased in the third period. In other words, as more and more Knights gained firsthand experience with organizing across the racial divide, the level of idealistic enthusiasm for interracial organizing dropped. This pattern of changing calculations of interest as the movement gained experience was common to the Knights and the Populists alike. In each case, the setbacks experienced—particularly as the movements turned to political organizing—led first to more matter-of-fact statements and later to more pessimistic views of interracial organizing.

What kind of sentiments do these letters actually express about race? In some, the question of interracial organizing was explicitly connected to material interest. As many sociological and historical accounts have suggested, employers began to use black strikebreakers to counter white labor organizing. A few letters suggested that the same happened to the Knights in many parts of the South.[53] Although reports of such problems were more apparent in the letters to Powderly than in the *Journal of United Labor,* many of the statements show white members of the Knights adopting the view of the movement narrative. Such statements did not simply parrot the leadership but rather emerged from perceptions based in particular local contexts. For example, Alabama was an early adopter of the Knights of Labor, especially in the coal mining villages (see Letwin 1998). As the workers began to organize in the early 1880s, employers began to bring in black workers to "blackleg" or undercut the white worker's established price of labor. Instead of calling to exclude black laborers, many white members argued that more should be done to organize them into the movement. This sentiment was echoed by others throughout the South. It was not an altruistic response—white workers were not happy to have their jobs threatened. Instead, their interests were articulated in material terms, sometimes within an explicit class language. This is not to say that racial tensions did not exist in these contexts, but rather that such tensions were mediated through practical understanding, which rested on a host of local conditions.

In many other contexts, however, whites were paternalistic in their relations with blacks. And throughout the South, whites resisted seeing blacks as social equals. Yet this response had more to do with status claims than with class per se. This distinction is important in understanding the complex calculations of the white workers of the era.[54] In class logic, whites should make common cause with blacks, since they were both being exploited. This did not mean that whites should accept blacks as their social equals. By contrast, the organizational rhetoric of the Knights of Labor pushed the equality and honorable treatment of brothers. Yet the unwillingness of working-class whites to give up the privileged social position they thought they deserved was evident, even when they were willing to join together as "brothers" in the movement.

Two views from Alabama speak to both the relatively close connections between white and black assemblies as well as the enforced social distance. A white official from Gadsden, Alabama, wrote to ask whether some separation of the local assemblies might be maintained: "The coloured men of this city are anxious to be organized . . . Some of our brothers have misgivings about the neges getting the same signs and passwords as are in possession of white assemblies. Could the password be given to them not be changed a little to prevent their getting admission to an assembly at work[?]"[55] This was echoed in a letter from a black member in Whistler, Alabama: "Dear Mr. Powderly i take it upon my self to ask you is it Wright that Colord Members can not speak in the White assembly. Last Meeting the White they was [discussing] Labor & one of the Colord Members ask the Master Workman could he speak a word or two on Labor [and] he told him he could not speak in this assembly and when they come to our meeting they speak as Long as they say in the meeting."[56]

Similarly, many of the racial conflicts inside the local and state organizations of the Knights between white and black members had to do not with the material concerns articulated in a language of class but with divided interests over politics. Political identification became a very deep issue by the late 1880s, as many whites felt that black allegiance to the Republican Party would doom their movement and lead to Republican victories.[57] One white organizer in Pine Bluff, Arkansas, complained that broader political divisions were disrupting the Knights' own elections: "The delegates at our annual meetings held in this place first Monday of the present month formed combinations and worked up combinations with the colored delegates, prejudicing their minds with partisan politics to elect the officers of the state assembly, and succeeded. . . . A real professional politician was elected State Master Workman over myself, the republicans including the darkies far outnumbering the Knights present."[58] A member from Charleston, South Carolina, indicated why the stakes were so high when it came to political control:

> This state has a large majority of Colored voters and they are Republican and held full control of the State municipal and County Governments from 1868 to 1876. During this regime, Corruption Robbery Plunder Bribery and everything vile, was the Ruling spirit and the White People made up their minds to redeem the State at all hazards and after a Campaign that was like a Revolution at a cost of many lives—we succeeded. The Democrats got control and have kept it since . . . The Politicians and the Press immediately branded [dissenters to one-party control] as Renegades and traitors who would again Place the Proud Old Palmetto state, at the mercy of the negro—and Carpet Bag Thieves and Plunderers who infested this state prior to 1876.[59]

Despite the widespread view within the Knights that class interests might indeed be best served by interracial organizing, some significant lines of division can be seen in the letters to Powderly, including the "status" concerns over social honor that are distinct from common class interest, and the split in party interests that led to conflicts over the political control of communities.

## CONCLUSION

In this chapter I have examined the question of how race was understood in an explicitly class-based movement. The Knights of Labor initially presents a puzzling case, since the organization simultaneously pursued racial openness and racial closure, justifying both on the basis of class interest. For the Knights, the connection between class and of race was made through three separate movement-level narratives, each of which tied the two elements together in different ways. The first linked black workers to an "interracial organizing" frame. The second tied new immigrants to a very different frame concerning competing interests. The third concerned a broader "slavery and social position" frame.

Understanding the connection between these narratives requires understanding what the Knights thought to be at stake in the labor struggle. Only one of the narratives concerned competition over material resources explicitly. Control over what might be called "civic virtue" was a central feature in each of the narratives, however. Civic virtue involved not only formal legal autonomy (being a "free" laborer as opposed to a slave or an indentured servant) but also the capacity and appreciation for maintaining republican institutions. This, in effect, was the lens through which the movement read the meaning of race and ethnicity.

These narratives thus provided both possibilities and constraints for interracial organizing. Both immigrants and black Americans were largely resource poor, and both competed with white workers to some degree in the workplace. To antebellum white workers, black workers had been "anticitizens" based on civic status. Even those who were formally free were not "free" in any civic sense of the term. For white Knights of the 1880s, the same class language portrayed black workers as sharing the view that civic virtue was central to the class struggle. For the Knights, the anticitizens became the new immigrants—particularly the Chinese and the southern Europeans who were outside of the democratic system and caught at the bottom of the economic system. The third narrative provided a way for the movement to discuss the civic position of whites. While this was a racially restrictive narrative in the sense that it was clearly driven by whites, it also provided a way to discuss common interests.

Other kinds of constraints came from the adoption and translation of the movement-level narratives to the local level. The analysis of the letters from the South to Terence Powderly suggested that at the local level the practical problems of interracial organizing were much more apparent. Active opposition to such organizing was one problem, but there was also the internal problem of status difference. While the movement-level narrative emphasized the class equality of all "producers," it did not make the same claim about status. The issue of social status, as well as the problem of political equality, is central to the next chapters, which examine the local organizing of the Knights in Richmond and in Atlanta.

CHAPTER 3

# THE KNIGHTS OF LABOR IN RICHMOND, VIRGINIA

Old Market Hall will seat 1,500 persons. It was there that I addressed the meeting last night. Every seat was occupied, and the standing room as well. There must have been 1,700 people in the room. A large part of the audience was of the colored persuasion. They were evidently impressed with what I said, for at their request I organized an assembly of colored men at the close of the meeting. At the close of my lecture I was subjected to a course of hand-shaking such as I have seldom experienced, except during a political campaign at home.—TERENCE V. POWDERLY

Early in 1885 Terence Powderly was excited about meeting a well-mannered and organized group of workers of both races during his stop in Richmond, Virginia, as part of his wider tour of the South. Despite the obstacles, Powderly thought that interracial cooperation was possible in Richmond, and so did the local activists. As William Mullen, the white local organizer of the Knights, wrote to Powderly soon after his visit, "We are getting on well. We have several colored Assemblies in good working order. I organized a fine one Saturday night in Manchester—a city across the river from here. Your visit has done us much good. If the honest workingmen are allowed to manage the affairs in our city without 'scabs,' 'rats,' and 'blacklegs,' we will succeed. If not, we will go under."[1]

In this chapter and the next I follow the practice of interracial organizing under the Knights of Labor in two concrete local contexts with very different levels of interracial success. This chapter examines Richmond, which was the clearest case of successful interracial coalition for the Knights. The relative success of the movement in breaking the color line in local settings hinged on the way that the movement narratives connecting race and class interacted with local social and economic structures and with the ongoing experience of organizing in the local settings. In the previous chapter I examined the movement-level narratives linking race and class, stressing in particular the importance of civic virtue as understood by the movement. Yet it is important to tie such broad analyses to local practice in concrete settings. In order for the Knights to make any headway at the local level, there had to be some acceptance of interracialism on the part of white workers. Because whites held most of the skilled positions in southern cities, they had some control over the success of labor actions at the local level. If white workers pursued labor activism only on the condition of racial closure, as was the case in many Southern cities, then they would rather desert the movement than organize with blacks. While the Knights of Labor could exist as a virtually all-black organization in some localities—and it did, particularly in some rural areas and especially after 1887—such a situation could not be meaningfully called "interracial." Movement narratives provided a basic framework for the acceptance of interracial action based on mutual interests as producers, but this acceptance rested in large part upon whites thinking that black workers were capable of civic virtue.

Such acceptance varied a great deal across local settings, depending upon local economic and social conditions and upon the ongoing experience of black and white workers in the course of local organizing. In some settings the movement narrative fit better than in others. In Richmond, Powderly and other white organizers saw black workers as at least potentially good republican citizens, able and willing to be organized and in step with both the material and civic goals of the movement. One factor that mattered a great deal was the black workers' capacity for autonomous organization in both the civic and labor realms. For whites, such organization was a sign of civic virtue. For blacks, it served a different function. The preexisting social organization—established neighborhoods and churches as well as a network of social and labor societies—provided resources that helped to initiate and sustain involvement in the Knights of Labor.

Most important for the present argument, the Knights sustained interracial cooperation more successfully in Richmond than in any other city in the nation. This is not to say that the Richmond Knights overcame the "color line" completely in either personal or institutional relationships. When the movement members had to confront the issue of race publicly—during the 1886 General Assembly and, later, in the city elections when the Knights ran candidates—it proved to be as much of a problem in Richmond as it was elsewhere. In personal interactions, white Knights were far more comfortable with notions of cross-race class coalition than they were with ideas of status or political equality. In institutional arrangements, the Knights were split by race in Richmond more than in most places. The black and white local assemblies were actually organized into separate district assemblies, an arrangement unique to the Richmond area.

Yet while the Knights fell short of the ideal type of interracial organizing in Richmond, they nevertheless came closer there than they did anywhere else, due in large part to the local structural conditions outlined above. Richmond's black population was relatively large, but it was also well established in the city's economy and in its civic life. As a result, white Knights in Richmond expected some black involvement in labor disputes and political activism—an expectation that was not shared in most of the South. The spatial and institutional segregation of the black community played an important role, too; in having their own institutions to rely upon, Richmond's black Knights had a greater degree of independence from their white colleagues than did the black members in most areas. Interracial labor activism did not spring fully formed from the organizational structure or the movement ideology of the Knights of Labor. Rather it developed imperfectly, in fits and starts, through a relatively long history of contact in Richmond's labor battles. Although these battles were not always successful, they did involve a significant amount of black organizing and cross-race coalition.

In the first section of this chapter I explore the local structural conditions that set the context for activity within the Knights and to which the movement's narratives were applied. I examine the economic organization of the city, including its industrial history and the occupational structure of white and black residents in the 1880s. I also consider the spatial ordering of the city and its importance for interracial interactions. In the second section I examine the development of the movement in Richmond and the success of its practical actions along with the longer history of labor organizing that set the context for the Knights. Interracial coalition was sustained more meaningfully and for a longer period in Richmond than in any comparable Southern city, but it nevertheless proved to be fragile. In light of this, the second section explores two related tensions that pulled the movement apart at the height of its success—namely, the issues of "social equality" and political allegiance.

### ECONOMIC AND SOCIAL ORGANIZATION

Unlike many cities of the South, Richmond had an established industrial economy and a relatively large population, and as a result it became a major center for the Knights of Labor. Richmond also had a large black population that was well established in its economic and community life. The result was a particular set of economic and social conditions that encouraged the development of the movement through the interactions of white and black workers.

The size and relative stability of Richmond's economy and population over the course of the 1880s was an important factor in the success of the Knights there. Richmond was the largest city in the South, boasting 64,000 residents in 1880. While industrialization was just getting underway in most Southern cities early in the decade, Richmond was already a center of trade, commerce, and manufacturing. Figures from the 1880 census show nearly six hundred manufacturing establishments in operation. The largest industry was tobacco production, which provided more than 10 percent of all the jobs in the city, but iron production and other manufacturing firms were also well established.[2] Despite its large size and its steady growth, the city was relatively stable during an extremely turbulent period. Many Southern cities changed drastically during the 1880s as industrial investment surged and city populations boomed. Richmond's population was also touched by these changes, and it grew roughly 27 percent over the decade. At the same time, the city retained a great deal of the insularity of the Old South. Its racial makeup remained stable at about 45 percent black during the 1880s, and it was overrun neither by northern "carpetbaggers" seeking investment opportunities in the New South nor by new immigrants looking for work. More than 90 percent of its residents were born in the state.

**TABLE 6** White occupational structure of Richmond, 1890

| | Men | | Women | | Total | |
|---|---|---|---|---|---|---|
| Category | Number | % | Number | % | Number | % |
| Capitalists/professionals | 700 | 5.1 | 0 | 0.0 | 700 | 4.1 |
| Merchants/shopkeepers | 1,748 | 12.8 | 8 | 0.2 | 1,756 | 10.4 |
| Salaried employees | 3,693 | 27.0 | 800 | 24.7 | 4,493 | 26.6 |
| Skilled trades | 3,629 | 26.6 | 1,022 | 31.6 | 4,651 | 27.5 |
| Industrial laborers | 2,274 | 16.7 | 836 | 25.8 | 3,110 | 18.4 |
| Unskilled laborers | 1,427 | 10.5 | 18 | 0.6 | 1,445 | 8.6 |
| Domestic/personal service | 182 | 1.3 | 552 | 17.1 | 734 | 4.3 |
| Total | 13,653 | 100.0 | 3,236 | 100.0 | 16,889 | 100.0 |

Source: Calculated from U.S. Bureau of the Census, *Eleventh Census of the United States*, 1890, vol. 1, 718–19.

Richmond's occupational structure was sharply split by race, but the distinction between "black" and "white" jobs was far more settled there than in cities like Atlanta where the population was changing quickly. Overall, Richmond's whites were predominantly employed as salaried employees (generally as clerks, bookkeepers, salesmen, and agents) and in skilled trades both inside and outside the major factories (see table 6).[3] The few white women working in industrial labor held jobs different from those of their male colleagues. There were two important sites of such work—in paper box factories and in tobacco factories. The box making factories in Richmond employed only white women. In the tobacco factories, white women were generally employed as cigarette makers. A number of white women also earned money as domestic and personal servants, either as regular household servants or hotel and boardinghouse keepers.

The job structure for Richmond's black residents was very different than that for whites (see table 7). Overwhelmingly, black jobs were at the bottom of the occupational ladder. The most common job category for black men listed in the period's census records was "laborer," which meant they were unskilled workers hired either into regular employment in factories and workshops or on a short-term basis on other job sites. In addition, many black men worked as semiskilled industrial workers in Richmond's tobacco factories, in the iron and steel plants, and on the railroads, though often in lower-pay and lower-skilled jobs than whites. Black women were almost as likely as black men to be

TABLE 7 Black occupational structure of Richmond, 1890

| | Men | | Women | | Total | |
|---|---|---|---|---|---|---|
| Category | Number | % | Number | % | Number | % |
| Capitalists/professionals | 56 | 0.7 | 0 | 0.0 | 56 | 0.3 |
| Merchants/shopkeepers | 227 | 2.9 | 5 | 0.1 | 232 | 1.4 |
| Salaried employees | 171 | 2.2 | 148 | 1.8 | 319 | 2.0 |
| Skilled trades | 1,068 | 13.6 | 300 | 3.7 | 1,368 | 8.5 |
| Industrial laborers | 1,535 | 19.5 | 571 | 7.0 | 2,106 | 13.2 |
| Unskilled laborers | 3,203 | 40.8 | 104 | 1.3 | 3,307 | 20.7 |
| Domestic/personal service | 1,600 | 20.4 | 7,021 | 86.2 | 8,621 | 53.9 |
| Total | 7,860 | 100.0 | 8,149 | 100.0 | 16,009 | 100.0 |

Source: Calculated from U.S. Bureau of the Census, *Eleventh Census of the United States*, 1890, vol. 1, 718–19.

in the labor force, and they were overwhelmingly employed as domestic servants and as laundry workers where they were likely either to work in their own home or in somebody else's. There were black women employed in many of the tobacco factories, but relative to their representation in the labor force such industrial employment was rare during the 1880s.

Despite this occupational stratification, there was a relatively long history of black involvement in Richmond industry, and this history led to a surprising degree of autonomy even before the Civil War. As one of the early industrial centers of the South, Richmond was also a center of industrial slavery, where slaves were hired out for work in skilled trades or in industrial production in the city (Tyler-McGraw and Kimball 1988). There were two basic patterns to the arrangement. In the first, owners (often country landholders) would hire out the slaves directly to the employer, collecting the wages and in turn supplying allowances for living costs.[4] In the second pattern, which became common in Richmond, slaves acted as their own brokers. They would contract with their owners to provide a certain amount of income, and then contract with an employer to work for specified wages. Any money earned in excess of the amount promised to the owner would be used for living expenses or saved (Tyler-McGraw and Kimball 1988: 22–25; O'Brien 1990: 20–44). The industrial slavery system—however onerous—thus involved a level of economic self-determination and autonomy on the part of the slaves that the more traditional plantation arrangements did not allow.[5]

The industrial slave's relative autonomy extended past the factory and into the home and surrounding community. Urban slaves were much freer than others to marry, worship, and set up homes as they wished, and their degree of autonomy approached that of free blacks. During the late antebellum period a vibrant black community life began to emerge in Richmond through neighborhoods, family ties, churches, and even secret benevolent societies. These communities were the building blocks for the emergence of black civic life after Reconstruction.

A particularly important institution in black civic life was the church. Records from the 1880s indicate that Richmond had relatively few black churches given its size, but they were unusually large and exceptionally well established.[6] Richmond's First Baptist Church provides an example of the degree of organization and autonomy that the city's black society could muster, even before the Civil War. When the church officially split from its white counterpart in 1841 more than a tenth of the city's black population were members. The black members purchased the building and renamed it the First African Baptist Church. Although a white preacher remained nominally in charge, the day-to-day functioning of the church, and a good deal of informal preaching, was in the hands of the membership (O'Brien 1990: 35–36). Four other black Baptist churches were founded before the war. A fifth, organized by a Richmond slave named John Harris, began to meet secretly in 1860 and was chartered officially in 1865 (Tyler-McGraw and Kimball 1988: 39).

After the war, a much more diverse set of community organizations bloomed. Schools were organized for black children while many adults took night classes to learn to read and write. Financial and legal autonomy spawned new institutions in the 1870s. As Peter Rachleff (1984: 71) notes, more than seven thousand black Richmond residents opened accounts in the Freedman's Savings Bank, notwithstanding the close-to-marginal existence that most of them faced. The bank held savings of well over $100,000 when it folded during the economic depression of the mid-1870s. As churches became fully autonomous from white control, the secret mutual aid societies that were initially attached to them began to operate more openly and independently. There were over four hundred black secret societies active at that time, many of them organized as mutual aid and benevolent societies to provide death benefits, poor relief, and other necessities to members of the community. Others provided moral and civic education for young people. Still others were more radical, functioning as de facto unions and political cells that organized strikes among black stevedores and coopers (O'Brien 1990: 282; Rachleff 1984: 24–27; 42–44).

By the 1880s, the emergence of the black community was evident in the spatial organization of the city and in rates of social contact across race.[7] Richmond's city directories provide valuable evidence for examining this organization, since they offer the equivalent of a census of adult permanent residents.[8] Richmond's six wards were distinct political units, but they were clearly differentiated social units as well. Jackson Ward, in the northwest, was the city's only majority-black ward and was predominantly working-class. Marshall Ward, at over 40 percent black, was closest in character to Jackson. Madison, in the center of the city, was overwhelmingly white and bourgeois in character. The populations of Clay, Monroe, and Jefferson wards were roughly one quarter black, and largely working class.

The degree of racial segregation within a city has traditionally been understood as a measure of oppression and exclusion, and for good reason. Yet it can also indicate meaningful neighborhoods, communities, and identities. One common measure of segregation is the index of dissimilarity ($D$),[9] which measures the difference between the population of white and black residents in a given spatial area relative to their overall population. Comparing wards, Richmond's racial segregation was only moderate in 1885, when the Knights were near their peak strength ($D = .31$). However, at the block level, there was significant segregation ($D = .65$).[10] In other words, even in the whitest wards there were some black residents, but these residents were concentrated into distinct blocks.

Segregated blocks can be isolated and dispersed or they can be concentrated. The establishment of a black community and its resulting strength depends, at least in some part, on concentration. Identities are formed through interaction with others, and much of the interaction that matters for community strength—such as political discussions, social support, and courtship—happens in neighborhoods. The second index reported for the wards is a measure of social contact ($P^*$) that approximates the likelihood of interracial contact at the block level across each ward (see table 8). The measure is here calculated to show the degree to which black residents were likely to come into contact with whites in daily life. While each ward had moderately high segregation, the contact measure varied widely across wards. Black residents

TABLE 8 Structural characteristics of Richmond's wards, 1885

| Ward | Black (%) | Working class (%) | Segregation (*D*) | Contact (*P**) |
|---|---|---|---|---|
| Clay | 26.5 | 69.6 | 0.69 | 0.33 |
| Jackson | 67.7 | 86.8 | 0.64 | 0.18 |
| Jefferson | 23.2 | 66.7 | 0.56 | 0.47 |
| Madison | 17.7 | 36.2 | 0.52 | 0.58 |
| Marshall | 41.5 | 85.7 | 0.52 | 0.27 |
| Monroe | 24.2 | 49.4 | 0.52 | 0.50 |

Source: Calculations are drawn from information in *Chataigne's Directory of Richmond, Va.*, 1885. Class composition figures are based on a 1/20 sample of the names index, all other figures are based on a full count of the address index (see appendix for details).

in some wards, such as Madison and Jefferson, were extremely likely to interact with whites on a daily basis. In Jackson Ward, by contrast, similar levels of segregation meant very little contact with whites and thus more interaction within the black community itself.[11]

This neighborhood clustering effect is clear on figure 1, which shows Richmond's blocks with the ward boundaries marked in heavy black lines. Each dot on the map indicates the placement of a residential block that was at least 90 percent black. There were isolated black residential blocks even in largely white wards, a pattern left over from the prewar years when most black tradesmen lived near their workplaces and domestic slaves lived in alleys behind upper-class homes.[12] There was an obvious concentration of black residential blocks in Jackson Ward, however, particularly in the western half. Part of Marshall might also be categorized as a black area, but it did not have the same dense clustering of blocks forming a distinct black neighborhood.

Jackson Ward was the heart of Richmond's black community and civic life. Historically speaking, Jackson Ward was a created community. Although most of its streets were laid out before the Civil War, its political boundaries were created afterward in order to concentrate the black population and to limit its electoral power. An 1867 annexation brought large areas of already settled land into the city boundaries. This led to the incorporation of the mostly white working-class Marshall Ward on the east end, and the largely black Jackson Ward on the north side. The boundaries of Jackson Ward were clearly gerrymandered by the white city council to contain the budding black electoral presence in Richmond. In 1870, the black residents were much more

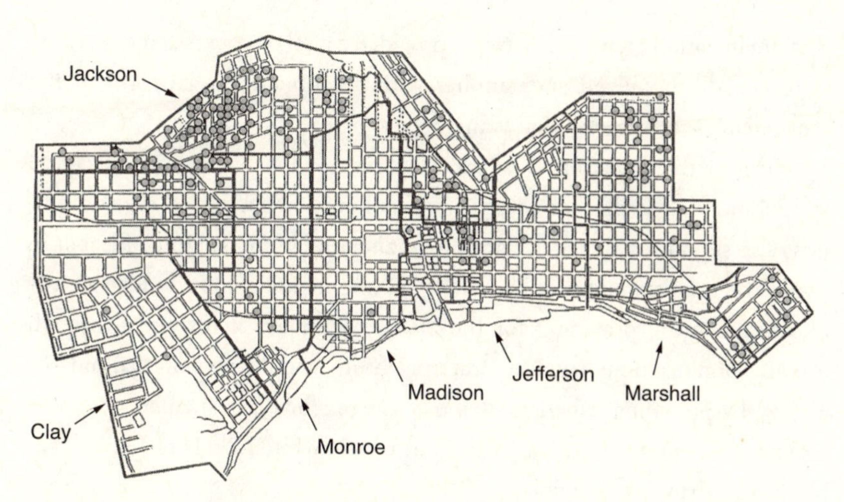


FIGURE 1. Black residential blocks in Richmond, Virginia, 1885. (Calculations from *Chataigne's City Directory of Richmond, Va.*, 1885. Map adapted from U.S. Bureau of the Census, *Tenth Census of the United States*, 1880, vol. 19, 82)

evenly spread across the city's wards, with some concentration toward the northern end of the city. Dividing up the land on the north side among the already-existing wards would have meant considerable black electoral power in each (Tyler-McGraw 1994: 173–74). This containment of black voting power was a double-edged sword, however: it meant reduced black influence on a citywide basis, but it also meant that black residents controlled Jackson politics.

The creation of Jackson Ward as a social unit was a more complex process. In addition to a "push" from white city planners there was also a "pull," as Jackson emerged as a social space where black residents wanted to live. Throughout the 1870s and 1880s, the black concentration in Jackson Ward increased steadily, and its community character became more apparent.[13] Jackson was not just an enclave for the poor but also the home of much of Richmond's small black middle class.[14]

## THE KNIGHTS OF LABOR IN RICHMOND

One of the basic points of recent scholarship on social movements has been that resources matter in the emergence of social movements.[15] In Richmond, the network of black churches, secret societies, and mutual benefit organizations that preexisted the Knights of Labor formed a grounding upon which that organization grew. The network provided a pool of potential recruits who were already mobilized and familiar with the organizational form of the movement as well as with more tangible resources.

The growth of Jackson Ward as a social and political center for black life in Richmond, and the web of civic associations that supported the community, also supported the later black organizing under the Knights of Labor in two ways. It bolstered the ability of black Knights to organize independently of white control, providing for the bloc recruitment of members through existing organizations (such as fraternal brotherhoods and mutual aid societies) by providing experiences and resources for black members to draw upon in the course of organizing.[16] It also gave white members a sense that black civic virtue was possible.

The development of an interracial labor coalition under the Knights had its own historical antecedents. There was evidence of formal labor activism by white tradesmen in Richmond starting from the early 1870s, as well as some working-class political organizing under the Greenback-Labor Party late in the decade (Fink 1985: 154). Black labor activism was first apparent around the same time. Black strikes in the early postwar years did not fare well, yet the fact that they were organized at all was evidence of the degree to which black workers were already bound up in Richmond's industrial economy. In April 1867, a self-organized group of black dockworkers calling themselves the Stevedores Society of Laboring Men of the City of Richmond began a strike for higher wages. Black coopers struck for the first time in May of that same year. In both cases, employers found replacement workers to break the strikes (Rachleff 1984: 42–44).

Using replacement workers to threaten striking workers (or workers contemplating a strike) was a common practice for southern employers. Studies of race relations have argued that the use of minority strikebreakers was one practice that kept black and white workers divided against each other. Yet in Richmond there was a twist: white strikebreakers were used several times to counter strikes organized by black workers. In the 1867 coopers' strike, the strikebreakers were local whites. An 1873 strike of black railroad workers was broken with newly arrived Italian immigrants. White workers also broke a later strike by the black Stevedores Society (Rachleff 1984: 42–44, 73, 80–81).[17]

Despite these cases of interracial strikebreaking, cooperation emerged in other cases, initially driven by overtures from self-organized black workers.

During summer 1873, the better-organized black trades made their first substantial contact with national labor organizations. The Coopers' Union No. 1 and the New Light Lodge of the Tobacco Laborers' Union in Richmond sent two black members to the first meeting of the Industrial Congress. The event, held in Cleveland, drew together prominent labor leaders from around the country in order to develop a national labor federation. Richmond's black delegates were able to claim seats in influential committees during that meeting, and Richmond's black trades sent delegates to the meetings in 1874 and 1875 as well (Foner 1974: 441; Rachleff 1984: 72–75). At the local level, the black coopers reorganized their union in 1877 and began a strike against the barrel shops of tobacco factories, where mechanization and competition with prison-made barrels had driven prices down. The strike, which lasted two weeks, included two hundred black and white coopers. Although they prevented strikebreakers from taking their jobs, they were not able to solve the problem of competition from convict labor (Rachleff 1984: 81–82). At the Tredegar Iron Works, skilled black workers organized in the Amalgamated Association of Iron and Steel Workers shortly after the union allowed black workers to join on an equal basis. The white local at the iron works was in fairly poor shape, but one black local had 125 members. The white and black locals, along with a number of sympathetic but nonunion workers at Tredegar, went on strike at the plant in an attempt to reinstate a white employee who had been fired. The strike was apparently undermined when the nonunion workers returned to work (Rachleff 1984: 106–7).

It was in this context that the Knights of Labor entered into the Richmond labor scene. The Knights of Labor were extremely successful in Richmond, both in terms of overall numerical strength and in the results of their practical actions. The Knights chartered 226 local assemblies across Virginia in 77 separate localities. There were significant clusters of local assemblies in only four cities—Richmond, Danville, Lynchburg, and Petersburg. With its 40 local assemblies, Richmond ranked far ahead of any other southern city and well ahead of many northern industrial centers as well.[18] Of the total number of assemblies, 26 were white (65 percent) and 14 (35 percent) were black. This was by far the largest number of black assemblies founded in a single location.[19]

In April 1884, a small group of white workers founded Eureka Assembly (LA 3157) of the Knights of Labor. The assembly was brought together by

William Cree, a German-born activist and long-time Richmond resident who had been involved in the city's earlier fraternal societies and trade unions. Eureka Assembly's history demonstrates one way that the Knights' organizing spread through the South in the years before 1885. Once the Knights had a foothold in the South, many smaller towns were organized through the efforts of an official lecturer or organizer of the Knights, who was commissioned to travel through the area bringing members into the Order. The second way that the organizing spread, which was characteristic of many of the bigger cities including Richmond, was through migration of already initiated members such as Cree, who had first been inducted in New York City. Richmond also had an earlier assembly of telegraph operators (LA 1856) that was likely organized in the same way but failed to survive (Rachleff 1984: 116–17; Garlock 1982).

With the establishment of LA 3157, the Richmond Knights began to expand beyond isolated networks. William Mullen came to be the de facto leader of the assembly in fall 1884. Mullen, a printer by trade, had himself been involved in Richmond's labor movement prior to the Knights. As the officially sanctioned local organizer for the area, Mullen began promoting the Knights through speeches to local workers. He primarily targeted his message to white skilled workers, and it proved to be effective. Mullen's speeches emphasized the importance of the Knights' broad, multitrade membership, which could overcome the trades unions' limits of solidarity (McLaurin 1978: 87; Rachleff 1984: 116–17). Under Mullen's leadership, six new assemblies were chartered by the end of 1884. All were listed in the Knights' records as "mixed," meaning they were not restricted to one occupational group although they were dominated by skilled workers (Garlock 1982).

Officially, there were no black assemblies in Richmond until January 1885 when a visit by Terence Powderly set off a burst of organizing in both the black and the white communities. Yet the official record hides a good deal of behind-the-scenes work. There were in fact a few black assemblies that had been meeting informally for several months prior to Powderly's visit. They had not been officially chartered, since they had to apply through the already-existing white assemblies, and Mullen was conflicted about how to proceed. Although he recognized the importance of organizing Richmond's black workers, he felt a great deal of pressure not to challenge too quickly the feelings of status superiority held by white members. He wrote as much in a letter to Powderly in late December 1884. In his local assembly, "the subject of organizing the colored men was discussed with much interest by members. Some [are] in favor of organizing them, and others opposed to it . . . You are well aware that there is yet in a large section of our country a strong objection on the part of whites to mix with the colored race. This objection may lessen as time goes on, but it cannot be gotten over all at once" (Rachleff 1984: 117).

At the same time Mullen saw the logic of organizing across the "color line," at least in terms of class if not status. "As to helping the colored man in any attempt to benefit himself or to advance the cause of labor or to call on him to assist us in time of trouble, we do not object" (Rachleff 1984: 117). It was not just the movement leaders who saw the logic of building a class-based coalition across racial lines—a white tobacco worker and member of LA 3545 named William Childress reported his own interest in doing so. As he stated in a letter: "I have been a hard worker for the benefit and interest of our beloved order and I have labored for and with our colored Brethren and I have completed my work up to this point . . . My colored Brethren are all tobacco worker[s] and I so far got them organised."[20]

The matter was settled during Powderly's visit to Richmond. The stop was part of a broader tour of the South that also took him through Raleigh, Nashville, Chattanooga, and Atlanta. Powderly addressed the Richmond workers at a large gathering at the Old Market Hall that included blacks and whites but was racially divided by seating area. Powderly presented the Knights as a movement that could overcome narrow interests for the benefit of working people in general. Before the speech, he held a private meeting with a few white activists, where he made the case that organizing black workers would not necessarily mean embracing social equality. Black workers could be organized into separate assemblies, he said, but with the same laws and privileges. The logic was apparently acceptable to the delegation, and he took a similar line in his speech. According to the account in the *Richmond Dispatch,* Powderly "did not expect the black men to be received in the homes of white men, but when their labor is exactly alike . . . then they ought to have equal wages. He asked the two races to stand side by side, 'to the end that wages shall not drop'" (Rachleff 1984: 119). By the end of the night, Powderly himself officially organized Richmond's first black assembly as LA 3564, comprised of twenty-four tobacco factory workers (Rachleff 1984: 119).

Following Powderly's visit, there was substantial growth in the movement.

The organization's 1885 records show 257 dues-paying members of LA 3564, the initial black assembly. Twelve new black assemblies were organized during the same year. Black women became organized in their own assemblies, LA 3929 and LA 4096. A great deal of growth occurred in the white assemblies as well—seven new white assemblies opened in 1885, including LA 4474 and LA 4684, both composed of white women (Garlock 1982).[21]

Full membership lists do not exist for Knights of Labor local assemblies, but summary records of individual assemblies were included in the records of the General Assembly until 1885. These records show that the Richmond assemblies were quite large. Of the twenty-four Richmond assemblies founded by that time, ten had a hundred or more dues-paying members. From 1886 to 1888, membership records were only reported for the regional district assemblies. Richmond was unique in having two functioning district assemblies covering the same territory, divided along racial rather than spatial lines. The first, DA 84, was white, while DA 92 was made up of black assemblies. This fact in itself was a testimony to the organizational resources of the black membership in Richmond. Figures from the movement show that the black and white memberships were nearly equal in number during the movement's peak years. In other words, although there were more white assemblies, the black assemblies were larger.

"Social equality" became a salient issue for white Knights as soon as there was a functioning black district assembly. As Rachleff (1984: 123, 144–45) observes, DA 92 became central to Richmond's black workers, but it was also directly tied to the city's black civic life.[22] This thorough organizational separation allowed the black leadership a degree of autonomy from white control that their peers in other cities would have envied. It also provided additional evidence to white members that Richmond's black workers were capable of such organizing. This separation did not prevent all conflict, however. In fall 1885, Mullen explained in a letter to Powderly the particulars of a local dispute between the two district assemblies: "The secret of the whole thing is that D.A. 92 is a colored D.A. and the court of D.A. 84 would have had to apply to it for a judge to fill the vacancy, and they did not want a colored judge in the court. They may sugar-coat the matter as they please, but this is the true pinch."[23] This was a minor matter as far as local organizing was concerned, but it was typical of the ways that concerns over social equality produced conflict, even when whites accepted the involvement of black members as fellow

TABLE 9 Knights of Labor membership in good standing, Richmond area districts

| Year | DA 84 | DA 92 | Total |
|---|---|---|---|
| 1885 | 1,619 | 1,285 | 2,904 |
| 1886 | 2,934 | 3,139 | 6,073 |
| 1887 | 1,645 | 909 | 2,554 |
| 1888 | 495 | 343 | 838 |

producers. The concern was fanned by the fraternal nature of the Knights—it was the granting of honors associated with "brotherhood" that bothered white members. Still, contact between the two district assemblies was regular enough for DA 92 to write to Powderly in spring 1887, asking for a "visiting password between District Assembly 84 and 92 located at Richmond."[24]

A broader organizational problem—one affecting black and white assemblies alike—was the lack of an organizer in the area during much of 1886. Due to the explosive growth of the organization, Powderly placed a nationwide hold on new charters for a period of several months. Although there were no new black assemblies in Richmond chartered after 1885, it was not from a lack of interest. Richard Thompson and Joseph Buswell, the heads of the black DA 92, wrote to Powderly to say that their former organizer was fully qualified under the new guidelines: "DA 92 do hope you will send him his commission just as soon as possible if you think it proper to commission him for we have a good many [assemblies] applying for chart[ers]. But no organizer here."[25] Mullen wrote to Powderly several months later with a similar plea. His own commission as organizer had expired and there had been no one commissioned to take his place. More important than filling the position, he said, was finding the right person to do it. "For heaven's sake, and for the sake of our order, be careful who you appoint as organizers in Virginia. If every precaution is not taken in this direction the order will be ruined in this section. There are some good, true men who will take commissions if a high standard of qualification is required, but they will not act if such men as have been commissioned in the past are put in the field in the future."[26] More than a year later nothing had changed. "While I would rather see someone else as organizer, I would rather have a commission than see the work so sadly neglected as it is at present," Mullen wrote.[27]

Despite these problems, the Richmond Knights followed the organizing boom of 1885 with a wave of labor activism. This took the form of strikes and boycotts, the establishment of producers' cooperatives, and a much greater contact between black and white activists than had ever previously occurred. The Knights' actions were not only numerous, they were also effective. Leon Fink (1985: 154) reports that of ten strikes in 1886 and 1887, nine were offensive actions for better pay and working conditions, and seven won.

One of the more important interracial actions was the Knights' campaign against convict labor, which had earlier motivated the black coopers' strike. The prison labor issue was a major concern of the Knights, and it registered often in the *Journal of United Labor.* When the nearby prison built a barrel factory inside its walls, the threat of large production at low prices threatened to put Richmond's coopers out of business. One of the first major actions of the Richmond Knights was an organized boycott of the Haxall-Crenshaw Flour Company over the issue of convict-made barrels. Although the mill was not itself a major center of employment, it was a large producer of flour for the region, and hence a large local purchaser of barrels. The boycott showed the importance of an interracial and intertrade organizational form such as the Knights; unlike the earlier coopers' actions, this boycott was supported not just by the coopers but by Knights of all trades throughout the city, and the resulting publicity gave an additional boost to recruiting.

Despite the backing of the local Chamber of Commerce, by the end of the year Haxall-Crenshaw pledged to stop buying convict-made barrels and gave a written promise not to discriminate against Knights in employment. Fear of a more general boycott forced many wholesalers to stop selling other goods made with convict labor as well (Fink 1985: 155; Rachleff 1984: 124–26). The victory was announced to Knights throughout the country by a short statement in the *Journal of United Labor:* "Governor Lee, of Virginia, has announced that all convict labor in the State has been withdrawn from competition with free labor, and hereafter no convict will be employed in shops, on railroads or in any capacity where it will interfere with honest labor."[28]

Delegates from Richmond also played a key role in the 1885 General Assembly, held that year in Hamilton, Ontario, even though most of the Richmond assemblies had been functioning for less than a year. Of the 142 official representatives listed in the proceedings of the General Assembly, there were eleven men sent from the Southern district assemblies. The two from Richmond were William Mullen and F. J. Reilly, a cigar maker. This number underrepresented the strength of the movement in the city—the combined black and white membership in good standing in Richmond and its surrounding area was reported to be 2,904 as of July 1, 1885. Only Boston, New York, Philadelphia, and Denver could boast more dues-paying members. One issue that caused notice was the presence of J. B. Johnson, a black barber from Manchester, Virginia, a city just across the James River from Richmond and part of the same district organization. Johnson was the first black delegate to the General Assembly of the Knights, and at one point was invited to join Terence Powderly on the stage.[29]

The crowning moment for the Richmond delegation and one of the highlights of the meeting was when Mullen presented Terence Powderly with a ceremonial gavel. In a short speech, he explained the symbolic significance of the gavel, which he claimed was made from three historic pieces of wood. Most of the handle was made from a piece of the sounding board of the Richmond church where Patrick Henry issued his famous "Give me liberty or give me death" speech. The top of the handle was made of wood from Yorktown, where Cornwallis surrendered to Washington. The head of the gavel was made from a pillar of the Old Libby prison where captured Union soldiers were kept during the Civil War. Mullen used these iconic references to liberty to make a showy but popular speech touching on race relations and the need to overcome the divisive memory of the Civil War. The prisoners at Old Libby, he said, "were firm in their opinion that all men should be free, and enjoy the sunlight of heaven provided by a kind of Providence, as men free and independent . . . That strike for liberty was successful, and to-day the race intended as the beneficiaries are enjoying the blessings of liberty." Mullen then tied this theme to class struggle in the South by drawing on one of the movement's central frames. "Can those who are now the slaves of monopoly and oppression be liberated as easily as was the African race in America?" he asked. "Yea, even much easier!"[30] The rhetorical theatrics worked in his favor, as it was decided that the 1886 meeting of the General Assembly would be held in Richmond.

In the interim, the Richmond Knights kept up their string of successes. During 1886, painters, coopers, typographers, cotton compress workers, hod carriers, and foundry workers all were involved in strikes. By May, several tobacco factories essentially became Knights of Labor closed shops. In one of them, workers won an eight-hour day with no pay reduction. In another, a local assembly of women cigarette makers was formed. After a protracted struggle, Richmond granite cutters won a nine-hour day. Even some of the losses suggested an unusually high level of solidarity in Richmond. In one case, cotton compress workers decided to strike because blacks were paid less than whites (Fink 1985: 155; McLaurin 1978: 65).

The movement reached the peak of its power in Richmond at the same time that it did so nationally. In several of its strongholds, including Richmond, the Knights of Labor attempted to turn its membership strength into political strength in city elections. In this arena, too, the Richmond Knights sought to build an interracial coalition. In this, both black and white members had to step across the party lines that divided them. Most white Knights had strong Democratic ties, if they also had growing independent sentiments. For black Richmond in the 1870s and 1880s, electoral politics remained yoked to the Republican Party.

The spatial concentration of Richmond's black population, although driven in part by gerrymandering intended to limit the political power of Richmond's black population in most wards, allowed for the establishment of an entrenched black political structure within Jackson Ward. Richmond's black Republicans concentrated on gaining a local foothold in the white-led party, and they began to win council seats in Jackson Ward by the mid-1870s (Rachleff 1984: 68). While the spatial segregation meant that black candidates were largely shut out of citywide elections, it also meant that third-party candidates often sought to create a coalition with black Republicans in order to succeed.

During the 1880s, the Knights of Labor followed the lead of earlier third party movements in Richmond. The Greenback-Labor Party made some advances in Richmond politics, but it was not able to build an interracial coalition. A more important example was set by the "Readjuster" movement, which was named for its advocacy of readjusting state war debt. Under the leadership of William Mahone, the movement built a racially mixed coalition of voters and became a powerful force in Virginia politics in the late 1870s. For a time the movement controlled the state legislature, but by 1883 it began to collapse under the weight of charges that it was promoting "social equality." By the time that the Knights began their own political organizing, several prominent Readjusters, including Mahone and John Wise, had become Republican leaders (Fink 1985: 153–54).

In spring 1886, the Knights of Labor began to build a political coalition, called the Reform Party, for citywide elections. The white DA 84 put forward its own candidates for the municipal elections in May, almost all of whom had been longtime Democrats (Fink 1985: 156–57). The Reform Party candidates campaigned on a number of labor issues designed to appeal to both black and white workingmen. Politically, the Reformers' coalition with black Republicans centered on a compromise. The Reform candidates promised to endorse the black Republican candidates for the Jackson Ward elections, thereby keeping the ward's black representation intact. White Republican leaders like Mahone also stood to gain if the Knights were able to undermine Democratic dominance in the city. In return, the Republicans pledged to support the Reform candidates for the citywide offices (Fink 1985: 157).

The result of this coalition work was a resounding victory for the labor candidates. Reform Party officials became a majority on the city council and took half the sets on the board of aldermen. Two black Republicans from Jackson Ward were elected to the board of aldermen and five blacks were elected to the city council (Fink 1985: 157; McLaurin 1978: 90–91). For a time, at least, this victory lent excitement to local Knights, and gave white and black assemblies a concrete reason to work in closer alliance through the spring and summer of 1886. All of the assemblies were invited to join into a Labor Reform Committee that would choose a candidate to run in the fall congressional election. The obvious candidate was William Mullen, who won the support of both black and white locals. The labor coalition seemed to hold solid, and the Republican leaders promised to back Mullen rather than field candidates of their own (McLaurin 1978: 87; Fink 1985: 159).

The General Assembly of 1886, held in the fall, proved to be the most tumultuous moment of the very busy year. The Knights' bland official report largely hid the fireworks over the question of "social equality" that the meeting had set off. Although the issue was nothing new for white Knights, it had been managed in Richmond by the movement's elaborate "separate-but-equal" provisions, as Powderly had promised during his visit the year before. The election had opened the question more publicly, however. The events of the General Assembly raised the issue in such a way that it was difficult for the Richmond Knights and the membership at large to avoid. The meeting marked a turning point by changing the way that both black and white Knights thought about their fragile coalition.

The tension began even before the doors of the meeting opened. The delegates from New York's socialist-led DA 49 announced that they would make a principled stand against the Southern norms of segregation that they were sure to encounter. The representatives further stated that if any of its members, including the well-known black radical Frank Ferrell, were not allowed the same accommodations as the rest of the delegation then they would all move to rooms in black homes and boardinghouses. After the Murphy Hotel announced that Ferrell could not stay, the representatives did just that. Several other delegations from around the country apparently chose to join the protest by taking the same kind of lodgings.[31]

On the opening day of the General Assembly, Powderly and Governor Fitzhugh Lee took the stage. Lee began the convention with a speech welcoming the delegates to Richmond. Powderly was scheduled to follow Lee's greeting with his own speech to open the ceremonies. In an unannounced change, however, Ferrell was also present on the stage. After the governor's speech, Ferrell stood up to introduce Powderly. It was a short introduction, but because of the governor's presence on the stage it carried great symbolic meaning. Ferrell stated: "It is with much pleasure that I introduce to you Mr. T. V. Powderly, of the State of Pennsylvania, who will reply to the address of welcome of Governor Lee. . . . It is with extreme pleasure that we, the Representatives from every section of our country, receive the welcome of congratulation [from Lee] for our efforts to improve the condition of humanity. One of the objects of our Order is the abolition of those distinctions which are maintained by creed or color. I believe I present to you a man above the superstitions which are involved in those distinctions."[32]

Ferrell's words, and indeed his mere presence on the stage, suggested that the governor's welcome implied tacit acceptance of the racial policies of the Knights. For his part, Powderly issued a fairly standard speech, but he ended it by turning toward Ferrell and remarking on his presence: "When it became necessary to seek quarters for a delegation in this city, and when it became known that there was a man among them of darker hue than the rest, it became evident that some of these men could not find a place in the hotels in this city . . . Rather than separate from that brother, [the delegation] stood by the principles of our organization, which recognizes no color or creed in the division of men. The majority of these men went with their colored brother. I made the selection of that man from that delegation to introduce me during the address of his Excellency, Governor Lee, so that it may go forth from here to the entire world that 'we practice what we preach.'"[33] In language that elided the enormous symbolic meaning of the moment, the official report of the proceedings stated simply: "On motion, a vote of thanks was tendered to Governor Lee for his kind address of welcome."[34] This was a brave moment for Powderly, but it also created a problem for him because he could not simultaneously praise the actions of DA 49 and hold to the separate-but-equal line that he had used to launch the movement in Richmond the year before. In publicly placing himself with DA 49, he took a stand for "social equality" and thus opened an extremely sensitive debate for Southern white members.

The controversy that followed these actions lasted through the rest of the two-week assembly. The intensity of the moment was heightened when Ferrell attended a production of "Hamlet" and sat in an area reserved for whites. This was considered an outrage to respectable opinion and it fueled the local opposition to the Knights. The incident was the basis of heated editorializing in the local press, and a local "Law and Order League" patrolled the area around the hall where Hamlet had been staged.[35] More importantly, the controversy also caused many white members to distance themselves from a movement that they thought was pushing too hard for social equality.

Powderly attempted to contain the damage on both fronts by backpedaling to his earlier, more conservative line on the issue. As he stated in a letter to the press: "Every man has the right to say who shall enter beneath his roof; who shall occupy the same bed, private conveyance, or such other place as he is master of."[36] For many white members in Richmond, this weak retraction was not enough. The local press included interviews with unnamed white Knights on the matter. Interestingly, these members were outraged about the issue of social equality, but they did not draw the color line so distinctly as to call for a totally segregated movement. One said, "I have yet to meet the first man, white or colored, Knight of Labor or otherwise, who has expressed anything but the severest condemnation of the action of [DA] 49. Indeed, all have some respect for Ferrell; for the others contempt." Another article quoted a white member arguing with a movement official: "The course you are pursuing will break up the Knights of Labor here. We have white and colored Knights of Labor here, and they are members of different assemblies. A colored man has all the rights of a white man except socially. They are satisfied with things as they are, and it is not right for you to come here and tear us all to pieces."[37]

The General Assembly was supposed to conclude with a triumphant parade of white and black Knights leaders, delegates, and members, all marching to the city's fairgrounds where there were to be speeches, races and games, a banquet, and a dance. Most white Richmond residents boycotted the event, but the black turnout was impressive. The local white delegations were also thinned, and although separate dance halls had been rented for white and black participants, most of the whites in attendance went home early (Rachleff 1984: 177–78).

It was at this point that problems began to emerge within the labor ranks that were Mullen's basis of support. There were some fissures appearing among the white Knights. Several assemblies announced that they would remain affiliated with the Democrats in the upcoming election. It was unclear how much this was driven by party loyalty, by personal animosity toward Mullen, or by some combination of the two. A splinter group of white Democratic Knights vowed to support their party's candidate, George D. Wise, a cousin of the Republican leader. Republican support was even less unified. The white leadership was split; Mahone was in favor of coalition with the Knights, while John Wise began to voice his discontent with what he viewed as a one-sided relationship. Black voters were split as well, even within the ranks of the Knights. Eventually, the Republicans decided to field their own candidate after all. The choice was Judge Edmund Waddill Jr., a white party leader from John Wise's camp (McLaurin 1978: 87; Fink 1985: 160–61).

The height of the election season coincided with the Knights' General Assembly in Richmond, and all of the controversy surrounding the event seeped into the campaign. Mullen and the Reform Party were in an extremely tight spot. Mullen wanted to avoid the seemingly intractable issue of "social equality" and concentrate instead on local issues that could unite white and black working-class voters. Leaders in the Democratic Party and in the Wise/Waddill camp of the Republicans began to attack the Reform Party platform on racial issues. The Democrats painted Mullen as a supporter of social equality, while the Republican leaders argued that he would take his black support for granted. Convinced that he could not win with his coalition in shambles, Mullen withdrew from the race and threw his support to the Democrat. Black Knights voted for Waddill, but the Republicans were defeated in the election (Rachleff 1984: 180; McLaurin 1978: 88; Fink 1985: 164–66).

Strangely, the 1886 election was not the last gasp for the Republican/

Reform coalition, although it was effectively the end of the grand vision of an interracial coalition on equal terms. The Reform Party mobilized for a state legislative election in 1887, as the Democratic Party became increasingly anti-labor in its platform. The ticket fell short of victory, however. After this point, Richmond's black Republicans had increasingly less influence while the color line was gradually imposed to a much greater degree (Fink 1985: 167–68).

The failure of Richmond's interracial electoral coalition was, of course, driven by a number of factors including personality, the contingencies stemming from the 1886 General Assembly, and political miscalculations. But the underlying problems of the coalition—the same ones that were also faced by the Populists in the following years—were essentially twofold. On the one side was the general problem "social equality." In Richmond, the political movement was not able to escape the controversy over social equality that entangled the events of the General Assembly. The second issue was that white and black workers had a particular reticence about breaking with their traditional party affiliations. This was especially true of black workers, centered in Jackson Ward, where the Republican Party was the only political instrument over which they had any real control. The dissolution of the coalition was not simply the result of white elite machinations but stemmed ultimately from a reluctance to give up the more or less independent institutions of a community.

### CONCLUSION

By 1888, both the black and white assemblies in Richmond were in serious decline. Mullen wrote to Powderly repeatedly to complain about the lack of an organizer and about the poor state of affairs in both district assemblies.[38] An official of the white DA 3675 wrote to Powderly asking to be excused from paying dues. "We are unable to pay the fifteen cent Assessment levied to Pay Teachers to Teach the principles of the Order[;] our membership Has Decreased in a short time from 380 down to 20 and they left us With a Heavy debt Hanging over us therfo[re] we ask you to Be Excused."[39] Another white assembly asked if members could at the same time be both Knights and members of trade unions. Dual membership would be best, they thought, "as the order here is not holding its own."[40] The black assemblies were in similar trouble. A Knight from DA 92 asked whether members, who had "through some cause become unfinancial," could be allowed back into the organization.[41] But for a time, at least, the movement had succeeded in Richmond. During its time, Richmond was among the firmest of the Knights' strongholds anywhere. It also had a relatively successful and sustained interracial coalition. What made this possible?

In the case of Richmond, two factors enabled sustained interracialism. The first had to do with the economic and population structures of the city, while the second had to do with its organization of black community life. As one of the oldest and most established industrial centers in the South, Richmond had a relatively settled population even during this period of turbulent growth throughout the region. In turn, a settled black community emerged in the city. The first part of this chapter examined community life both spatially and organizationally. Richmond's black community life influenced the ability of black workers to organize and the reception that white workers gave to them. The community provided resources and experiences that supported organizing. The organization of the black community also influenced the view of white Knights. The prominent existence of black unions, self-help societies, and other organizations made the prospect of class alliance seem feasible in practice to white workers, even while they distanced themselves from the issue of social equality. In fact, informal alliances in Richmond between white and black workers predated the Knights in several industries and were especially prominent among tobacco workers and coopers. Having experienced this history, white workers in Richmond expected black involvement in the movement to a degree that did not occur in most places. It also fit with the emphasis that the movement narratives placed on civic virtue and self-organization as a central symbolic resource.

By turning community resources into organizational strength, Richmond's black Knights were able to maintain some independence both from hostile employers and from the white Knights. Segregation played an interesting and ironic role in this. The degree of residential segregation in Richmond was part of the emergence of the black community there, as it led to a concentration of organizational and political power. The segregation of local assemblies, and ultimately of district assemblies, also allowed black Knights to remain relatively free from white control. A movement that is segregated to the degree that white and black members were organized into different local assemblies and administrative units might be better termed "biracial" than "interracial." However, one of the points that emerges from this chapter is that the biracial structure was important for keeping the movement interracial in the more important sense of working together on relatively equal grounds. One measure of this was that the segregated structure of the district assemblies was imposed as much at the instigation of the black members as the white. Segregated assemblies allowed black members to have their own officials and set their own agenda. It also meant that the white members could not completely dominate the movement at the local level.

Interracial activism in Richmond eventually crumbled. Particularly important in its demise were the divisive issues of "social equality" and political interest. These issues came to a head during the 1886 General Assembly and the elections that followed soon thereafter. While Richmond's white workers were willing to accept the logic of interracial organizing in class terms, they were on the whole not willing to give up their status distinctions in interracial contact. When the issue was broached during the 1886 convention, the result was the unsettling of a delicate balance that had been struck in 1885 when black assemblies came into the order for the first time. The second limitation was the divergence of political interests among white and black members of the movement, a factor that foreshadowed the problems of race in the Populist political movement in the South several years later. Although an interracial coalition was successful in the municipal elections of spring 1886, the failure of the fall elections showed the problem of political action. Black workers were largely unwilling to abandon the Republican Party, which through the electoral base of Jackson Ward they were able to keep intact. White workers, faced with the collapse of the independent movement, themselves generally proved willing to return to the Democratic fold.

CHAPTER 4

# THE KNIGHTS OF LABOR IN ATLANTA, GEORGIA

In Atlanta we find the colored man in about the same condition as when the war closed. The trouble with the colored man here is that he is too well contented, too well satisfied with his lot to make any strenuous exertion to change it, and as it requires exertion to keep abreast of the times in Atlanta, [that is] why the black man is at all times a straggler, bringing up the rear of the army of progress. He will work for little or nothing so long as he gets enough to keep body and soul together, and as a consequence is regarded by his white brother as a stumbling block. There are, of course, exceptions, and some of them display a remarkable degree of push and energy, but it is too much to expect that the effects and teachings of two centuries of slavery could be forgotten and eradicated in twenty years.—TERENCE V. POWDERLY

During his tour through the South in 1885 Terence Powderly traveled from Richmond, where he had personally organized the city's first black local assembly, to Atlanta, where he had a remarkably different reaction to the city's prospect of interracial organizing. In Richmond, Powderly saw black workers as an orderly, organized group already mobilized and ready to enter the

Knights. In Atlanta, he saw them as an unorganized mass. In Powderly's eyes, and in those of the white Knights in general, the black workers in Atlanta were collectively a "stumbling block."

The difference between Richmond and Atlanta was related to the economic and social organization built into the history of the two cities, as well as to differences in the taken-for-granted assumptions about race that provided the base for social identity and for organizing. Atlanta had no settled and well-defined black community. For that matter, it had no settled white community either. As a new city, strong communities had not formed spatially or culturally. This meant that the black residents did not have the cultural and organizational resources to foster and sustain organizing, such as those held by Richmond's black community. It also meant that Atlanta's white Knights of Labor did not view black presence and involvement in the labor movement as a historical given over which they did not have an active say. As a result, white workers did not think that creating a coalition with black workers was important and necessary for the continued survival of the movement there.

In this chapter I examine the Knights of Labor in Atlanta by placing the movement's experience with the "color line" in the context of the economic and residential structure of the city and its history of labor organizing. My argument is essentially a negative one. The Knights of Labor, examined as an interracial movement, stalled in Atlanta. In the absence of an organized black community, there were few resources to sustain black organizing in the Knights independent of the white assemblies. Moreover, in the absence of a history of independent black organizing, white workers reacted warily to interracial cooperation, even on a limited "separate but equal" basis. In other words, white workers viewed blacks as potential competitors rather than as potential allies and, as a result, interracialism stalled. Early on a few black assemblies were organized, but they did not last for long.

In examining this issue it is much easier to trace the path of the things that happened than the things that did not. It is important to examine the case of Atlanta in conjunction with that of Richmond, however. In the South there were a few other places like Richmond with its settled black communities and its history of significant and sustained interracial involvement in the labor movement. Yet there were far more places like Atlanta, where despite important structural similarities, interracialism was limited or nonexistent.

The structure of this chapter closely parallels that of chapter 3. First, I outline the economic and social conditions of Atlanta that shaped the growth of the labor movement there. Like Richmond, Atlanta was a major industrial center of the South, and despite a few differences the two cities had very similar occupational structures. Atlanta was a new city, however, and it was not until the 1860s that Atlanta's population or industry became significant. Moreover, Atlanta's black residents were unable to draw on the collective cultural and material resources that the more centralized and historically rooted Richmond community had at their disposal. In the second section of this chapter I give an overview of the Knights of Labor in Atlanta. The movement was not as strong as it was in Richmond but it was reasonably well established, thus ranking Atlanta among the better-organized southern cities. There was also some black involvement in the Atlanta Knights; the major difference was that in Atlanta interracialism failed.

## ECONOMIC AND SOCIAL ORGANIZATION

The most important thing about Atlanta was the pace of social change. By the 1880s, it was one of the largest cities in the South, but it was also very new. Atlanta was a railway boomtown and a city of migrants. The oldest Atlanta families had settled there only two generations before, and the vast majority of the city's residents were recently arrived. Like Richmond, almost all of Atlanta's residents were born in the United States, but only three quarters of them were born in the state of Georgia. By way of contrast, nine out of ten Richmond residents were native Virginians.[1]

There was nothing but forest on Atlanta's site in 1837, when the location was incorporated under the name "Terminus" as the end point planned for the new Western & Atlantic rail line. The town was known as "Marthasville" when the first train stopped there in September 1845, but the population had only reached about one hundred residents. When a junction was made with the Macon & Western Railroad a few years later the population had grown to about five hundred, and a city charter was granted for the place now called Atlanta. Additional rail lines were connected to the city in 1846 and in 1853.[2]

The city grew at a much more rapid rate after that point. At the time of the 1850 census, the first for which Atlanta was listed, the population stood at 2,752. By 1860, it was more than three times that size. With the population growth came the establishment of city institutions and businesses, and thus more migrants arrived from the surrounding country. The new city dwellers seemed like a rough bunch to visitors, who noted what they politely termed a "frontier spirit." The city's summary in the 1880 census recalled the same thing about the early residents: "There was a large class at this time [1850] composed chiefly of workmen employed on the various railways, and adventurers, usual with new and thriving places, which was lawless and disposed to disorder. There were occasional conflicts between this class and the better citizens reinforced by the law; but the lawless element was gradually suppressed by the influx of better classes."[3]

Despite the city's significant damage during and after the Civil War, it continued to grow.[4] Atlanta became a central supply point for the Confederate troops and a manufacturing center for arms and ammunition. Although the Atlanta rolling mill was owned by northern-born men, it was renamed the Confederate Rolling Mill as its productive capacity was turned to making rails as well as cannon and armor for Confederate ships (Russell 1988: 47). A somewhat romantic myth has developed about the burning of Atlanta at the hands of Sherman's troops in November 1864. Much of the city was indeed left in ruin; contemporary accounts state that three-quarters of Atlanta's buildings were entirely destroyed. Yet this new city was not devastated in any meaningful way. Most of the prewar residents soon returned and began rebuilding, and by the end of 1866, Atlanta's population was larger than it had been before the war. Northerners began to invest capital into Atlanta businesses, although most remained relatively small in the immediate postwar years. The combination of rail lines and cotton production in nearby areas allowed Atlanta to grow as a site of cotton shipping (Taylor 1973: 47, 54, 92). To accommodate all of the newcomers, the city boundaries were expanded to a radius of one and a half miles from the rail depot at the town center, where they remained through the 1880s.

The 1880s were especially turbulent years for Atlanta's population. The city remained about 44 percent black over the decade, but both the black and the white populations exploded in size. At the 1880 census, the city was home to 37,409 residents. By 1890, the population had grown to 65,533—thereby increasing 75 percent in one ten-year span. While this decade was a time of industrialization and city expansion throughout the South, Atlanta's growth was unparalleled in the region. The bulk of the new residents came from the farms and towns of Georgia, and most of the rest came from other parts of the South, especially South Carolina, Alabama, Tennessee, North Carolina, and Virginia.[5]

Such rapid growth, combined with the level of existing industrialization,

TABLE 10 White occupational structure of Atlanta, 1890

| Category | Men | | Women | | Total | |
|---|---|---|---|---|---|---|
| | Number | % | Number | % | Number | % |
| Capitalists/professionals | 845 | 7.4 | 236 | 12.1 | 1,081 | 8.1 |
| Merchants/shopkeepers | 1,288 | 11.3 | 33 | 1.7 | 1,321 | 9.9 |
| Salaried employees | 3,997 | 35.1 | 283 | 14.5 | 4,280 | 32.1 |
| Skilled trades | 2,819 | 24.8 | 902 | 46.3 | 3,721 | 27.9 |
| Industrial laborers | 1,844 | 16.2 | 41 | 2.1 | 1,885 | 14.1 |
| Unskilled laborers | 430 | 3.8 | 5 | 0.3 | 435 | 3.3 |
| Domestic/personal service | 159 | 1.4 | 449 | 23.0 | 608 | 4.6 |
| Total | 11,382 | 100.0 | 1,949 | 100.0 | 13,331 | 100.0 |

Source: Calculated from U.S. Bureau of the Census, *Eleventh Census of the United States*, 1890, vol. 1, 634–35.

allowed the city's business boosters to adopt the image of the phoenix and to advertise themselves in the North as a city "rising from the ashes" of the Civil War. The vision put forth was that Atlanta was a thoroughly modern city, one unfettered by the past legacy of the South and the racial burdens still carried in other parts of the region. The city's industrial capacity lent some support to this claim, particularly in its principal industries of cotton textiles and railroads. Although the cotton mills have been at the center of a good deal of research about Atlanta's industry, the railroads were much more central to the employment of Atlanta's residents. Many worked for the railways directly, but many more worked for related industries such as rail car building and repair, iron production and casting, and railroad-related white collar jobs—especially as agents, clerks, and copyists.[6] There were two central cotton mills in Atlanta in the 1880s: the Fulton Cotton Spinning Company, which opened in 1881, and the Exposition Cotton Mill, opened the following year. A related industry, the Southern Bag Factory, produced cotton bagging for various commercial uses (McLeod 1989: 11). Although the cotton mills were smaller than the rail industry in terms of their scale of employment, they were the major industrial employers of women and of children under sixteen. Initially, all of the cotton spinning and manufacturing mills employed whites only; by the 1880s, however, there were a few blacks employed in the mills, generally as custodians and general laborers.

As in Richmond, occupations in Atlanta were divided by race and by

TABLE 11 Black occupational structure of Atlanta, 1890

| Category | Men | | Women | | Total | |
|---|---|---|---|---|---|---|
| | Number | % | Number | % | Number | % |
| Capitalists/professionals | 66 | 0.9 | 109 | 1.6 | 175 | 1.2 |
| Merchants/shopkeepers | 150 | 2.0 | 40 | 0.6 | 190 | 1.3 |
| Salaried employees | 246 | 3.4 | 15 | 0.2 | 261 | 1.8 |
| Skilled trades | 1,505 | 20.5 | 203 | 3.0 | 1,708 | 12.0 |
| Industrial laborers | 556 | 7.6 | 7 | 0.1 | 563 | 4.0 |
| Unskilled laborers | 3,224 | 43.9 | 24 | 0.4 | 3,248 | 22.9 |
| Domestic/personal service | 1,596 | 21.7 | 6,442 | 94.2 | 8,038 | 56.7 |
| Total | 7,343 | 100.0 | 6,840 | 100.0 | 14,183 | 100.0 |

Source: Calculated from U.S. Bureau of the Census, *Eleventh Census of the United States*, 1890, vol. 1, 634–35.

gender within each race.[7] Atlanta's whites were largely either salaried employees or skilled workers, although men were much more likely than women to be salaried. Since Atlanta had been made Georgia's state capital, and since it was at the center of rail linkages in the state, a large proportion of white men were employed as clerks, bookkeepers, and agents (McLeod 1989: 13). Most of the male skilled workers were employed as carpenters and joiners in the building trades (especially as plasterers, painters, and glaziers) and in related industries.

By contrast, blacks in Atlanta were concentrated into lower-status jobs, particularly as unskilled workers and as workers in domestic service (see table 11). A sizable minority of black men worked in skilled trades, however. Common among them were carpenters, stonecutters, blacksmiths, boot and shoemakers, and plasterers. The black men in industrial labor were mostly employed on the railroads as brakemen, stokers, and other laborers of various sorts. Although it was almost as common for black women to hold employment as it was for black men, they were overwhelmingly employed in the domestic and personal service industries as servants and laundry workers.

The distinction between "black" and "white" jobs was no less clear in Atlanta than it was in Richmond, but it was the point of much more contention because Atlanta did not have a long history of industrial contact across the color line. Organizing across the color line was easier in Richmond in part because long-standing experience taught white workers to expect such contacts

TABLE 12 Structural characteristics of Atlanta's wards, 1885

| Ward | Black (%) | Working class (%) | Segregation ($D$) | Contact ($P^*$) |
|---|---|---|---|---|
| Ward 1 | 43.4 | 71.8 | 0.72 | 0.23 |
| Ward 2 | 26.2 | 50.8 | 0.83 | 0.22 |
| Ward 3 | 50.9 | 81.8 | 0.72 | 0.19 |
| Ward 4 | 58.1 | 81.9 | 0.65 | 0.20 |
| Ward 5 | 24.5 | 63.1 | 0.67 | 0.37 |
| Ward 6 | 29.2 | 44.0 | 0.76 | 0.27 |

Source: Calculations are drawn from information in *Weatherbe's Atlanta, Ga., Duplex City Directory*, 1885. Class composition figures are based on a 1/20 sample of the names index, all other figures are based on a full count of the address index (see appendix for details).

and to expect black involvement in the labor movement. In Atlanta, however, no such expectation had emerged because there was no such history to rely upon and no established black community to support such involvement.

The spatial organization of Atlanta was very different from that of Richmond, owing to its more recent history, its different patterns of economic development, and its different political structure. As a result, there was no unified working-class experience in Atlanta, and neither was there a centralized black community. Without common experiences, there did not emerge a coherent, locally led labor movement in the workplaces or in politics.

Atlanta in the 1880s was divided into six wards, as was Richmond. The most prominent "natural" boundaries in Atlanta were the various rail lines that divided the southern wards (1, 2, and 3) from the northern wards (4, 5, and 6). The unusual numbering of the northern wards (5, 6, and 4, moving clockwise) resulted from the fact that Ward 6 was formed by carving a section each from Ward 4 and Ward 5 (see figure 2). These wards were partially racially distinct, with the black residents somewhat more concentrated in Ward 4. Atlanta's white working class was spread fairly evenly across all of the city's wards, with the exception of Ward 6 which was more distinctly bourgeois. Atlanta's black residents were similarly spread across the city, with the "whitest" ward nearly 25 percent black. Because of the extremely small size of the black middle class in Atlanta, each ward's black population was overwhelmingly working class, and none contained the bulk of the small middle class.

Atlanta's levels of racial segregation compare in interesting ways to those of Richmond. Whether Atlanta can be called more or less residentially segre-

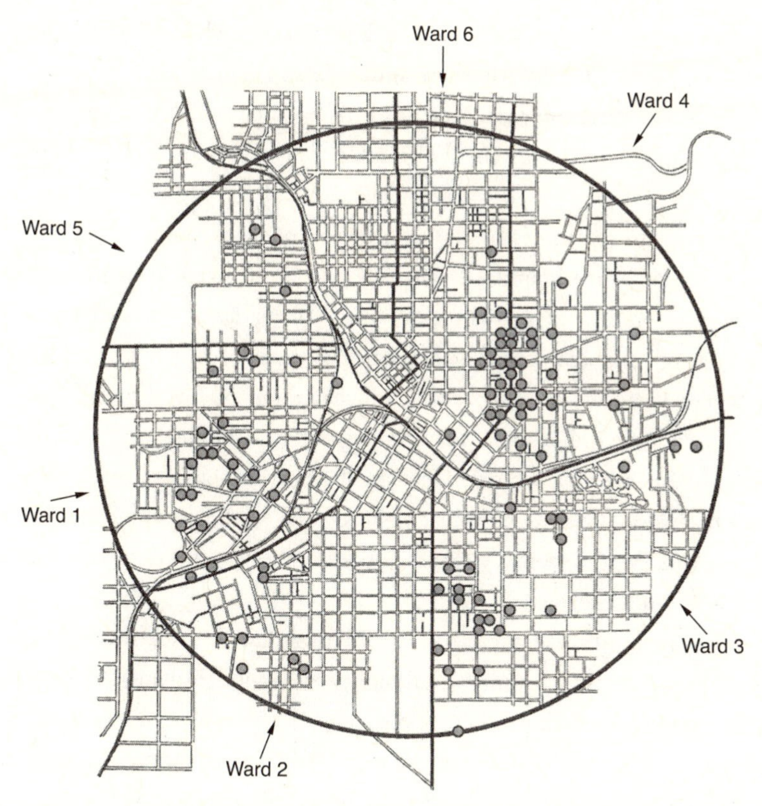


FIGURE 2. Black residential blocks in Atlanta, Georgia, 1885. (Calculations from *Weatherbe's Atlanta, Ga., Duplex City Directory*, 1885. Map adapted from U.S. Bureau of the Census, *Tenth Census of the United States*, 1880, vol. 19, 158)

gated than Richmond in terms of race is largely a function of how segregation is measured. Calculating by ward, Atlanta's segregation appears lower than that of Richmond ($D$ =.25). However, when measured at the block level, segregation appears much higher than in Richmond ($D$ =.73). What this means is simply that Atlanta's pattern of segregation was quite different. The level of segregation by block remained high in each of the city's wards, although it was highest in Ward 2 and lowest in Ward 4. There was an uneven distribution of the black residents of the city across the wards as well, but it was not nearly as dramatic as the division in Richmond.

The interracial experience in the city was also much different, a fact that becomes evident in the measure of contact that black residents were likely to have with their white neighbors ($P^*$). In Richmond, the ward with the largest black population (Jackson Ward) had the lowest score, while largely white, middle-class wards such as Madison and Jefferson had very high scores. There was far less variation across the wards of Atlanta, with the sole exception of Ward 5, which had the smallest black population in both relative and absolute terms.

Another way to see this is by the distribution of black residential blocks through the city. Ward boundaries and the city limits are shown in heavy black lines superimposed on a map of Atlanta's streets. Each dot on the map indicates a residential block that was at least 90 percent black. Unlike Richmond, where there was a clear spatial concentration of black blocks that formed a visible neighborhood, there is a great deal of dispersion in the placement of Atlanta's black blocks. Instead of one clear neighborhood, there are two loosely organized strips of black blocks, one on the west side of town spanning across Wards 1, 2, and 5, and the other on the east side of town across Wards 3, 4, and 6.

All of this meant that it was much harder for Atlanta's black residents to see themselves as part of a common community, even though there were some culturally recognized black neighborhoods. The black residential area on the east side of town on the border of Ward 6 and Ward 4 was known as Shermantown, and the area to the south of it in Ward 3 was called Summerhill. Much less clearly demarcated were Jenningstown and Mechanicsville, the black areas on the west side of town, largely in Wards 1 and 5 (Thornbery 1977: 36; Maclachlan 1992: 265–66). In the 1880s, however, these were "neighborhoods" only in a very loose sense. By 1900, the black residential areas were much more clearly demarcated in Atlanta, but they were still scattered in different sections of the city (Maclachlan 1992: 278–80).

To be sure, there was some degree of organization among Atlanta's black residents, as evidenced by the community organizations that began to spring up after the Civil War. As in all Southern cities, the church was a central institution for the black community. There were several black churches in existence during the 1870s, some with antebellum roots. After the war, many of the churches began to develop greater independence from their white counterparts. Several were located in and around Shermantown, including Bethel Church, which ran its own school (Taylor 1973: 185–87; Thornberry 1977: 28, 143). By the mid-1880s, there were twenty-two black churches scattered throughout Atlanta in proximity to the various black settlements.[8]

Schools also were an important point of interest for the black community. They remained more important for community organization as a political demand than a reality, however. After the war, several black schools were opened, staffed mostly by whites associated with charitable societies. There was continual squabbling over ever-elusive funding for black schools, however. By 1885 there were only four black grammar schools in Atlanta, each in different parts of the city. Three of these schools were run by the city while the fourth was under the auspices of the American Congregational Missionary Society. Atlanta's four black colleges and seminaries (Atlanta University, Clark University, Atlanta Baptist Seminary, and Spelman Baptist Female Seminary), despite their importance to the region as a whole, were inaccessible to the vast majority of the city's black residents.[9]

There was thus a degree of black community life in Atlanta, as in every city of the South. There was even some black involvement in fraternal orders such as the Masons and the Odd Fellows (Thornbery 1977: 188–89). The question at hand is the degree to which it sustained independent organizations, especially activist organizations, that could in turn foster Knights of Labor organizing. While there were some instances of black civic and religious organizations in Atlanta, they were neither particularly activist in orientation nor especially independent. By contrast, Atlanta's black churches were quite numerous and autonomous. Yet there is no indication that there was anything like the dense network of secret societies active in politics, mutual benefit services, or unionism that emerged in Richmond.

This pattern of residential and civic organization led to very different results in Atlanta's history of class organizing in general and in the development of the Knights of Labor specifically. Without significant community resources to rely upon, black workers in Atlanta were not able to launch their own involvement in the labor movement. White workers, in turn, had little experience in dealing with an organized black community in their daily lives and with organized black laborers in their workplace demands.

### THE KNIGHTS OF LABOR IN ATLANTA

The Knights of Labor were relatively successful in Atlanta, and yet the degree of interracialism within the organization never approached that of Richmond. Whether measured in terms of the numbers of black assemblies, or in terms of labor activism and practical alliances between black and white workers, interracialism stalled in Atlanta. There was some black involvement in the Knights, as there was in virtually every Southern city of any size, but it was limited in degree as well as rather short lived. In Richmond, the crises involving politics and the question of "social equality" divided an already well-organized movement. As a result, the Knights of Labor failed in that city among both white and black workers simultaneously. In Atlanta, support simply did not exist to foster black membership in the first place. White members did not see a compelling logic to organizing black workers, while black workers did not have the resources to organize themselves. White assemblies continued to come into existence and to thrive, even while the black assemblies failed.

The Knights of Labor established 147 local assemblies in Georgia, which were spread across sixty-fve different localities. Only three cities—Atlanta, Augusta, and Savannah—had more than 10 assemblies.[10] Atlanta was the only major city in Georgia with more than one known black assembly. In Atlanta, 14 local assemblies of the Knights of Labor were established. The first, an assembly of white telegraph operators, emerged in 1882 but did not last the year. In 1883, two new assemblies were founded. Both were mixed-trade assemblies, one was white and the other black. The following year, the same pattern was repeated. Thus, before there even were regularly appointed organizers in the region, the interracial project in Atlanta looked quite promising. Atlanta seemed to support the movement's claim that it could overcome the color line.

Yet by 1885 the interracial project began to falter in Atlanta even while the overall membership expanded.[11] In that year, there were four new assemblies founded, but all of them were white and three were organized among specific trades—carpenters, railroad workers, and cotton mill workers (an industry that was almost completely white). There were five more assemblies founded in 1886, all of them mixed trade but all of them white. Despite the relative longevity of the movement in Atlanta—the last assembly in Atlanta functioned until 1892, several years after the precipitous decline in the movement's membership nationwide—the two black assemblies folded quite early. Local Assembly 2992, founded in 1883, disintegrated in 1886 despite the fact that its membership (fifty dues-paying members in 1884, with seventy-seven the following year) was on a par with the white assemblies. Local Assembly 3428-a, chartered in 1884 with only seventeen members, disappeared from the

Knights' official records after a year (Garlock 1982). A member of DA 105 recommended a man named Andrew Allen "as (colored) organizer" in 1886, but it is not clear whether he was ever appointed. If he was, he was either not active or not successful in Atlanta itself.[12] In fact, black organizing in Atlanta had stopped by the time of Powderly's visit in January 1885. His assessment of black workers in Atlanta as a "stumbling block" rather than as potential coalition partners was very likely in accord with that of the white Knights who hosted him. Given that outlook, white Knights had very little incentive to organize new black assemblies, and Atlanta's black workers had few resources to organize their own.

Before the establishment of DA 105 in 1886, the expansion of the Knights in and around Atlanta generally occurred under the watch of the white LA 2514. Unlike Richmond, where there were groups of workers ready to join the Knights, LA 2514 felt that the duty and the burden of getting up new assemblies fell upon its shoulders. One official of the assembly wrote to Powderly in 1884 to say that the members had "determined to take vigorous action toward organizing Local assemblies throughout the State."[13] Although the assembly reported a total of only 70 members in 1884 and 1885, it had a huge turnover, adding 139 new members in 1884 and losing 90, then quickly adding and losing another 143 new members in 1885 (Garlock 1982). This was most likely the result of the assembly taking on new members until a new assembly could be formed for them.[14]

Local Assembly 2514 was itself in some financial difficulties despite its active membership. The officers of the assembly asked to be excused from paying a special assessment in support of a miners' strike in Pennsylvania. "2514 is the pioneer assembly here and has taken the whole responsibility of organizing and superintending the order in this section," they wrote. "Its members are poor and the times are fast reaching starvation point here, which of course makes extra assessments very unpopular . . . Many of our men are out of work one third of the time and then get only $1.00 to $1.50 per day."[15]

The history of class organizing in Atlanta provides some clues as to why the Knights of Labor never reached across the color line in that city to the extent that they did in Richmond, despite the similar proportional size of the black population and the similar occupational profiles in the two cities. The accumulated history of cross-race interaction in labor actions that made black involvement seem a given in Richmond was simply not present in Atlanta.

What was lacking for workers was, according to one study of workplace dynamics in Atlanta, "an alternate experience providing them a vision of an inclusive working-class collectivity" spanning across race (McLeod 1989: 59).[16] The lack of such alternate experiences was reflected in the history of labor organizing in the city. Union activity in Atlanta often highlighted, rather than elided, the city's racial divisions.

Isolated cases of white and black labor organizing could and did arise, but they were neither sustained nor particularly coordinated with each other. The strikes that occurred in Atlanta were generally wildcat strikes, and they often occurred over perceived breaches of the color line. This happened both in the railroads and in the iron mills, which were two of the major sites of interracial employment. In both industries, there was a history of largely unsuccessful trade union activity in the 1860s, which was revived in the 1870s over the pressure of declining wages due to the depression. In both industries, the labor organizations that existed served the interests of skilled (and thus mostly white) workers. Although there was some organized protest by black workers, such protests did not become a part of a unified response against common problems. In other words, while in Richmond interracial cooperation was pursued in the name of class interest even before the Knights, in Atlanta racial interests and class interests were mutually entangled.

In Atlanta's railroad industry, labor organization prior to the Knights was sporadic and largely ineffective. There were some early cases of black collective organizing in Atlanta's rail lines, but they were without tangible success. As early as 1867, black railroad workers in Atlanta petitioned the federal army in charge of the area for greater employment of freedmen on the Western & Atlantic rail line. By the 1880s, however, blacks were employed on the rail lines generally as unskilled laborers. Even the position of brakeman, a dangerous but skilled job that had formerly been open to blacks, was by the 1880s almost completely white. A more cohesive action occurred in 1871, when black workers organized a strike of the Western & Atlantic line over the issue of "death warrants." The railroad, in an attempt to scale back its financial obligations to employees, forced all workers to sign contracts waiving their rights to compensation in the event of accidental injury. Black workers walked off the job in a self-organized strike, but the railroad replaced them with white workers who were willing to sign the contracts.

White workers on the railroads had much more contact with national labor groups but were generally no more successful in their attempts to organize. The unions that existed before the Knights of Labor among white railroad employees were organized strictly according to skill and job. The first railway organization in Atlanta, the Brotherhood of Locomotive Engineers (BLE) Local No. 69, was founded in 1867. Locomotive firemen formed a chapter of their own union by 1877. The railway conductors finally organized under the Brotherhood of Railway Conductors in 1874, and their own national convention was held in Atlanta in 1875. These unions were reluctant to form alliances with less-skilled workers, however, and they espoused only modest goals. The conductors' association, by the later 1870s, banned strikes altogether. The BLE's leadership rejected alliances with both the Knights of Labor and other national labor organizations.

Despite such conservative organizations, railroad employees did organize strikes during the depression years of the 1870s. Such actions tended to underscore the lack of unity across skill lines even in the same industry. In 1872, shortly after the failed black strike, white mechanics on the Western & Atlantic line began to plan a strike to oppose wage cuts. The railroad announced that it would replace the workers immediately if they decided to strike, and the plans were called off. In late 1876, the Atlanta BLE organized and conducted a strike over a major wage cut that was proposed on the Georgia Railroad. The strike had enormous popular support among employees. The conductors, however, who were in their own union and were not threatened by the wage cut, refused to walk out. Many went so far as to guard the trains from the striking workers. The following year, railroad firemen threatened another strike over wages but the engineers refused to go along.

By the 1880s, Atlanta's railroad unions were in disarray. The BLE had collapsed in 1881, and the others had faded significantly. By mid-decade, railway men turned their interest to the Knights of Labor and built a local assembly of railroad workers, LA 4335. Most likely, this was an assembly of skilled tradesmen in the tradition of the earlier unions. Its official designation by the Knights as a "mixed" assembly meant only that it brought together different kinds of skilled tradesmen—conductors, firemen, car builders—which the earlier trade unions did not. There is no direct evidence that the local assembly admitted unskilled laborers, whether black or white (Garlock 1982). Nor is there any evidence that the assembly waged any sustained work stoppages or boycotts, despite the fact that the Knights were at the center of the national labor upheavals on the railroads during 1885 and 1886. By the early 1890s, skilled railroad workers were again organized into narrow trade unions.

Workers in the city's iron mills did not fare any better in their history of organization. Instead of forging links across racial lines, as in several of Richmond's industries, Atlanta's metal trade workers organized into craft organizations that actively maintained racial divisions. In 1869, William Sylvis, head of the Iron Molders' Union (IMU) and the National Labor Union, visited the city as part of a larger organizing drive in the South. Before he left, a new local of the IMU was organized. Blacks were excluded from the Atlanta locals of the IMU and later from the Amalgamated Association of Iron and Steel Workers. The turbulent economic times of the 1870s brought these skilled workers into conflict with the mill owners over wages as well as control of the labor process, which was being wrested away from skilled workers.

The protracted labor struggles at the Atlanta Rolling Mill beginning in 1875 set an interesting example of the consequences for a divided workforce. The management withheld a promised payment of back wages and attempted to institute instead payment in "scrip"—company checks good only at the company-owned store. Although scrip payment was not uncommon in mining and mill towns throughout the South, it was far less ordinary in cities, and the mill workers refused to accept the plan. When soon afterward the manager of the mill fired three skilled tradesmen who were active in the IMU, workers at the mill began a strike—which quickly collapsed. Later strikes were no more effective at the financially troubled mill, and the new management installed by the court after the mill's bankruptcy imposed a contract that precluded union activity altogether.

In 1881, workers at the plant defied the contract by joining into a broader organization that bridged different crafts—namely, the Amalgamated Association of Iron and Steel Workers. The Atlanta Lodge No. 1 included roughers, heaters, and rollers. Rollers were traditionally skilled workers, but they were in a trade that was gradually being mechanized and deskilled. Heaters were semiskilled workers, while roughers were unskilled. Although the Amalgamated stretched across traditional shop-floor barriers of skill and craft, the union excluded black workers. In July, the management of the mill fired a union member, and a major strike was organized. As with the other mill strikes, this one had enough support to stop production for a time. The management sidestepped the problem by hiring more than two hundred black workers, and then announced that the company would from that point on continue to hire blacks as skilled and semiskilled workers (Thornbery 1977: 210–11; McLeod 1989).[17]

Some interracial activity did occur in the building trades, the one industry in which there were blacks in both skilled and unskilled work. A strike of both black and white construction workers occurred in 1875. In reaction to a proposed wage cut, the crews stopped work on the new U.S. Customs House building. Replacement workers—at least some of them black—were hired on to take their places. As in Richmond, the black strikers tried to keep them out by appealing to their moral sense as well as to racial solidarity. When at least two of the scabs decided to continue, a fight broke out and the police arrested the black strikers. A similar pattern happened the following year, when hod carriers and their assistants walked off the job during the building of a new cotton factory in 1876. The skilled workers never stopped work in support, and employers hired new men to take their places.

For the most part, however, black organizing and strike activity occurred separately from white organizing. Some of the grassroots organization among domestic and personal service workers in Atlanta suggests that the black community, while less organized than in Richmond, was not completely devoid of organizational resources. The case of washerwomen is particularly interesting, since it was a major source of employment for black women yet also largely informal. There was some organization among washerwomen in Atlanta beginning in 1877, and in July 1880 there was an attempt to set standard minimum prices for laundry. In summer 1881, a much more coordinated effort came about. Nearly two dozen washerwomen and a few male supporters met in a church in the black Summerhill neighborhood to plan an effort for standard wages. Organizers appealed to local ministers, who in turn appealed to black congregations.

About three thousand women eventually joined in the action, and they managed to raise a strike fund of $300. Although this was a sadly small sum to rely upon, it was a surprising amount for women who earned so little; in fact, it was significantly more than the average yearly wages for a domestic worker in Atlanta. The strike itself began in July as the women called for a minimum rate of one dollar per twelve pounds of wash (McLeod 1989: 103). The results of the strike are not clear from existing records, but we must assume that it failed. Several landlords threatened to raise the rents of the women who did their wash, and the city government considered imposing business taxes and licensing fees on washerwomen (Thornbery 1977: 215–19). Also in the early 1880s were two cases of strikes by black waiters. The first was against the National Hotel in 1881. In this case, the waiters won their demand for a monthly wage of $14. The second strike, which was precipitated by the firing of a worker, was organized at the Markham Hotel in 1883. No gains were made in this case (Maclachlan 1992: 196).

In this way, the history of labor divisions along the lines of skill and trade—as well as race—left the Knights few resources for building unity in Atlanta. Several of the trade unions continued to keep a tight hold on some industries, despite the fact that they were not terribly successful in forcing the demands of their members. Many Knights in fact held dual memberships in their trade organizations and in the Knights. As a result, the local assemblies took on the same territorial battles of the trade unions. In their strikes and boycotts, they found themselves opposing other skilled unions in several cases. One division that did not continue to trouble the practical activity of the Atlanta Knights was that of race. After the two black assemblies folded, the movement operated in the same way as the earlier trade unions had—that is, they represented skilled white workers almost exclusively.

One sense in which the history of exclusive trade union consciousness continued to pervade the Knights was in the local wrangling over the exclusive nature of the local assemblies. By design, Knights of Labor assemblies were meant to reach across divides of trade and skill, but some white workers considered them to be more like trade unions. Three of the four assemblies chartered in 1885 were organized by trade or industry. Railroad employees and car builders made up LA 4335, LA 3854 was composed entirely of carpenters, and LA 4455 included only cotton mill employees. In search of advice, E. L. Lafontaine, the secretary of DA 105, wrote to Powderly to say that the issue of trade-based organizing was becoming a divisive one in Atlanta. His concerns surrounded the carpenters' LA 3854: "Their charter is worded like all other charters, but they wish to control all carpenters. Now there has been several Assemblies organized since theirs and they [also] take carpenters in. 3854 has never succeeded in doing much. Now it is a very serious question whether you should prohibit other assemblies from taking in carpenters when it is well known that they won't unite with 3854 . . . I think it would be better to let all assemblies spread their selves and take in all branches of trade . . . For instance, Gibraltar assembly no. 4335 is very popular [and] increasing very fast. They can get plenty of carpenters that otherwise would not join 3854."[18]

A letter from District Master Workman N. E. Stone explained the matter a little differently. He made clear that the issue was not whether assemblies should exist exclusive to trade, but rather to which assembly the carpenters could belong: "Among the L.A.s that goes to make up D.A. 105 is one that is a trade as[sembly], namely . . . no. 3854. All the others are mixed as[semblies]. Now the question is can the mixed as[semblies] take in carpenters or must all such applications be referred to L.A. 3854. Atlanta a[ssembly] 2514 has long cesed to take in carpenters and I think all the others would be willing to do the same with one exception. That is L.A. 4335 who were chartered as R.R. Imployees and car builders. They claim that under their charter they can take them (carpenters) in. The L.A.s meet in the same Hall and you can see it weakens one considerably."[19] The dispute reveals the degree to which the earlier history of white trade-based organization continued under the Knights of Labor. While the Knights adopted brotherhood as their watchword and touted the importance of organizing across race, occupation, and skill boundaries, the assemblies in Atlanta were fighting over who would get to control a single trade. Simply put, historical conditions in Atlanta did not favor solidarity.

The Knights' one major boycott in Atlanta was begun in cooperation with the International Typographers' Union (ITU). The relations between the two organizations soured in the course of the matter, however. In Richmond and elsewhere, ITU members became Knights. In Atlanta, the organizations remained separate. In 1885, ITU members began a boycott of Henry Grady's newspaper, the Atlanta *Constitution,* demanding that the paper pay union wages and institute a closed shop. The action emerged from a long battle between the union and the paper, which had resulted in the firing of several union members during an earlier strike. The Knights entered the boycott, but at the request of Grady and the other owners, DA 105 officials acted as arbitrators for the dispute. The Knights hammered out a settlement that included some benefits for the union, but which fell short of the typographers' demands. At this point, the Atlanta Knights considered the boycott to be over. The typographers, however, accused the Knights of selling out.[20] The most important labor action for the Knights in Atlanta during this period thus turned out to sharpen and maintain the divisive tendencies of the local labor scene.

Bitterness between the Knights in Atlanta and the trade unions continued to be apparent in the railroad industry as well. One Atlanta railroad worker expressed his local frustrations in a letter about a strike on a distant rail line that was being waged by the Brotherhood of Locomotive Engineers. "It is true that we can't all serve in the capacity of Engineers or even firemen when called upon. But a man can serve in honor and justice if he is not too selfish and imbued with the principles and ideas that Chief Arthur and his organization appear to have on hand ready for use at all times against the K of L," he wrote, referring to Peter Arthur, the head of the BLE. He then suggested that the Knights should offer to break the strike by taking the places of the BLE men as just return for the union's control of high wage jobs: "[I]t is not their skill or ability that keeps them solid[;] they shovel coal for a few years [then] they join the B.L.E. and think they are better than all employees around . . . No doubt they draw the most money. . . are they entitled to it as much as a mechanic[?] I say no . . . [T]he company can't afford to pay fair wages to the mechanic or laborer or never will as long as the B.L.E. gets the lions share of it."[21]

Black workers in Atlanta did not have the organizational power to make their inclusion into labor activism seem necessary to the white Knights. The same was true in the field of politics. While the Richmond Knights needed black support for their political endeavors, the Atlanta Knights did not. Political interests proved to be divisive in Richmond, but such coalitions were never even formed on a stable basis in Atlanta. Although there were some manifestations of labor politics in Atlanta, there was never a strong or especially promising coalition between black and white working-class voters during the 1880s or in the crucial period leading up to it.

There were several important limitations on black voting power in Atlanta. The first was the system of citywide elections, which was instituted to limit potential black electoral power. The elected councilmen of Atlanta represented particular wards, but the votes for these offices, like those for mayor, came from across the city (Thornbery 1977: 230–31; Watts 1978: 13). The only year that city council elections were based on ward votes was 1870, when the Radical Republican city government held power. In that year, the first full Republican ticket in the city's history held three black and seven white candidates. The two winning black councilmen (a tailor and a carpenter by trade, respectively) were elected in Wards 3 and 4, where black residents were in the majority (Russell 1988: 177–78, 181; Watts 1978: 21).[22] Citywide elections diluted black votes and prevented the kind of limited but effective political power that Richmond's black voters held in Jackson Ward.

But the lack of black political influence was also due to the divisions within the black public itself, and the way that Atlanta's white working-class voters took this public for granted. As a result of structural restrictions, Atlanta's black vote was both numerically unstable and internally divided. After 1873, a city ordinance required that before an Atlanta resident could vote, he was required to pay all taxes for the year. Subsequent versions of the ordinance gradually made this more restrictive—all back taxes had to be paid for previous years as well (Russell 1988: 181; Watts 1978: 14). The obvious goal of this policy was to reduce the potential power of black voting, although it surely also reduced the numbers of poor whites at the polls. In the years from 1883 to 1886, blacks as a percentage of all registered voters ranged between 19 percent and 39 percent (Watts 1974: 268, n.2). The voting restrictions thus did not uniformly destroy the black vote. Instead, the figures suggest that black voters were particularly important in specific years (1883, 1885, and 1888). In those years, black voting remained at least as substantial as it was in 1877, when the restriction was temporarily lifted (Watts 1974: 271, n.7). Yet the black vote was internally divided as well as numerically unstable. There was a resurrection of the Republican Party in the 1880s, but the black vote was not solidly behind the party (Watts 1978: 21).

Through much of the 1880s, the only significant political choice in Atlanta politics was between the pro-business and pro-labor Democrats. Several different "tickets" were nominated in any given election, sometimes by unknown sources and often without the consent of the candidates. Despite the ephemeral nature of most of the tickets, they often had a latent class character as the white working-class "wool-hat boys" opposed the wealthy "kid gloves" (Watts 1978: 19–21).[23] In these elections, the black vote was still split, although it leaned toward the business faction (Watts 1978: 24–29).[24] There were a few isolated cases of independent labor campaigns in Atlanta during Reconstruction, but from the late 1870s through the mid-1880s, the white working class largely remained within the Democratic Party, albeit in a faction opposing the business-led Democrats.

Before the 1880s there were two important but isolated cases of labor involvement in independent political activity in Atlanta. The first unsuccessful attempt was in the 1869 election. Atlanta's Labor Union No. 1, representing unskilled workers, selected its own candidates for the city offices (Watts 1978: 18). The second attempt, under the Greenback-Labor Party, was more promising. It was also the first organized labor effort in Atlanta politics to broach the possibility of an interracial alliance by directly appealing for black votes. The appearance, however, of a black candidate running as an independent for city council divided the potential black supporters. Two Greenback-Labor candidates were successful in their bids for council seats from Ward 1 and Ward 3, but these successes did not carry over into the next election (Russell 1988: 207).

The emerging class-based factions of the Democratic Party began to take more definite shape in the election of 1884. Arrayed on the one side was the economic elite of the city, which was organized into a faction known as the Citizen's Reform movement. Reacting to the alleged corruption of city officers, the Citizen's Reform movement nominated the city's "best people" for office (Russell 1988: 184–85, 208–9; Watts 1978: 26–27). In opposition, a "People's Ticket" supported by the white working class was nominated at a second rally. The People's Ticket lost the election resoundingly, except for one candidate for the board of aldermen. The People's Ticket also failed to gain black support. The Citizen's Reform ticket gained the support of prominent white Republicans and was favored by black voters as well (Russell 1988: 209–10; Watts 1978: 27–28).

Thus, by the time that the Knights of Labor began organizing politically in Atlanta, some examples of prior class-based campaigns existed, but without any hint of interracial coalition. Although black votes were pivotal in several earlier elections they consistently favored the conservative tickets, and the white working-class efforts to oppose those tickets consistently ignored the black voters.[25] The 1886 election was heavily shaped by the Knights of Labor. Despite the internal split over the prohibition issue in 1886, the pro-business Citizens' Fusion Ticket offered a few prominent blacks (two prohibitionists and two antiprohibitionists) a place on the nominating committee, even while denying them a place on the ballot itself. The People's Ticket, now organized under the Knights of Labor and including a number of antiprohibitionists, did not hold out an offer for black representation at all.

The white Knights of Labor were not unified on political matters, either. Writing during the 1886 elections, the recording secretary for DA 105 suggested that past organizers had not been careful in who they accepted into the Knights, thereby "allowing all the political 'hacks' to creep in who desired.

The result is we are so split up on candidates for congress that nothing can be accomplished." He then summarized the congressional campaign of that year. In seeking to capitalize on white working-class votes, Knights were put onto many tickets. The Knights thus wielded significant symbolic power during this election, but they were not unified enough to rally behind a single candidate. "Two men are in the field from this distict (5th Ga.) and K. of L. men are on each ticket as electors. Mr. Hammond is again offering. He has been in Congress eight years and has never voted for a measure looking to the benefit of the poorer classes, but has defiantly voted against bills introduced at the solicitation of our order. Knights are on his ticket."[26]

When black candidates were denied direct representation on the Citizen's Fusion Ticket, some black voters began to support the People's Ticket anyway. The working-class ticket was defeated, but it carried Ward 4 (Watts 1974: 277). The issue of black representation continued to simmer in Atlanta elections, and the prohibition issue offered Atlanta's few black political leaders a chance to demand more notice in return for their votes (Russell 1988: 210).

The election of 1888 was the most important potential turning point for electoral coalitions in Atlanta. The Citizens' Reform ticket was particularly conservative in that year, and it contained neither blacks nor token working-class whites. Black support of the ticket seemed unstable, and black leaders present at the meeting to select candidates voiced their complaints about the lack of black representation. There was even some discussion about reviving a Republican Party ticket for the election. The People's Ticket of that year was one of the most broad-based coalitions in Atlanta's electoral history. It was composed of members of the Mutual Aid Brotherhood, white antiprohibitionists, and several leaders of the old regular Democrats. The nomination committee of this coalition included eighteen black men, three of whom later withdrew. Although the announced ticket included no blacks and only two manual laborers, this was the most extensive that the black voice had been in any of Atlanta's working-class coalitions (Russell 1988: 210–12).

The election of 1888 was also one in which class was especially salient. Walter R. Brown, the People's Ticket nominee for mayor, pursued the issue of municipal improvements especially, pointing out that the city water line extended only to the wealthy neighborhoods. Brown promised educational expansions for white and black residents and better streets and sanitation in the poorer areas of Atlanta (Russell 1988: 212). But the most important part of the political calculation was that black political leaders remained independent by reinstating the Republican Party. The party's leaders formed a committee dominated by blacks to discuss the possibility of a separate black Republican ticket. Moses Bentley, a leading black politician, made it clear that any Republican support for the labor coalitions would be contingent: "If we get reasonable representation, we will not put out a ticket, but will support that ticket which allows us representation" (quoted in Watts 1974: 279). The People's ticket responded by immediately inviting blacks to sit on the committee that would select its nominating committee of seventy.

At this point, the Republican committee itself was divided into those who favored putting forth a straight ticket and those who favored coalition with the People's Ticket. The core question was whether the anti-Conservative forces would honor their promises. The group decided to withhold its decision until the People's Ticket slate was nominated. When no blacks were included, the Republicans again pushed for representation, but with little effect.[27] The People's Ticket was soundly beaten at the polls. It is unclear how much white working-class support was actually behind the coalition, but most observers indicated that the bulk of black voters remained with the conservatives. Brown also lost the mayors' race throughout the city, and narrowly lost even Ward 4 (Russell 1988: 212–13; Watts 1974: 281).

These events spelled the end of practical attempts at independent, labor-oriented political alliances between whites and blacks in Atlanta. Although the Knights of Labor was still active in Atlanta, there was no independent political movement. The former People's Ticket mayoral candidate, Walter Brown, joined with the Citizens' Reform movement, and he even called for the resurrection of the white Democratic Party in local politics (Russell 1988: 213). In 1890, the residual Democratic machine ran a white-only primary. In response, Atlanta's black leaders drew up an all-black ticket, but kept it secret. Word of this ticket leaked out to the press the day before the election, and Atlanta's white voters turned out heavily to reject it. After that point, white-only primaries were the rule, but there were no more efforts at independent black political organization (Russell 1988: 214–15; Watts 1974: 271).

## CONCLUSION

While the interracial labor coalition eventually failed in Richmond, in Atlanta it stalled before it ever got off the ground. Atlanta and Richmond were the only two southern cities to host the annual meeting of the General Assembly of the Knights of Labor. In Richmond, the 1886 assembly exploded in racial fireworks that shook the local unity of the order. In Atlanta's 1889 meeting, there were no such fireworks because there was no significant interracial activity to fuel them. By that date, Atlanta had not had a black local in operation for three years. In Richmond, the presence of Frank Ferrell, a black man, on the stage with Powderly and Governor Lee caused a stir that rattled the coalition of black and white workers in the Knights. In Atlanta, the highlight of the meeting was a visit from Leonidas F. Livingston, an ardent Democrat, president of the Georgia State Farmers' Alliance, and later opponent of the interracial political organizing of the Populist Tom Watson.

While Atlanta's General Assembly was in session, two members of the city's burgeoning educated black elite wrote to Powderly to ask how they could best become involved in helping with the black organizing efforts in the city. Charles Taylor, an attorney and former U.S. minister to Liberia, offered his services in helping to organize the black community. "Your grand order is able to do more good for them than any organization I know of on earth . . . I have pledged myself to spend the rest of my life in the work of trying to free my race from the mental slavery which now so grievously afflicts them."[28] C. E. Yarboro, the editor of the *Southern Appeal,* a short-lived black publication in Atlanta, wrote, "I send with this letter copies of my paper. If you deem that it can prove beneficial to the order amongst the Negroes in Georgia, I would be glad to have it made the official organ for the Knights of Labor for the state."[29] Neither offers received a response; by that point, they hardly mattered.

It is worth recalling Powderly's wildly divergent claims about black workers in Atlanta and Richmond. Although he was in Atlanta only shortly after his visit to Richmond during his southern tour of 1885, Powderly saw no advancement of the "colored man" since the Civil War. According to Powderly, Atlanta's black population was too contented to change its own circumstances, and was willing instead to settle for just enough to get by. As a result, it was a stumbling block on the road to progress. In short, the black workers of Richmond appeared to Powderly's eyes akin to the new immigrants, unorganized and unorganizable. This is not to say that there was no organization within Atlanta's black community; rather, it was the social, economic, and historical differences between Richmond and Atlanta that made such organization seem particularly slight.

CHAPTER 5

# RACE AND THE POPULIST "HAYSEED REVOLUTION"

The opponents of the People's Party profess to see in the division of the white people of the South the direst calamity . . . The hypocrisy is apparent to a blind man. A very large number of our people have no fear of the negro supremacy so much as they do greatly fear for the very life of the republic if the present system is permitted much longer to survive. If those who profess to consider every question but that of the negro as insignificant had any sincerity, they would hasten to join the People's Party, for according to their own testimony they would be doing no violence to their principles and the white race would remain unified. On the other hand those who believe in the principles of the People's Party can no longer remain in the Democratic party.—*PEOPLE'S PARTY PAPER*

Although Populism is often hailed as the pinnacle of southern agrarian radicalism, its racial legacy remains a subject of considerable debate. To a degree, the Farmers' Alliance and the People's Party, like the Knights of Labor, opened the possibility for interracial organizing in the South, but the movements remained ambivalent about the project. The Alliance barred blacks from membership even as it worked in close contact with the Colored Farmers' Alliance and went to great trouble to point out that its goals would benefit whites and blacks alike. The People's Party promised to support black voting rights and to fight for economic reforms that would benefit all farmers, and many Populists faced ostracism, violence, and ultimately defeat in defending these promises. At the same time, many were perfectly candid about the fact that between the races they wanted as little social contact as possible.

In this chapter I examine the movement narratives that organized the discussions of race in the Farmers' Alliance and in the People's Party. Populism was deeply intertwined with the same tradition of civic republicanism that motivated the Knights of Labor. For the Knights, the otherwise divergent movement narratives were each given shape by a common logic that saw civic virtue as a fundamental resource that the labor movement needed to defend. For the Populists, too, labor republicanism and its emphasis on civic virtue were expressed in a language of "patriotism, race, and rights," thereby giving organizational form to the movement narratives.

These narratives provided a foundation for interracial activity at the same time that they provided boundaries for such action. First, as was the case in the Knights of Labor, there was a distinct difference between the movements' reaction to foreigners and to Southern blacks. The class understanding of the movements, which framed the foreigners as outsiders and the black farmers as potential insiders, again drove this difference. The Populists were not generally concerned with foreign immigrants so much as with the foreign investors who they feared were conspiring to drive them into landless poverty. Thus, the xenophobic bent of the Populists was not a reaction to the unorganized mass below but to the malevolent "money kings" they perceived to be above them. This rhetoric was particularly pronounced in the Alliance, which was most focused on the economic plight of southern farmers.

Second, the cultural reaction of the white Populists to Southern blacks was also deeply ambivalent. Scholars of Populism have debated the degree to which the Alliance and the People's Party were actually committed to racial inclusion as opposed to exclusion, and whether such a commitment, if present, resulted from altruism, paternalism, or craven self-interest. The movement narratives suggest that such commitment, when it existed, was genuine and was based in an honest belief that such organizing would benefit both races. Yet at the same time, the Populists drew the color line much more distinctly than did the Knights of Labor, and they rejected "social equality" out of hand by setting a limit on the degree to which interracial organizing could extend. The Populists also confronted the latent racial competition inherent in politics much more directly than did the Knights. While the common interests suggested by emerging class identities opened the possibility for interracial organizing, the social and political identities tended to close it.

### THE ORGANIZATIONAL UNDERSTANDING OF RACE

This chapter parallels my discussion of the Knights of Labor movement narratives. The analysis I present herein is developed from over eight hundred items culled from movement journals during the most active period of both organizations.[1] In the case of the Alliance, the data are from the organization's official paper, the *National Economist*, which was edited by C. W. Macune. I collected and coded data from issues of the *National Economist* from early 1889, when the paper began distribution, through early 1893, when it ceased. The People's Party data are from the *People's Party Paper*, edited by Tom Watson.[2] The data span the available run of the paper, from late 1891 through late 1894, with scattered issues in fall 1895 and 1896.[3] Both papers were weekly editions.

Both papers served as a voice for their respective organizations and as such were important sources for seeing the movement narratives linking race to economic and political interests. Despite the fact that these papers reflected their respective editors more than did the Knights' journal, both of the Populist papers were the product of many different voices—the *National Economist* included many of these voices in its guest essays while the *People's Party Paper* achieved the same diversity by reprinting items from the smaller, regional Populist papers. Both included many letters and notices from local activists. The Populist movement narratives are defined by the same basic elements that defined those of the Knights of Labor—the racial or ethnic "others" and the frames of interest that organized the discussions.[4] Although the movement goals were clearly class based, for obvious reasons political goals were often more salient than economic ones in the Populist discussions. Because of this, I included both material and political interest frames.

The *National Economist*, published by the Alliance in Washington, D.C., was "devoted to social, financial, and political economy" according to the masthead slogan. For the one dollar annual subscription price, readers found a wealth of political and economic essays, lessons on the principles of the movement, and commentaries on current events. In addition to providing a forum for the movement as a whole, the *National Economist* was also devoted to the education of rural farmers in the matter of political economy. A typical edition began with short editorial comments sandwiched between longer editorial essays by well-known figures in the organization—"The Power of Money to Oppress" by N. A. Dunning was a typical example, using movement wisdom and long lists of figures to connect the contraction of the money supply to the increase in mortgage foreclosures and thus demonstrate that the crisis that the Southern farmers found themselves in resulted from structural rather than personal failure.[5]

The *People's Party Paper* ("Equal rights to all—special privileges to none") was similar to the *National Economist* in format, although the emphasis was shifted from economic to political education. The paper included political news and essays on the "money question" in addition to reports of Populist organizing across the South and news from other labor and political organizations. The People's Party saw itself as the united expression of the great labor movement broadly conceived, but the paper also included essays on the party's evolving platform, on its election advances and setbacks, and on the general state of the movement.

The first defining element in the movement narratives was the racial and ethnic "others" that the movement confronted. The Farmers' Alliance and the People's Party identified very similar groups of relevant "others."[6] One central category for both organizations was black Americans ("negro," "colored," or less often "black") but far more than in the Knights' communications, the Populists also made use of specifically Southern labels that illustrated the taken-for-granted nature of the color line in the movements. The term "nigger" was used with some frequency (seven times in the Alliance communications, twenty-four times in the People's Party newspaper). Generally the term was enclosed by quotation marks to indicate that the author was using it ironically—for example, against Democratic charges that the movement was promoting "nigger supremacy."[7] However, at certain times the term was used without such self-consciousness, as were other terms such as "darky" and "cuffee."[8]

The second category referred to various ethnic and national groups. The

TABLE 13 Racial/ethnic "others" in Populist papers

| | *National Economist* | | *People's Party Paper* | |
|---|---|---|---|---|
| Group | Number | % | Number | % |
| Black | 132 | 29.1 | 316 | 63.8 |
| Ethnic/national | 205 | 45.3 | 97 | 19.6 |
| Foreign, not specified | 74 | | 17 | |
| British/English | 42 | | 12 | |
| Indian | 23 | | 14 | |
| Jews | 13 | | 9 | |
| Italians | 7 | | 7 | |
| Chinese | 12 | | 13 | |
| Other | 34 | | 24 | |
| General | 111 | 24.5 | 68 | 13.7 |
| White | 5 | 1.1 | 14 | 2.8 |
| Total | 453 | 100.0 | 495 | 100.0 |

Note: Because some communications named more than one "group," the total exceeds the N of communications.

Alliance and People's Party communications made scattered mention of many different groups—particularly the English and unspecified "aliens" and "foreigners." As in the Knights of Labor communications, these statements mostly made broad references to slavery, race, or race relations without specifying particular groups. In the final category, "white" was used as the relevant "other" term in several communications penned by black correspondents. In the third category, there was no specific racial "other" mentioned.

While the terms used were quite similar for the two movements, the distribution of their usage differed markedly. The *National Economist* communications linking race and class dealt first and foremost with the ethnic and national "others" and only secondarily with black Americans. The *People's Party Paper* communications concentrated on blacks, and only to a much lesser extent on "aliens" and other foreigners and immigrant groups. The Alliance communications also made more extensive use of discussions of slavery in their rhetoric than did the People's Party.

The second defining element for the movement narratives involves the movement frames linking race to discussions of the movement's interests (see table 14). For the Populists, one major frame had to do with interracial

TABLE 14 Frames of interest in Populist papers

| Interest frame | *National Economist* Number | *National Economist* % | *People's Party Paper* Number | *People's Party Paper* % |
|---|---|---|---|---|
| Interracial organizing | 70 | 18.7 | 98 | 21.9 |
| Positive evaluations | 35 | | 80 | |
| Neutral evaluations | 25 | | 9 | |
| Mixed/negative evaluations | 10 | | 10 | |
| Material interests | 82 | 21.9 | 44 | 9.8 |
| Economic competition | 77 | | 35 | |
| Economic similarity, etc. | 5 | | 9 | |
| Political/social interests | 49 | 13.1 | 201 | 44.9 |
| Political Competition | 36 | | 167 | |
| Status Competition | 13 | | 34 | |
| Slavery and social position | 104 | 27.7 | 41 | 9.2 |
| Wage slaves like chattel slaves | 41 | | 12 | |
| White slaves like chattel slaves | 10 | | 4 | |
| Money slaves like chattel slaves | 35 | | 14 | |
| Party slaves like chattel slaves | 18 | | 11 | |
| Other | 70 | 18.7 | 64 | 14.3 |
| Total | 375 | 100.0 | 448 | 100.0 |

organizing. Within this frame, there were very few statements that made an outright argument against such actions. There was a difference in how the two organizations presented the issue, however. The Alliance rhetoric was divided between those statements that explicitly supported interracial organizing and those that discussed or reported instances of such organizing but remained normatively neutral. By contrast, the People's Party communications that took up this discourse were overwhelmingly positive.

While the Knights essentially had one interest frame that was centered on the role of intergroup competition, the Populists had two such frames. One surrounded class interests per se—discussions of the conditions of the small farmers, essays on the problems of cotton debt and the crop lien system, or debates about proposed remedies in the sub-treasury plan or in local cooperatives. As the movement began to consider a political mobilization as an outlet for its class interests, the political interests themselves became an issue, for reasons more central to the People's Party than to the Alliance.[9]

The Alliance, by contrast, was much more concerned with the rhetoric of

TABLE 15 Movement narratives of race/class, *National Economist*

| Discourse | Black | Ethnic/Nat'l | General | White | Total |
|---|---|---|---|---|---|
| Interracial organizing | **54 (40.9%)** | 3 (1.5%) | 11 (9.9%) | 4 (80.0%) | 72 |
| Material interests | 8 (6.1%) | **120 (58.5%)** | 1 (0.9%) | 0 (0.0%) | 129 |
| Political interests | **36 (27.3%)** | 11 (5.4%) | 8 (7.2%) | 1 (20.0%) | 56 |
| Slavery and social position | 13 (9.8%) | 21 (10.2%) | **77 (69.4%)** | 0 (0.0%) | 111 |
| Other | 21 (15.9%) | 50 (24.4%) | 14 (12.6%) | 0 (0.0%) | 85 |
| Total | 132 (100.0%) | 205 (100.0%) | 111 (100.0%) | 5 (100.0%) | 453 |

Note: Lambda = .532, approx. sig. = .000; Uncertainty coefficient = .368, approx. sig. = .000.

slavery as it applied to the class-based demands of the organization. Like the Knights' use of slavery as a trope for their class discussions, the Alliance also adopted the imagery of the declining position of white labor in their discussions of the social position of laboring people. However, the Populists elaborated upon this frame in ways that the Knights did not. The Alliance in particular pressed the frame into the areas that most concerned the southern membership—the increasing indebtedness of farmers who were being tied by mortgages to land that they did not control, and the control that the Democratic Party had over white southerners.

For the Populists, as for the Knights, the two elements were connected together into stable movement narratives.[10] The structure of the resulting narratives was similar to those of the Knights of Labor, but there was also an important difference. The Populist discussions of black workers were clearly more bifurcated than those of the Knights of Labor. There were two separate narratives—one tied black Americans to a discussion of class-based interracial organizing and the other tied them to a discussion of political and status competition. The third narrative tied various ethic and national "others" to the material competition frame, while the fourth linked general mentions of race (i.e., those that did not mention a particular group) to the "slavery and social position" frame. There were also some significant differences across the two Populist movement organizations. Most important was the tradeoff between the first two narratives. The discussions in the Alliance newspaper put more emphasis on the first narrative, relatively speaking. The People's Party discussions, by contrast, shifted more emphasis to the second narrative.

TABLE 16 Movement narratives of race/class, *People's Party Paper*

| Discourse | Black | Ethnic/Nat'l | General | White | Total |
|---|---|---|---|---|---|
| Interracial organizing | **68 (21.5%)** | 2 (2.1%) | 19 (27.9%) | 11 (78.6%) | 100 |
| Material interests | 18 (5.7%) | **37 (38.1%)** | 0 (0.0%) | 1 (7.1%) | 56 |
| Political interests | **183 (57.9%)** | 20 (20.6%) | 11 (16.2%) | 2 (14.3%) | 216 |
| Slavery and social position | 11 (3.5%) | 11 (11.3%) | **25 (36.8%)** | 0 (0.0%) | 47 |
| Other | 36 (11.4%) | 27 (27.8%) | 13 (19.1%) | 0 (0.0%) | 76 |
| Total | 316 (100.0%) | 97 (100.0%) | 68 (100.0%) | 14 (100.0%) | 495 |

Note: Lambda = .184, approx. sig. = .000; Uncertainty coefficient = .226, approx. sig. = .000.

Understanding the structure of the Populist movement narratives is important, but understanding the way that the narratives linked race and interests requires examining the content of each. In what follows I examine each of the narratives in greater detail. This more culturally sensitive analysis shows how a separate structure of interests led the Alliance (and to a lesser extent the People's Party) to use a rhetoric of economic competition to different ends than did the Knights of Labor when it came to discussions of various ethnic and national groups. The result was a framing process that brought together the racial "other" terms "alien," "British" and "Jew" with the class terms "banker" and "aristocrat." In addition, it shows the ambivalent approach to black involvement and interracial organizing in the Populist communications. The Alliance attempted to walk a fine line in expressing to white members and black followers alike why racial egalitarianism in class action was beneficial to all, even while denying that "social equality" was a desirable goal. The People's Party was even more deeply ambivalent in their discussions about both the social and political consequences of interracial organizing.

The following sections examine the internal logic of each of these narratives in turn, beginning with the "economic competition" and "slavery and social position" narratives. These establish most clearly the role of the Populists' republican notions of civic virtue. The remaining two movement narratives are treated together, since they were in effect competing ways that the movement understood the role of black Americans. These narratives were also underlined by the importance of civic virtue, but they diverged on the issues of whether blacks were able to appreciate and support such goals and what black involvement would mean for the position of white Populists.

## ECONOMIC COMPETITION AND RACE

The Populists followed the pattern set by the Knights in tying the discussion of several ethnic and national groups to an interest frame about class competition. In some cases, these discussions followed the same path as the Knights of Labor by examining the role they felt that European "pauper laborers" would play in the wages and conditions of American laborers. In a few cases, the Alliance recognized that while the new immigrants would not threaten the farmers who owned their own land, they might eventually cause problems for those who were not landowners. Here, as in the Knights of Labor discussions, the threat of economic competition and its impact on the conditions of native-born working people was a central concern. Here, too, the concern was not just about material conditions but also about the social conditions of liberty and civic virtue: As the *National Economist* put it: "In the United States the question of immigration is one of startling importance, and threatens the direst evils to American industry, both agricultural and mechanical. In this riffraff of European vagabonds lies a power servile and mercenary ready to the hand of arrogant plutocracy that would murder liberty at a nod. It is time for Americans to beware."[11] Yet such discussions remained tangential for most Southern farmers who did not compete with immigrant workers directly and rarely if ever came into contact with them.[12] Instead, such statements reflected the concerns and language of the broader labor press.

Far more common for the Populists was the argument that the competition from foreigners was coming from above, not from below. Particularly in the Alliance discussions, it was foreign investment and control of the money supply, much more than foreign immigration, that caused the declining condition of farmers. This narrative took several directions, each feeding the Alliance's political demands in a different way. The most direct of the Alliance claims was that "alien" investment was causing a concentration of farmlands that would eventually turn small farmers into tenants. Here too the issue of liberty was front and center: "The truth of the matter is that foreign citizens owning lands or having capital otherwise invested in this country means subjection to them . . . so that in the course of time, if it is allowed to continue, they will get to own so much of the wealth that it will prove disastrous to our liberties. For instance, the foreign land-owners are gradually instituting a system of tenantry similar to that in their own country."[13]

Here, the ideal felt to be slipping away was not that of a republic of independent artisans but one of smallholding yeomen. Indebtedness, monetary contraction, and foreclosure, in the eyes of the movement, all came to symbolize a threat not just to individual farmers but to the Jeffersonian tradition of independent farmers as a pillar of American civic freedom. The negative image was European serfdom: "The title-deeds held by alien aristocrats to American lands are the transfers of the liberty of American citizens and evidences of their thralldom" claimed one article. "By those patents the Government of the United States pledges itself to enforce the demands for tribute made by these foreign lords upon their subjects in this country. Can Americans remain content while such facts exist?"[14]

Such claims were the movement's response to the growing debt crisis among farmers. In this narrative, the crisis was not simply a product of abstract market institutions but the active doing of "aliens." In particular, it was the English investors ("capitalists" and "speculators") that the Alliance worried about—and about whom they tried to warn others: "English capitalists are visiting the south, and they speak in the highest terms of their treatment at the hands of the southern people, says the Kentucky *State Union.* It is all right to treat them nicely as visitors, but there is another side to be seen. Our visitors are prospecting for places in which to invest their surplus money, and this is what we object to. We do not want our land or manufactories or transportation owned by foreigners."[15]

It was within this narrative that the Alliance made their otherwise curious demand that the "alien ownership of land" be abolished. It was not a free-floating jingoism that created the demand, but reaction to the experience of growing farm debt and the resulting land concentration. Others in the Alliance tempered this argument by pointing out that there was little difference between English speculators buying up foreclosed land and American capitalists doing the same thing.[16] If it were true that the English capitalists took as much profit from their American investments as the native ones, then "there can be no doubt that the capitalists of both countries are associated together for the purpose of living at the expense of American farmers and laborers."[17]

The analysis may have been incorrect, but it was consistent with the broader republican sentiments of the movement. The falling status of the small farmer was one side of this issue. Another side was the demand for democracy in economic institutions. A central thread of this narrative was that it was through unfair control of the American money supply that the English capitalists were gaining control of the land and political machinery of the country.[18] It was here that the essentially class-based analysis became distinctly racialized. The English capitalists were linked to long-standing stereotypes about the Jewish bankers. After arguing that the struggle against English investors was a second stage in the fight for independence, one editorial made this claim explicit: "The first move of those wiley English Jews was to work on Congress through Wall street agents and direct to get control of this nation's currency . . . The next step was to obtain possession of our farming lands and people them with tenant farmers, that the rental might contribute to English support." Even amid this explicit anti-Semitism, the essentially civic nature of the Alliance narrative was clear in the editorial's conclusion: "The Alliance demands that those aliens become citizens, or that after five years their lands shall be sold to citizens and the proceeds handed over to such aliens, with the invitation to 'git.'"[19]

While this narrative was much less prominent in the People's Party communications, the argument about competition between Southern farmers and foreign speculators was developed in the same way. The People's Party also adopted the Alliance's use of long-standing racial conspiracy theory.[20] As one editorial from the paper put it, in reference to the outcome of the 1892 election won by the Democrat Grover Cleveland: "I don't see why the southern people go wild over the election of Cleveland, he is nothing only an Eastern Yankee with all the oppressive ideas of a London Jew . . . We will have to form an alliance for self protection against the plutocrats of this country and the London Jew. That is if we want to leave an inheritance for our children. If we don't, we will leave a bond[ed] and mortgaged country for them to live in."[21]

Thus for the Populists it was not merely abstract forces that were to blame for the agrarian economic crisis, but concrete institutions and actors that worked for the interests of the bankers rather than "the producers." While the anti-Semitism was clear, it was also an expression of a broader republican nationalism. The image of the foreign Jewish banker was clearly racist, but it was also a stock image for a general and nefarious "money power" standing in opposition to Jeffersonian sensibilities and to democratic control. Regardless of the external validity of this assessment, the movement's internal logic saw the "London Jew" as a problem as much because he stood for foreign money power as because he was a Jew.

## SLAVERY AND THE SOCIAL POSITION OF FARMERS

The concern that the Populists felt over what they saw as the erosion of a republic built on independent small farmers, and the consequent decline of democracy in economic life as well as political life, were also factors that drove the narrative relating to "slavery." As in the Knights of Labor discussions, this narrative was an important window on the construction of whiteness in that it revealed the status fears of white farmers as well as the use to which the movement leaders put these fears in framing their approach to their political and class-based demands. Much of the discussion of slavery proceeded in the same manner as it had for the Knights of Labor—that is, with a focus on the concepts of "wage slavery" and "white slavery." Although the farmers might not be paid a wage for their work, the "slavery" beginning to envelop them was argued to have the same effect on all producers. "The success of the Farmers Alliance means the emancipation of the farmers' and laborers' wives, daughters, and mothers from the isolated slavery that now environs them," according to one editorial. "No intelligent people has ever been enslaved, no ignorant people have been found in any other condition."[22]

The Alliance reminded white farmers that such slavery was not unthinkable for them. According to this narrative, slavery was not a matter of race but of condition. Nor was such slavery—or at least indenture—unknown in white civilization: "It might be well while boasting of the dignity of our race and the unconquerable Anglo-Saxon spirit to remember that the vaunted liberty of our ancestors was enjoyed only by the upper classes, the favored few of fortune, to whom the inferior classes were slaves."[23] The goal of the Alliance was to preserve the proud and independent status of the farmer that the movement felt was slipping away. One editorial summed up the achievements of the Alliance in the following manner: "I would say that the Alliance found the southern farmer in a worse condition than the African previous to 1860, and to-day we find that it has succeeded in placing him on his feet, making him realize that he is still a man and not a slave; and if he is an Alliance man he can boast of an amount of independence and self-respect that hasn't prevailed in the southern and southwestern States in a generation."[24] The editorial obviously exaggerated the farmers' condition and the Alliance's role in changing it. But it does give a sense of the fears of southern farmers concerning their changing social status, and the sense that the Alliance was a vehicle that could help them formulate a solution.

The Populists also elaborated the slavery narrative in ways that the Knights of Labor did not. Particularly vital to the narrative were two additional tropes, which might be labeled "money slavery" and "party slavery."[25] These tropes were linked to the movement's twin goals of monetary reform and political involvement. The first issue involved the control of the money supply and the resulting control of land. The bind that farmers felt was expressed in several discussions of increasing debt and foreclosure. As one editorial stated, "The annual interest on this debt has entailed an actual tax upon the farmers . . . which amounts to more than five-sixths of the value of the entire crop last year." All farmers felt the result in their changing relationship to the local merchants. Even if the farmer had no liens on his crop, he was forced to sell at the going rate to finance his mortgage: "I want to see the day come when the farmer can carry his cotton to town, and when the merchant prices his goods, the farmer can have the privilege of pricing the fruits of his honest toil. As it is now, the farmer is at the mercy of the man who sells him his goods and buys his crops. As a rule of law it requires two persons to make a contract, but there is a glaring exception when the farmer walks into a store with his cotton sample. The merchant alone settles all the particulars of that transaction, and to that extent the farmer is a slave."[26]

Unfreedom thus was defined by a fundamental inequality of power. The Alliance rhetoric played the subservience of farmers to market forces and commodification against its ideal of independent yeomanry: "Interest, earnings, rents, and profits are the shackles Americans have to fear," remarked one editorial. "They are the modern development of the collar, the gives, the manacles, and the clanking chain."[27] But the Alliance also gave this dissatisfaction a direction, through a sense of who was to blame and how the situation could be fixed. Ultimately, the Alliance argued, it was the contraction of the monetary supply that was behind the declining market price for farm products and the increasingly expensive credit that the farmers faced. The bankers and "land sharks" were thus the ones enslaving the producers, not abstract market forces. The way out of such bondage was to increase the supply of money: "The sub-treasury plan would do for the producer what the emancipation act did, or was intended to do, for the African slave. It would give him liberty and permit him to retain the just rewards of his labor. It would release his family from the bonds of poverty, and himself from the thraldom of debt. It would remove the vampire speculator from his throat and permit him to enjoy the blessings of an honest industry. The sub-treasury idea might fitly be named the second abolition agitation, and it will as surely succeed as did the first. Justice and right will prevail, and though the time may not appear here just now, it will come sooner than its opponents expect."[28]

This analysis of money slavery was also linked to an argument about the influence of political power. To the extent that the money interests controlled the established political parties, the Alliance was faced with a deep problem. As one account put it, "To-day shylock can stalk through the halls of Congress and influence the guardian of the sacred blood-bought rights of a free people to fasten the manacles of white slavery upon 20,000,000 freemen, and it is not called high treason. It is called business."[29] To address this, the Alliance also began to develop a critique of "party slavery." While the money slaves could not change their condition simply by willing it, the party slaves were as much slaves to their own minds as much as to the "bosses": "A man can take an ear of corn and with one grain at a time, tole a pig into a pen, just where the pig does not want to go. The 'bosses' of the two old parties, with grains of prejudice and promises, dropped alternately, one at a time, are toling the voters of this country into the pen of slavery, built and owned by the money power."[30]

"The day is past for 'whipping them back' like slaves" into the party ranks, argued the Alliance in the months leading up to and immediately following the St. Louis convention that officially endorsed the third party.[31] The Populist communications used the metaphor in the same way, although they relied upon it less than did the Alliance. "We publish this paper for Freemen, and not for slaves," stated the *People's Party Paper*, "and if you are going to be a slave to a party it would only make your chains feel heavier to read a paper published by freemen for freemen."[32] A local Populist club then picked up the language: "Resolved, That while we still hold to the teachings of Jefferson, Jackson, Calhoun and Benton, in our opinion, the time has come when it behooves the farmers and laboring men of America to lay aside party prejudice, break loose from party shackles and cast their votes for the preservation of their homes, and the protection of ourselves and our children from the power of money to oppress and enslave."[33]

It is important to note that while the emphasis had shifted in the People's Party from reform within the existing parties to independent political action, much of the class analysis of the Alliance—and the ethnic connotations that went along with it—was retained: "We, the People, have the same right to

Driving the Two Old Parties to the Polls.

FIGURE 3. Populists view the "money king." (*People's Party Paper*, May 4, 1894)

join hands, for an old-fashioned or a new fashioned country dance and to thresh the floor with the gang that now controls the entire labor and wealth producing element, as we have to get on the fence, pray to the gold-bottomed gods, or to Jew-usurers, and other slimy agents, and see our wives stripped of their clothing and our children legislated still deeper into slavery to the money kings."[34]

If the republican concern with patriotism and rights was preserved in this narrative, the anti-Semitic race thinking was also preserved. A cartoon in the *People's Party Paper* neatly tied together the arguments about money slavery and party slavery, along with the claim about the power of the Jewish "money kings." Titled "Driving the Two Old Parties to the Polls," the cartoon showed a stereotyped "Jewish" figure herding cattle (the "old party voters") to two packing houses representing the two parties.[35]

### INTERRACIAL ORGANIZING AND ITS LIMITS

The movement's reaction to blacks was organized into two partly competing discourses—that of the logic of interracial organizing, and that of the political competition between (and within) the races. The ambivalent approach to race that was present in the Alliance and glaring in the People's Party resulted from the tension between these two moments. These two narratives overlapped, but they should also be seen as partly sequential. The first was more central in the *National Economist,* while the *People's Party Paper* emphasized the second.

In these narratives, the issue of republican liberty and civic virtue remained fundamental, but in different ways. These constructions had implications for the way the movement understood the role of southern blacks. The interracial organizing narrative followed from the same tradition as the Knights' discussion of interracial organizing. This narrative suggested that as fellow producers, black farmers and farm laborers deserved a place in the agrarian movement and should be seen as potential allies. Moreover, these producers should have access to the same political rights that the white farmers thought to be so central to their own independence.

The other narrative suggested limits to this project of organizing having to do with political and social interests. While black workers may have been seen by white Populists as potential class allies, the movement was equally clear that they were not social equals. Moreover, the movement dealt explicitly with the problems defining common political interest, even as it tried to organize a political movement with black support. While the "organizing" narrative was predicated on the movement's view of black voters as able to appreciate and support a vision of republican freedom, the "competition" narrative questioned this civic maturity. Instead, this narrative focused on the fact that black voters were at the center of intense efforts by Democrats to control election outcomes, and thus in this narrative they came to be seen as competitors, challenging white political freedom.

The organizing narrative focused on the role of the "bankers," "capitalists," and "speculators" as working against the producers. This analysis suggested that the class interests of the white and black Southern farmers were alike. The narrative about the conditions of "slavery" gradually engulfing the white farmers suggested the same. White Populists had no desire to fall into the place of rural blacks—the majority of whom already were tenants by 1890—but neither did they identify black tenants as the cause of their immiseration. In line with these claims, both the Alliance and the People's Party issued frank calls for interracial organizing, albeit ones that sharply drew the color line in social affairs. For the Alliance, this meant organizing in separate but parallel orders. For the People's Party, this meant courting black votes and making promises of political inclusion while explicitly rejecting the possibility for equal treatment in social life.

In both of its political and economic goals, the Alliance recognized the importance of collaboration if not consolidation. This was an uncomfortable but important point for the organization and its members. There were some outspoken racists in the Alliance, and most members were uneasy about any social contact between the races that could be thought of as bringing about social equality. In other words, few if any white Alliance members were willing to espouse racial egalitarianism. All the same, the economic analysis at the center of the Alliance rhetoric recognized a common cause that trumped racial interests.[36] As one editorial in the *National Economist* asserted, "The prevailing discontent, coupled with a desire for better material conditions, are precursors of radical economic changes in the country. The motor power [behind] labor agitations and party upheavals, is the recognition of the individual as above class, party, sect, or race." Overcoming these divisions was necessary for building social power. "We want to use, not be used, control, not be controlled, to work for ourselves, our own dear ones, instead of being immolated on the unholy alters of ambition and sordid lust."[37]

At a distance from such lofty rhetoric, the Alliance also realized that cooperation in local economic goals was important. Such an effort could only help the white Alliance, and would at least do no harm to the black organization. A notice in the *National Economist* in early 1890 reflected how such cooperative agreements were brokered:

> To the Colored Farmers Union of Louisiana:
> Arrangements have been made with T. A. Clayton, State Agent of the Farmers Union of Louisiana, by which the Colored Union of Louisiana can trade through the [white Alliance] agency and receive all the benefits of cheap goods without the expense of a separate agency, and thus unite the financial strength of both orders. It will certainly be to the advantage of both, and as both organizations are working for the same objects, the Colored Farmers Union will co-operate with the Farmers Union whenever it is possible to do so."[38]

Occasionally, the Alliance leaders led themselves to believe that through cooperation in their economic and political goals, the Alliance could provide the solution to the "race problem." This was an incredibly naive argument, but it was one that showed how an incipient class consciousness could begin to erode color consciousness. "There is no negro problem, there is no race issue, except such as is hatched up by designing politicians to further their ends," stated one argument sent in by the Marion County Farmer's Alliance in

Georgia. "And a brotherhood of men knowing no North, South, East or West, only asking justice, with a common cause, are and should be invincible if they prove faithful to the end."[39] A comment reprinted from an Alliance paper in Texas made a similar argument. "There is but one conflict between the white and black races of the South, and that is justice. Give the negro justice under the law and he will soon learn to not only appreciate it but defend it."[40]

It was important that such claims came not just from the national leadership but from the local level, too. In a report from a state meeting in South Carolina, the same argument was put forward that the Alliance had overcome racial problems in favor of a class alliance. Of course, this was not strictly true, but the fact that native white Southerners could adopt this narrative was important for setting the stage for organizing:

> The fact that the Alliance, white and colored, saved the State of South Carolina from the horrors of a bitter race conflict, should teach us the necessity and importance of cultivating the closest fraternal relations with our brethren of the colored Alliance; they stand with us in support of Alliance demands, and should receive from us all possible aid and encouragement; the interests of the races are identical, and we should, by fair treatment of our colored brethren, bury out of sight all political race antagonisms. That there was no race conflict in South Carolina last year was due to the Alliance bond of brotherhood, which was too strong and too serviceable to both races to be broken or disturbed by the political upheaval, and to-day the two races in that State stand nearer together in sympathy and interest than they have ever done before.[41]

In more sober moments, the Alliance realized that the racial divide was real and was reinforced by differences of condition. Despite these differences, this narrative provided reasons for white farmers to bring blacks into the cooperative movement, if not into the white Alliance organization itself. "The Alliance movement in the South has demonstrated more clearly than was before realized, that the farmer, in order to prosper, must take with him all engaged in that occupation" one editorial argued. "He must take the poor man who is in debt and the renters, both white and colored, along and enable them to secure like prices, or he can not himself get them."[42] Another item combined a deep paternalism with its economic analysis to make the same point:

The idea of conflict of interest between the whites and blacks of the South is a great absurdity. The fact is, that they are to a great extent mutually dependent upon each other, and therefore that the most perfect harmony and unity of interest must exist. The southern farmer knows and feels it his duty to protect and assist the poor colored people who are his neighbors. No one realizes better than he, if he allows sharpers to swindle the colored man by paying him excessively low prices for his cotton, by taking advantage of his necessity for money, that the flooding of the market with cotton at such low prices will tend to keep prices low until others whose necessity for money was less at the beginning of the season are also compelled to sell at the same low prices, and their sales will tend to perpetuate the low prices until all the crop is sacrificed on the same rock. The fact is, that the law of self-preservation compels the southern white farmer to take the southern black farmer by the hand and hold him out of the clutches of the exploiter who every year manipulates the volume of money so as to develop the "power of money to oppress."[43]

The Alliance also began to formulate these arguments in terms of political organizing. If the white and black farmers could vote together on the basis of common interest, the Alliance economic demands would surely gain a hearing in the state assemblies and in Washington. In practice, such plans often meant that the white Alliance would set the political course and expect that the Colored Farmers' Alliance would follow along. Still, the white order noticed with appreciation the occasions when this strategy seemed to work. "The campaign in South Carolina is becoming complicated to a degree that perplexes outsiders. A wonderful thing to the uninitiated seems to be the notice from the Colored Alliance that its members will support the candidates agreed on by the white farmers," stated one editorial in 1890. "It is, however, a natural result of the teachings of the Alliance, that all farmers, and indeed all producers, have common interests, which should be a stronger bond between them than mere party ties."[44]

The idea of economic and political coalition resonated with at least some black southerners as well. One letter, reprinted from the Colored Farmers' Alliance journal, remarked that for South Carolina blacks, the order was like "a grand second emancipation."[45] The pages of the *National Economist* featured summaries of the workings of the Colored Farmers' Alliance as well as mentions of meetings and speeches that brought blacks and whites together. These were for the most part normatively neutral accounts, but they revealed the delicate ways in which interracial organizing occurred in these parallel but segregated organizations.

In many cases, the paternalism of the white Alliance was much clearer to the black members than it was to the whites themselves. James Powell, a black state agent for the Colored Farmers' Alliance in Mississippi, made this clear at the same time that he voiced his support for the broader political demands of the Alliance. "The colored farmers are watching with a single eye the leaders of this great organization (who claim that superiority in management), and who have made so many failures at striking the key-note or the true letter of the organization."[46] Several months later, Powell wrote again. Once more, he put the white order on notice about taking for granted the political allegiance of black farmers even while supporting the broader coalition of southern farmers for political and economic ends. "The Colored Alliance in the State of Mississippi was organized for the common good and benefit of the farmer and [for] national reform. This we expect to obtain by legislation brought about through our choice of candidates," he wrote.[47]

As the movement into third party politics became more certain, the Alliance enthusiasm over the opportunities for an interracial coalition of voters was carried over into the People's Party. Much of the racial tone of the party was set by the remarks of Tom Watson. Particularly on the campaign trail, Watson articulated the reasons that such a coalition should be made. Always careful to denounce social equality, Watson argued that southern blacks deserved equal and fair treatment in the political realm. This served the interests of white Populists as well as those of black supporters, since otherwise Democratic control of black votes through fraud and force would only block the movement. The white Populists of Oconee County, Georgia, openly asked for black support on such pragmatic grounds in the *People's Party Paper*: "Now, we don't come to you with any visionary tale of forty acres and a mule, but we come telling you that your race to-day, like ours, is groaning under the oppression of taxation and the low estimate placed on labor, and that, under the present administration, the fruits of your labor, like the fruits of ours, instead of going to make our homes happy and comfortable, go to pay tithes to the money lords of Wall street. We also come telling you that our interest is one, and to better our condition means to better yours. So, as true citizens, let's work harmoniously for the redemption of our country."[48]

By the time that the People's Party got underway, the Colored Farmers'

Alliance had all but disappeared. Several sub-alliances evidently reorganized as black political clubs. Of course, the Populist sources were unlikely to report on the cases where black Alliancemen such as Powell did not support the movement. They did point at that by 1892 there were some self-organized black Populist clubs. One correspondent reported that a black Republican convention in one Georgia county dissolved into a Populist rally. He noted that when "several of the boys rose to their feet and said they were for the third party" the convention chairman tried to keep order by rapping his gavel and stomping on the floor. When the meeting was finally called back to order, a vote was called on the issue. "Two thirds was for [the] third party including one of the delegates."[49] "A Colored Voter" wrote in to say that he could accept exclusion in social matters so long as his race was given a fair shake in political matters: "Now, let me tell you, Mr. Editor, we don't want to rule the government; we don't want to come into your family; we don't want to enter your school-houses or your churches. But I tell you what we do want! We want equal rights at the ballot-box and equal justice before the law; we want better wages for our labor and better prices for our produce; we want more money in circulation to pay for our labor or our produce; we want to lift the mortgage from the old cow and mule which they have carried till they are sway-backed; we want to school our children, and we want a chance to earn a home."[50]

Linking Democratic Party leaders with landlords, the People's Party urged political cooperation and economic solidarity. "When Democrats say poor white men and negroes will have to vote their tickets or leave the farm, it is a good idea to tell them you will leave at once and let them gather the crops. That will bring them to their senses."[51]

Like the corresponding Knights of Labor claim, the Populist narrative linking black farmers and voters to an "interracial organizing" frame presumed common interests. At issue was how such organizing would work out. Neither the Alliance nor the People's Party was willing to suggest that social equality should be part of the bargain. Instead, both organizations claimed that economic and political cooperation were the first and most important steps toward a solution to the problems that they faced. Yet this view was countered by a separate narrative that recognized the potential costs of political competition. It was the tension between the two narratives that created the ambiguity of the Populist approach to the "color line."

In moving into independent politics, the Alliance and the Populists moved beyond a coalition justified in terms of narrow class interest. They asked white and black voters to leave party structures that had become a central element of identity in the post-Reconstruction South. The bind was not a superficial one. On one side, attempts to form local coalitions with black Republicans meant potentially alienating their white supporters. The Populists took very seriously the Democratic charge that an interracial political movement would lead to "nigger supremacy" akin to a second Reconstruction. The problem was not the truth of the claims but the fact that such charges could erode the movement's standing with white voters. On the other side, to maintain the movement as a white party would mean alienating black support, and the attendant danger that black votes would be co-opted by the Democratic Party. The political competition narrative was concerned with the fact that black votes could be mobilized against them as easily as for them, a fact made more likely by Democratic election fraud.

Within the Alliance, the complaints of racial or ethnic political competition took the form of arguments that the political system pandered to every group but the (white) farmers of the South and their allies. According to one editorial, "Congress has time to listen to the demands of the soldier, the Indian, the negro, the bondholder, the national banker and manufacturer, but the farmers and laborers, who support them all, must look out for themselves."[52] As the Alliance moved into the third party, the organization began to warn its white members of the arguments that would be leveled against them. The "old parties" would try "to cripple the new move [into politics], arousing by every possible device fear of black supremacy."[53]

But it was in the *People's Party Paper* that the opposition between the organizing and competition narratives became most apparent. For the People's Party, racial competition in the political realm centered on the Democratic taunts of "negro supremacy" that threatened to break up white support for the third party, and on the forms of Democratic fraud that used black votes against the movement. In discussing the loss of Reuben Kolb in the Alabama governor's race in 1890, one editorial argued that it was the fraudulent black votes that had kept the Populist out of office. Ill gained or not, the black votes posed a challenge to the Populists and to "white supremacy," a goal that the movement did not entirely oppose: "The people of Alabama have been laboring under the impression that when republicanism was dethroned that white supremacy would be the result. From what the *Age-Herald* says, [the election outcome] was not the assurance of white supremacy, but of the organized democracy. What does it mean by organized democracy? It means that the black belt counties, by fictitious strength acquired by manipulation of the negro vote, has become supreme in the control of the state."[54] The Populist discussions of black supremacy indicated that, despite claiming it a canard, the issue was taken very seriously by the movement. One editorial noted that the political enemies of the party were using the issue of black supremacy to shout down any substantive proposals that they offered. "The hypocrisy is apparent to a blind man," the Populist paper pronounced.[55]

The hypocrisy was that the Democrats openly manipulated the black vote and at times even campaigned for it yet at the same time they condemned the Populists for their own efforts to organize black voters. This brought caustic comments from the Populists, who pointed out such ironies whenever they could. "Frank Holt, a prominent Democrat and well to do former ex-merchant, and county commissioner of Macon county, says he will bring all of his negroes over to Montezuma on election day and make them vote his way or they'll have to leave his place" one Populist wrote in. "Still the Democrats [say that they] do not want the negro votes."[56] How to deal with the problem was less clear. In an editorial entitled "Who Says Stay?" one Populist attempted to refute the arguments of a hypothetical white Allianceman who hesitated in leaving the Democratic Party. Despite elaborate arguments in response to most reservations, when he turned to the Allianceman's concerns about the racial divide, the author's consternation was apparent: "But, the nigger! I acknowledge he is a puzzling problem to solve: but, as much as I have heard of dividing the white vote, I have not heard a single word about dividing the negro vote. Left to themselves we have nothing to fear. Very many of them have caught on to the idea that what is good for the white laborer is good for the black. But rest assured that money and whiskey will play an important part in the coming election. Old monopoly is not going to give up its hold without a struggle; not going to lose its occupation for a few paltry dollars when it controls the whole amount."[57]

From the point of view of this narrative, the failure of white Democrats to switch party allegiance was one thing, but the fact that the Democrats received help from southern blacks was another. Whether such support was coerced or voluntary, the People's Party argued that the "negro Democrat" traded votes for patronage. The Populists' realization that they had little influence to spread around made for a number of bitter comments about this new character: "The negro democrat is a source of inspiration and joy to all who know him. He holds an office. Of course he does—that's what he came for. The purpose of life is to get a higher and better one . . . The negro democrat . . . cares nothing for the poor and the oppressed of his race. Having sold out his own color in order to get a democratic office, nothing better could be expected of him. He treats the black laborer precisely as the white office-holder treats the white producer—with gushing fondness during the campaign and with contemptuous indifference after the election."[58]

But it was not only those who got offices from the Democrats that felt the ire of the People's Party. The desperately poor blacks who were paid to vote for the Democrats were not accorded any more sympathy. Even though the "honest colored voters" went for the Populists, others did not. Reports of black votes bought with cash or whiskey were common in the *People's Party Paper* coverage of elections. "The evening before [the election] the train brought up all the Negro filth of Woodstock and Lickskillit districts," claimed one report from Georgia's 1894 election. "Accommodations and whisky were furnished Tuesday night by 'the men who control' . . . The new 'coined' silver half dollars [were] brought to bear in deluding the uneducated and buying their votes. One continued deluge of Negroes and deluded white men [were] passing to and from the drinking cesspools, then [were] hugged and armed to the polls and voted by the bosses."[59]

### CONCLUSION

This chapter has examined the narratives linking race to frames of interest in the context of the Farmers' Alliance and the People's Party. Like the Knights of Labor, these movements held open the possibility for an interracial alliance to emerge. While the same republican concern for civic autonomy and social standing drove the Populist narratives, there were distinctly different narratives linking race to class interest in these organizations.

The first dealt with foreign economic competitors. The farmers' movements did not confront Chinese and European immigration as a problem, but the class-based discussion of those above them also relied on ethnicity, particularly in focusing on the perceived threat from "Jews" and "English aristocrats," both understood to be "money kings" in control of the currency and therefore a threat to independent farmers. The same threat to economic and political independence also supported the second narrative, which relied on the tropes of "money slaves" and "party slaves" to describe the condition that Populists feared they would fall into.

The Populists were also much more ambivalent than the Knights about the prospects for interracial organizing. The remaining two narratives provided different takes on the role of blacks in the Populist movement. What these partially opposing narratives suggest is that the Populist interest in interracial organizing was sincere, as far as it went, but also that it had limits. One narrative affirmed the importance of interracial organizing on the basis of the economic and political equality of the producers, even as it drew the color line much more sharply in terms of social equality. The emphasis on social and political rights that was so central to this narrative was countered by the next one, which focused on interracial political competition.

The movement's emphasis on the latter two narratives also shifted as the Alliance gave way to the People's Party. It was the Alliance, the more racially closed organization, that emphasized the interracial organizing narrative more clearly. The problems of political organizing became particularly clear in the People's Party as the agrarian movement made electoral politics its central arena for protest. This reconstruction of the movement narratives necessarily steps out of historical time, however. The following chapters trace this interaction in Virginia and in Georgia, where the negotiation of interests can be seen more clearly. The sincerity and the limits of the Populists' approach to southern blacks was more apparent at the local level, where the movement narratives were placed in interaction with concrete political, social, and historical conditions.

CHAPTER 6

# RACE AND THE AGRARIAN REVOLT IN GEORGIA

> Now the People's party says to these two men [white and black], "You are kept apart that you may be separately fleeced of your earnings. You are made to hate each other because upon that hatred is rested the keystone of the arch of financial despotism which enslaves you both. You are deceived and blinded that you may not see how this race antagonism perpetuates a monetary system which beggars you both."—TOM WATSON

Financial and political despotism were, in the Populist discourse, conditions that endangered the ideal of a republic of independent yeomen able to decide their own economic and political futures. This vision of independence had scant connection with historical reality for most of the South, but it had undeniable cultural resonance. Although the Populist vision initially extended only to white owners of property, Populists such as Tom Watson began to argue that economic and political despotism was supported by a system of racial separation and animosity, and that the road to independence had to involve coalition. However, the power of this claim to motivate local activism and the degree to which that activism became tied to an interracial project varied a great deal across the South.

The degree of interracial opportunity under the Populist banner in the South was influenced not only by the broad movement narratives that drew a connection between race and class interests but also by the local economic and social conditions of white and black farmers and by the reactions of local actors to events and experiences as they unfolded. In the preceding chapter I described the dual nature of the movement narratives regarding blacks, particularly in the case of the People's Party. What I could not show there, however, was the way that local conditions provided possibilities and limits for local organizing, or the way that the experience of local struggles shaped the way that calculations of political interest were made regarding the interracial coalition. In this chapter and the next I investigate the local practice of interracial organizing under the Farmers' Alliance and the Populist Party in two contrasting sites. This chapter contains an examination of Georgia, a state that was a Populist stronghold and one where the movement is said to have come closest to being truly interracial in character. The next chapter provides an investigation of the case of Virginia, a state generally considered a failure for the movement.

Support for the movement was uneven across the South, and local conditions had a good deal to do with its appeal. In states where the movement narratives matched relatively well with material and social conditions, the movement achieved much more consistent support than in other areas where the movement demands did not resonate so well. The fit also varied within states. In the first part of this chapter I outline the alignment between the movement narratives and the economic and social conditions in Georgia at the beginning of the 1890s. In areas where there was a close fit, particularly in Tom Watson's tenth congressional district, there was also heightened Populist fervor. Where the fit was good, the movement narratives opened a space in which interracial organizing, justified on the basis of class interest, became possible.

In the foreground of this chapter is the connection between the movement narratives and the changing calculations of interest in the course of organizing. Even in the areas that were disposed toward Populism, ideas about the wisdom of interracial coalition were far from static. The tenth district campaigns, particularly Watson's, are worth close attention. Because of their qualities of passion and outspokenness on racial matters, these races set the tone for the movement as a whole. In the core of this chapter I trace the changing internal ideas about racial coalition based on the election coverage in Tom Watson's *People's Party Paper.* Watson's position on racial matters offered a direct challenge to the political status quo, but it was also more divided than has been noticed by later observers, and it shifted significantly over time. Within election cycles, the Georgia Populists moved between optimism at the prospects of interracial organizing and despair over what they perceived as political competition from black voters. Over the course of repeated elections, the emphasis shifted decidedly from the former to the latter as Watson and other white Populists met with massive vote fraud and struggled with the question of what an integrated party meant for them.

### RACE AND THE REFORM APPEAL

Populism did not take root evenly across the South, but rather it grew in areas where the economic and social conditions fit the movement's central narrative claims. Studies of the movements have emphasized the role played by economic pressures relating to the lien system and to falling prices for farm products in general and cotton in particular.[1] Both trends resulted in the same outcome for southern farmers: mounting debt and increasing tenancy. A more controversial argument is that the farmers' movements were motivated by anxiety over their falling social status (see Hofstadter 1956: 26). The fast-changing economic circumstances lent a particular salience to the backward-looking romanticism of the yeoman tradition as rendered by the farmers' movements. This vision was one that was extended to black as well as white farmers—at least for a time. Georgia stood out among Southern states in terms of both the strength of its Populist organizing and the degree to which it approached a truly interracial character.

By the early 1890s, most Georgia farmers felt the forces of economic change keenly even if they did not always understand them. One change in particular reveals a great deal about the fears of Georgia farmers. In 1880, over half (56 percent) of the farms in the average Georgia county were cultivated by their owners, while the remainder (44 percent) were farmed under various kinds of tenant arrangements. Most common were the arrangements by which use of the land was traded for a "share" of the eventual crop, but cash rents were sometimes collected instead. By 1890 these statistics had reversed. Tenants worked roughly 53 percent of the farms in the average county while owners worked fewer than half.[2] This shift in the aggregate statistics offers a

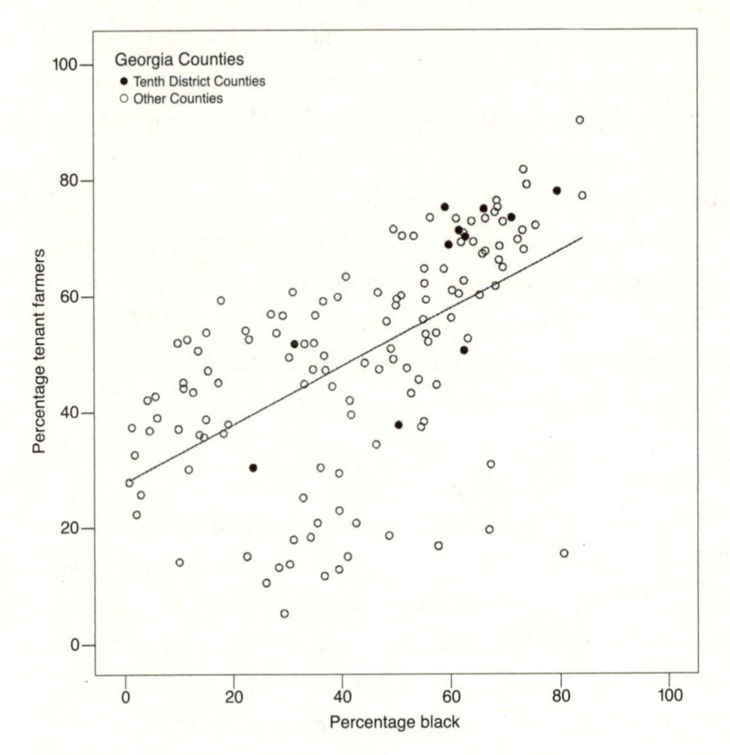


FIGURE 4. Race and tenant farming in Georgia counties, 1890.

glimpse of the changed conditions that farmers saw reflected in the well-being of their families, the lives of their neighbors, and their changing position in relation to their creditors.

Tenant farming in Georgia was, of course, a much more common status for black farmers than for white ones. The average county in Georgia was about 44 percent black, but the population ranged from virtually all white in some of the upland counties in the north of the state to more than 80 percent black in some of the Southern counties. Tenant farming arrangements similarly varied across the state.[3] The relationship was clear: the more black the population of a county, the more likely that tenant arrangements predominated.[4]

Despite the fact that it was Georgia's blacks who were most tied to tenant farming, these trends were a source of concern to Georgia's white independent farmers who could not shake the unpleasant thought that they too could be pressed into tenancy.[5] From an economic perspective, they feared that their increasing debt burden would soon push them into tenant farming. From a social perspective, the status of the small independent farmer held a particular significance as a symbol of republican virtue. By 1890, even in the counties that were virtually all white, as much as 40 percent of all farms were occupied by tenants. When a Georgia farmer claimed in an open letter to President Cleveland that "the farmers . . . have been turned over to merciless Shylocks and their homes shingled over with mortgages," his hysteria was rooted in the changes he saw around him. He also saw these changes as cause of the growing political revolt. "In 1884 not a white farmer in this county voted against you; to-day it would be difficult to find a dozen who would not scratch your name from the ticket," he said. "I ask your candid consideration of some of the reasons that cause the yeomanry of Georgia almost solidly to oppose your renomination."[6]

For black farmers too, the fall of the independent farmers was a cause for concern. Although the vast majority of rural blacks were not independent, the status was symbolic of their aspirations. The self-help philosophy embodied in the Colored Farmers' Alliance statement of purpose was one reflection of this. While few black farmers could realistically hope to own their farms, they could dream of crawling out of debt and perhaps owning their homes and equipment. By spring 1890, the Colored Farmers' Alliance was beginning to form several land investment companies across the South, with the newest in Atlanta. The *National Economist* noted approvingly that "the Colored Alliances recognize that the colored farmers must help themselves, and it is wonderful how self-reliantly they are getting about doing it."[7] Despite the patronizing tone, the white Alliance's endorsement of black efforts toward economic independence deserves notice. It fit with the same republican framework in which white Populists saw themselves ("If every man in America owned his own home what a glorious country this would be!" one of Georgia's Populist papers proclaimed),[8] but it also envisioned the same status as possible and desirable for black farmers.

Certainly the numerical strength of the Alliance movement in Georgia is some indication of the success of the movement's appeal under these conditions. The Colored Farmers' Alliance claimed 84,000 members in Georgia in late 1890 (Saloutos 1960: 81). At about the same time, the white Farmers' Alliance in the state reported roughly 100,000 members. In short, over half of all eligible people in Georgia were affiliated with the Alliance (McMath 1975: 165). The membership was statewide, but the organization had particular strength in the central and western counties (Shaw 1984: 24). The relationship between the two orders was close enough that the secretary of the Colored Farmers' Alliance in Georgia could report that "both white and colored are going on together."[9] To be sure, the white Alliance was not proposing to help the Colored Farmers' Alliance in any positive way when it endorsed black economic independence, however striking that was in its time. During the Alliance's early work of organizing, lecturing, and building cooperatives, the issue of race could largely be avoided so long as the orders remained officially separate.[10] The white Alliance could maintain a rhetorical allegiance to the economic equality of conditions while keeping the status distinction of separate fraternal organizations. As the Alliance moved into politics and then dissolved into the People's Party, white Populists were forced to confront the issue of integration more directly. The process was not uniform. Instead, the political side of the farmer's revolt took different patterns in different parts of the state, and its racial implications varied.

The upcountry counties of Georgia had been the ones most quickly transformed by the expanding cotton market and the threat of tenancy. The hill country areas of the South were also central to the earlier political uprising of the 1870s and 1880s. Driven by their changing relationship to the market, as well as tension with a new class of town-based political and economic elites, upcountry yeoman farmers across the South flocked to Independents, Greenbackers, and other dissident Democratic candidates.[11] Georgia was no exception. The upcountry counties were the only ones to support Independents and breakaway Democratic candidates in the 1874 and 1876 congressional races, and they continued to lead the independent movement as other piedmont areas joined the cause in 1878 and in later elections. The independent movement set a precedent for the later Populist revolt, emphasizing the same republican ideals and producerist claims (Hyman 1990: 31, 42; Hahn 1983: 2–3). The Georgia upcountry counties began adopting the Alliance in 1887 and soon became a core area for the movement in Georgia, with a relatively established cooperative structure.[12] The region mustered support for the electoral stage of the Populist revolt as well, but it ceased to be a center for the movement and instead provided only average support for the People's Party.

In the majority-white upland counties, however, neither of these revolts was overtly colored by race. Georgia's upland Independents of the 1870s and 1880s did not have to seek coalition with Republicans or court black voters,[13] unlike Virginia's Readjuster movement or the urban political revolts of the same period. The same was true for electoral Populism. Indeed, recent studies have placed political debates over grazing rights, rather than debates about race, as the hallmark of upcountry Populism.[14]

In other contexts, the issue of race had to be more directly confronted by the white Populists, and by their potential black supporters. The eleven counties that made up Georgia's tenth congressional district, marked in black on figure 4, were particularly open to the Populist laments. Located in the northeastern section of the state, the tenth district was well above the rest of the state both in terms of the relative size of its black population and the prevalence of tenant farming arrangements.[15] The tenth district counties had not been part of the independent political movement of the 1870s and 1880s, nor had they been a stronghold for the Alliance (Shaw 1984: 96). However, the district became the driving force behind electoral Populism by consistently voting Populist at a rate well ahead of other districts. In the key governor's race of 1892, for example, only one of the district's counties had less than a third of its votes go to the Populist candidate. In that election and again in 1894, the tenth was the only district that averaged more than 60 percent Populist votes.

The tenth district also differed from other areas in the degree to which the Populist project explicitly confronted the issue of race. In this majority-black area, Watson and his white Populist followers argued forcefully for an interracial political coalition. That there was some difference in the economic and social positions of Georgia's black and white farmers was undeniable. Yet the Populists insisted that tenants, yeomen, and even larger planters shared economic interests as producers, that they shared political interests as dispossessed voters. Nowhere was this claim made with such force or met with such support as in the tenth district. Watson, a quick-tempered lawyer and perennial candidate, built a loyal following among white Georgia Populists without retreating from the issue of racial coalition. Repeatedly calling for blacks and whites to work together to throw out the "two old parties," Watson argued that preserving the political and economic rights of the poor and the uneducated required reaching across the color line.

Such a view did not guarantee success for an interracial coalition, but it did allow interracial organizing to make sense. At the same time, white Populists did not give up their equally taken-for-granted assumptions about race. The sincerity and scope of Watson's own views have formed a particular point of contention. C. Vann Woodward's biography of Watson paints a picture of a man who made an earnest attempt to unite Georgia's black and white farmers during the 1890s, even though he was an apologist for disfranchisement and even lynching later in his life. For Woodward (1963), the later moment was the bitter reaction of a man who history had passed by. Other observers have portrayed Watson quite differently. Barton Shaw (1984, esp. 200–201), for example, suggested that the later moment more clearly reflected Watson's true convictions while the earlier egalitarianism was simply a veneer designed to attract black votes.

In the rest of this chapter, which is focused on Watson and the tenth district, I develop a different argument. Watson's views about black voters did change, even within the active period of the movement itself. But Watson's appeal for coalition was always both sincere and strategic. It was also limited. Although much of Watson's rhetoric was about the need for "political equality," he and most other white Populists maintained that "social equality" was out of the question.[16] In this, Watson was in step with the movement in general. The movement-level narratives of the Alliance and the People's Party were deeply ambivalent in their approach to blacks, as I have shown in the previous chapter. The white Populists' appeal for black support was not simply a veneer, but neither was it motivated by a naive dream of racial equality. The Populists' sincere attempt to build an interracial coalition on the basis of economic and political interest was always limited by an equally sincere belief in white supremacy motivated by deeply held racial identities, and it coexisted with a more defensive narrative about blacks as political competitors.

### RACE AND THE POPULIST SCHISM, 1891–1892

The Georgia Alliance began to pursue its political goals by pressuring the regular Democrats to subscribe to the Alliance principles. "The Alliance does intend to make itself felt in politics. It intends to see that its members vote for no man who will not pledge himself to our policy," stated Georgia's Alliance paper.[17] The optimism extended to the question of race. "There is no negro problem, there is no race issue, except such as is hatched up by designing politicians to further their ends," the Marion County Alliance claimed. "And a brotherhood of men . . . with a common cause, are and should be invincible if they prove faithful to the end."[18] The optimism seemed justified as the election season got underway. "The Farmer's Alliance *is* the Democratic Party," the *Atlanta Constitution* declared.[19] In the gubernatorial race, Leonidas F. Livingston, president of the Georgia Alliance, squared off against another Alliance leader, William J. Northen, for the Democratic nomination. Northen's victory was secured after Livingston dropped his candidacy to focus on a congressional race in the fifth district instead, where he won easily. In the tenth district, Tom Watson won a tight contest with his Democratic rival in the primary, and then easily won his own congressional seat in the general election. Alliance Democrats won in four additional districts, forced significant concessions from the four other regular Democratic winners, and won control of the state legislature (Arnett 1922: 105–16).

The ballots had barely been counted when the third party question began to be more seriously considered in Georgia and around the country. Many white Alliance leaders, Livingston most prominent among them, wanted to remain within the Democratic Party. Watson and others argued that Alliance principles should come before party loyalty, and that a third party was the best way to achieve those principles. Both sides agreed that the third party route would mean facing the issue of race more directly since the Democrats would charge that they were traitors to the white man's party. Those advocating the break thought that their sheer numbers could overcome the Democratic appeals for white solidarity. "If the Alliance does decide to go into the new party, the old politicians had just as well stand aside," announced the *National Economist*. "The old bosses may crack their whips over the farmers and yell 'nigger supremacy;' . . . but they just can't stay the stampede. Georgia Alliancemen are going to stand together, work together and vote together."[20]

The personal relationship between Watson and Livingston was never warm, but their mutual dislike turned into a movement schism at the beginning of the new session of Congress. The Alliance congressmen from across the country met at the Washington office of the *National Economist* to decide on a strategy for the caucus. Watson stood with the representatives from western and midwestern states who wanted to officially bolt from the regular Democratic caucus and hold their own. Livingston stood with other southern Democrats who felt that they should remain in the caucus. Watson and Livingston began to argue about where their loyalties should lie, with each accusing the other of selling out his constituency. A fistfight between the two was narrowly averted when other Alliancemen intervened. The split between the two groups was plain, and they entered Congress under different party caucuses (Woodward 1963: 190–93; Arnett 1922: 128–31).

The differences between the two central figures in the Georgia farmers' movement involved more than personal animosity. Watson and Livingston represented two sides in a broader cultural battle over black involvement in the political movement. The debate over the third party strategy polarized the racial rhetoric of the two leaders who were otherwise fellow heirs of the same reform tradition and who shared nearly identical political biographies (Goodwyn 1976: 249–53; Shaw 1984, chapter 2). With separate organizations it was easy for the white Alliancemen to accept black support when it suited them and to distance themselves from the Colored Farmers' Alliance at other times. The political question was much more divisive, even though Watson and his followers drew the color line on social grounds every bit as assiduously as did Livingston.

The fight at the *National Economist* headquarters was the most explicit moment of the schism, but the racial implications were more apparent in the aftermath of the St. Louis convention of reform organizations in February 1892. The Colored Alliance in Georgia, as elsewhere through the South, was in disarray by this point, and there were few black delegates present despite the large number of seats they were allotted. A white Alliance lecturer named J. J. Gilmore, who had also been inducted into the Colored Alliance as an organizer, represented Georgia's black delegates. In proxy for them, he cast the vote in favor of independent political action.[21] Back in Georgia just days after the convention, Livingston was irate. He began to publicly chide both the blacks who were willing to follow the third party and the whites who would accept black support. In the words of a press report: "He said if the negroes wanted to follow Gilmore, who was a foreign Georgian and a deserter from the English army, they could do so, but if they did, he hoped God would have mercy on their souls."[22] Watson contended that whatever the legitimacy of Gilmore's action, it made no substantive difference in the outcome. "The statement being made that the vote of Georgia was controlled in the conference by negro votes, is absolutely false."[23] Gilmore himself felt it necessary to recount his legitimate ties to the Colored Farmers' Alliance, and to state that "not a negro paid a cent of my expenses. I hear that it has been said that they did. If [Livingston and his supporters] said so they lied."[24]

The tension was not abated when, soon after, Livingston reportedly threatened to revoke the Alliance charters of those groups that had supported the People's Party at the St. Louis convention. Reacting to Livingston's charges that the People's Party meant "negro supremacy," Watson shot back that Livingston had not been afraid to support independent political activity before the St. Louis convention: "[Livingston] was not afraid of negro supremacy then. He was not afraid of a black nation inside of a white one then. He was not afraid of a plague spot in the body politic then. He was not of the opinion that it was unconstitutional for Alliances to endorse or condemn this or that policy, this or that man, this or that party."[25]

The friction continued during the fall 1892 campaign. Livingston taunted the Populists for seeking black support. On the stump for reelection as a Democrat, Livingston brought up the Populist call for black political involvement and fair elections. "It would cause warfare, for the people of this land just wouldn't submit to federal interference" he said referring to the unpopular proposal for electoral reform known as the Force Bill. In reaction to Populist promises for black economic improvement, he stated: "Why do you fellows tell these poor, ignorant negroes these lies?"[26] At one point in a debate with Watson, Livingston lost his temper, threatening a black heckler that he would pull more "wool out of [the] negro's head than he had in it."[27] Watson, in front of a mixed race audience, began to recount a plan that Livingston had allegedly endorsed to resettle Southern blacks in a separate territory to be carved out of Texas.[28]

These charges and countercharges were driven not only by personal animosity but also by political interests. It is worth remembering that Livingston, while never a friend to southern blacks, in less passionate moments made the claim that they were not class competitors, and earlier in his career at the helm of the Georgia Alliance, he had addressed the Knights of Labor at their 1889 convention in Atlanta. His speech showed a deeply paternalistic attitude, but it also pointed out that blacks were not the cause of the white farmers' problems: "There are people who think that the negro is at the bottom of our trouble. This is not so; the negro has not been at all in the way . . . The negroes are a happy, contented people, and as long as they can jingle some silver in their pockets they are as satisfied as a mortal can be . . . No, the negro is not the cause of our trouble. Some of you are from Ohio, and your state is covered with mortgages. Surely, the negro is not the cause of your troubles . . . . We are all in the same boat, and must endeavor to save it as best we can."[29]

It was the question of political involvement, rather than interracial class cooperation generally, that proved to be a lightning rod. For his own part, Watson's early understanding of the color line was far less clear-cut than it might appear from his later statements. Watson's views on the relationship of southern blacks to the Populist movement developed in his campaign speeches during 1892. The most famous statement of the position that emerged was laid out in his article in the Populist-friendly journal *Arena.* A deeply important piece, the article frankly recognized the uncomfortable position of poor whites caught between racial identities and class experience: "You might beseech a southern white tenant to listen to you upon questions of finance, taxation, and transportation; you might demonstrate with mathematical precision that herein lay his way out of poverty [and] into comfort; you might have him 'almost persuaded' to the truth, but if the merchant who furnished his farm supplies (at tremendous usury) or the town politician (who never spoke to him except at election times) came along and cried 'Negro rule!' the entire fabric of reason and common sense which you had patiently constructed would fall, and the poor tenant would joyously hug the chains of an actual wretchedness rather than do any experimenting on a question of mere sentiment" (1967 [1892]: 60).

This arrangement, Watson argued, did not help the tenant and yet served the politicians well. "If we were dealing with a few tribes of red men or a few sporadic Chinese, the question would be easily disposed of," Watson claimed, echoing the Knights of Labor. "But the Negroes number 8,000,000. They are interwoven with our business, political, and labor systems. They assimilate with our customs, our religion, our civilization. They meet us at every turn,—in the fields, the shops, the mines. They are a part of our system, and they are here to stay." To remedy the problem, Watson proposed to remove the political obstacles that kept the races apart. Essentially, Watson was arguing that white Populists had to engage black voters not because it was morally right but because there was no alternative. Toward this end, he argued that the People's Party should speak to the common economic interests of both, help secure a fair vote count, and ensure the voting rights of blacks.[30]

Although the Colored Alliance in Georgia initially rejected open involvement in the third party, a handful of colored Populist clubs were springing up in several black belt counties by 1892.[31] The ingrained racial beliefs of Georgia whites set some limits to the scope of any potential coalition, however. Some remarkably honest statements of the sentiments of white Georgians on the subject made their way into the reform press from time to time. "We are not in favor of wiping out any color lines, yet, we are strongly in favor of the negro having his rights under the Constitution. He should be allowed to vote freely and openly as he likes . . . he should have full protection of life and property, and justice in the courts," claimed *Hale's Weekly* of Conyers, Ga. "[B]ut we do not think he is yet competent to fill the offices and run the government or any part of it."[32] A Populist lecturer in the tenth congressional district made a similar argument: "We are not going to put the nigger on top but we are going to give him the advantage as a laborer and a wealth producer that comes of laws enacted in the interest of laborers of the land, be they white or black. We are going to do justice, and when the white man gets a better price for his labor and his cotton the colored man will get a better price for his cotton and his labor."[33]

## WATSON ON THE STUMP, 1892

The development and demise of this limited potential for coalition was worked out on the campaign trail. The 1892 elections were the first in Georgia to pit the new party as an independent entity against the Democrats. By July, 99 of the state's 137 counties were reported to be "organized for the People's Party," although the degree of that organization was undoubtedly varied.[34] The beginning of the race saw a full slate of ambitious Populist candidates, but it was also a tangle of personal and professional association. In the governor's race, the Populists nominated William L. Peek, a onetime head of the state Alliance Exchange, against the Democrat William Northen, originally elected on the Alliance platform. Watson ran for Congress in the tenth district as a Populist against James C. C. Black in a stormy campaign that commanded statewide attention. As with Livingston, Black and Watson had once been political comrades (Woodward 1963: 98, 104). These were the most closely watched campaigns, but the Populists ran candidates for congress in every district and for a host of state positions as well.[35]

This election was also the first in which the Populists faced squarely the issue of whether and how far they would pursue black support. Both sides were split on the matter. The Democrats and the Populists alike claimed allegiance to white supremacy and racial purity, at least in social matters. The Populist candidates' histories were not necessarily more promising for black voters. Northen's opposition to lynching was a matter of public record, for instance, while Peek had once sponsored a bill that would have jailed tenants who did not meet their obligations to their landlords.[36]

Watson's race in the tenth district was crucial. It was there that the issue of race was debated most openly, and there that its limits became most apparent. Other sources have discussed Watson's campaign speeches in detail, but none have adequately highlighted both the consistency and the dual nature of Watson's stump sermons (cf. Woodward 1963; Reinhart 1972; Shaw 1984). The presentation changed from speech to speech, but two basic elements never wavered. First was Watson's open appeal for black support and demand for political equality. Second was his equally open rejection of social equality. Watson stuck to the first position in his campaigns, thus taking steps that were radical for his time, place, and audience. He spoke directly to mixed-race crowds of Populists, in which he often addressed part of his speech to his black supporters.

There were also black Populist lecturers with whom Watson sometimes shared the stage. The most well-known of these was H. S. Doyle, a young black minister. Doyle's life was threatened several times during the successive Watson campaigns in the tenth district. In Jefferson County, a bullet that was probably meant for him instead killed a white Populist standing nearby.[37] During the 1892 campaign Doyle was threatened with lynching, and he fled to Watson's farm near Thomson, Georgia. Armed Populists from around the state—by some accounts, as many as two thousand—flocked to Watson's land to stand guard.[38]

Yet it is equally important to realize that Watson remained resolute in his rejection of "social equality" in any form. Doyle, his loyal supporter, was not given access to Watson's house, but rather was hosted in a "negro" tenant house on his property while a fugitive from the Democratic mob.[39] Watson was not coy about these beliefs on the stump. Although Populist speeches and meetings were often biracial affairs and were advertised openly as such, there was usually an area set aside for the black audience, and if a picnic dinner was served there was either a separate area for blacks or they were seated after the whites had finished.[40] The campaign speeches themselves addressed the topic of social equality. A speech of 1892 was typical of Watson's statements during this period. After a long harangue about the monetary policies of the Democrats and the need for government to support the rights of the "farmers" against the "monopolists" and bankers, Watson turned to the issue of black involvement. In this moment, both sides of Watson's thought were unveiled for the audience:

> They say that I am for social equality between the whites and the blacks. I most emphatically say that it is untrue . . . I say here and now that social equality is not a good thing for either race. You colored people, as well as the whites, are better apart. You go to your churches, without any interference, as we will go to ours.
>
> I have said that what injures the black tenant injures the white tenant. What injures the black farmer injures the white farmer. That we should live under a system of just laws where the laborer, the farmer, or the mechanic will be treated right. That the farmer, the mechanic, the tenant or the laborer ought to be treated with the same consideration as the national banker or bondholder; the railroader or the capitalist. Thus I said that this new spirit infused by the People's Party had great things for you black men as well as for white men.[41]

Watson declared that social equality was an issue that "every citizen settles for himself," not one that can be imposed by law. Still, he argued:

> Why should not a colored farmer feel the need of the same relief as the white Farmer? Why is not the Colored Tenant open to the conviction that he is in the same boat as the white tenant; the colored laborer with the white laborer?
>
> Why cannot the cause of one be made the cause of both?
>
> Why would this be dangerous?
>
> I can see very well where it would be dangerous to Ring Rule, to Bossism, but I can see no reason why I am any less a white man—true to my color, my rights, my principles—simply because the black people are convinced that our Platform is a fair one, and vote for me upon it.[42]

Watson, in advocating for equality on political and economic grounds while at the same time defending social inequality, led himself into sometimes glaring logical inconsistencies.[43] This basic contradiction faced the southern Alliance as well as the Knights of Labor. But the People's Party, particularly in Georgia, was forced to do so more openly than either of the earlier organizations. Here it is worthwhile asking how black followers of the movement reconciled this obvious division in Watson's thought. The evidence is scanty, but one important perspective came from H. S. Doyle himself, who figures centrally in sympathetic accounts of the Georgia Populists. In reflecting on his support for the party, he stated: "The Populists made no secret promises to the negro . . . The only argument that they offered was that, with an increase of currency and with a triumph of the principles of the Populist party, would come increased prosperity to the country, in which prosperity white and black alike would share." He noted that the Populist primaries were open to black voters, unlike the Democratic ones. But he also noted that there were more practical reasons why black supporters felt the need for coalition: "The negro had learned by twenty-five years' experience, that single-handed he was not able to cope with the Democratic party. As a general thing all white men in Georgia were Democrats, all negroes Republicans, and in an issue between a solid black and a solid white vote, no one doubts the outcome, regardless of the relative principles of each. So, realizing the helplessness of his condition, he welcomed the Populist party, not so much from the actual belief in its principles—he did not stop to debate them—but from the political liberty and the right of franchise [for] whose practical exercise the Populist party voted."[44] In other words, one of the most ardent black supporters of the reform movement, when called upon to defend his position, did so in terms of political expediency rather than in terms of ultimate belonging or deep conviction. As Doyle himself noted, although the vast majority of black voters thought of themselves as Republicans, there was no longer any viable Republican party in Georgia.[45]

Summer 1892 saw a flurry of positive assessments of black support for the Populist cause from around the tenth district and adjoining counties.[46] It was easy for the Populists to believe that they could hold a good portion of the black vote. The Populist candidates, especially Watson, met with enthusiastic black crowds at most of their speeches. At regular intervals, local organizers would write in to report that not only the whites but the blacks were "with us." Black Populist supporters also delivered some upbeat assessments, such as that of one man from Sparta, Georgia: "The majority [of colored voters] go for the People's Party, regardless of whatever may be said about the grand old party, and we are not bought, but are going on principle, and on that principle we intend to live and die."[47] In one Populist stronghold, black voters were reported to be skeptical about promises that the Democrats were making to them: "On Saturday last the Democrats of this (McDuffie) county had a barbecue and public speaking . . . Two or three colored men also made short speeches, but the colored voters would shake their heads and be heard to say: 'That negro has Democratic money in his pocket; we are not going to let him sell us out; we are free men, we are.' "[48] When Watson came to town later the same day, the black audience, after being "filled with Democratic barbecue," deserted to the Populist meeting. Other white Populists, such as the correspondent calling himself "Peeping Tom," appealed for solidarity in the face of Democratic attempts to woo black votes. "You who suffer as we suffer . . . don't be fooled by these rascally town foppish negroes who are bought by Democratic leaders to catch your vote."[49]

### THE INTERRACIAL APPEAL AND ITS LIMITS, 1892–1893

While the Populists set out to capture black votes, the Democrats wanted to make them pay for their efforts. The period leading up to the 1892 elections was a relatively innocent and idealistic time in the Populist racial rhetoric. It was a time when they thought that an interracial alliance of small farmers and tenants would be a viable coalition, and that black voters might stay with them. This assessment of interests was not completely reversed by the outcome of the election, but the experience did alter the tone of Georgia Populism's racial rhetoric.

The optimism began to vanish in the early part of October as the first election results were being counted. At that point the *People's Party Paper* noted that it was clear that the black voters had not supported the Populists as a mass. It reserved judgment about the reasons "until definite reports of the election are accessible."[50] In fact, the election of 1892 was a painful loss for the Georgia Populists. The two most prominent candidates, Watson and Peek, both lost their races. Democratic fraud was widespread, including the "repeat voting" of some blacks. The total vote tally in several counties was higher than the number of registered voters, according to Populist reports. It is likely that Watson was cheated of his victory by such tactics, but the Populists were not free of suspicious practices either. There were even reports of the use of Ku Klux Klan–style "night riding" in some Populist areas (Shaw 1984: 75–77, 87–88).[51] Such practices make it impossible to tally the actual level of black support for the Populists, but it certainly was not what Watson and others had hoped.

While the dual nature of Watson's campaign rhetoric did not change, the overall emphasis placed on the two sides did change. This shift has been recognized in the literature on the movement, but studies of the Georgia Populists have had a hard time pinning down the exact nature or meaning of

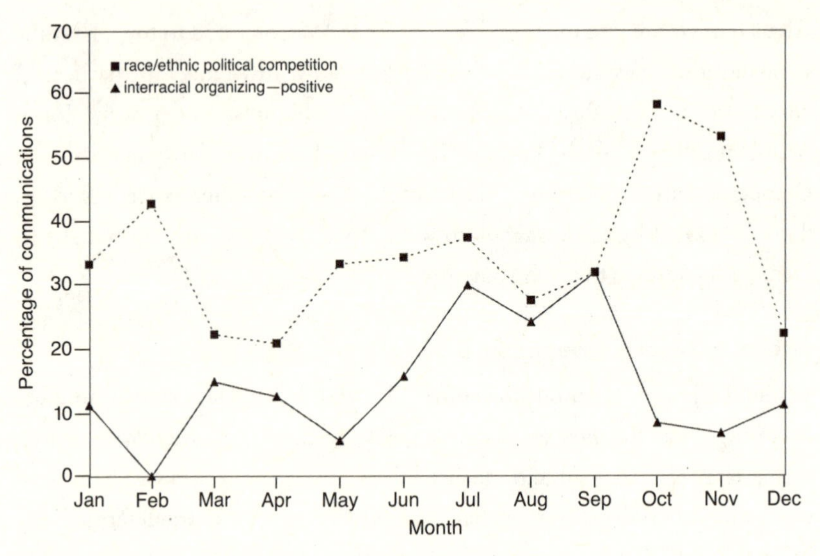


FIGURE 5. Seasonal trends in interest frames, *People's Party Paper*.

this shift. There were actually two sets of changes that were intertwined. On the one side were regular fluctuations in the annual political cycle of campaigns, elections, and their aftermath. On the other side was a longer and more linear trend away from the white Populist's early optimism about the prospects of interracial coalition.

The cyclical changes can be seen through a careful analysis of items in the *People's Party Paper* relating to both race and to economic or political interest over the key campaign years of 1892 and 1893. This coverage focused primarily on the congressional campaigns in 1892 and the local and state elections in 1893, which kept the columns lively. They included many of Watson's speeches and editorials as well as editorials and letters of other Populists in the tenth district and across the state.

The Populist rhetoric was shaped in large part by the repeated cycle of hope and failure that accompanied elections in Georgia and elsewhere. Figure 5 does not show the development of the Populist racial frames in Georgia over "real time"; instead, the pooled months show the changes in relation to the "campaign time" of the election cycle.[52] The solid line in the figure represents the communications that supported interracial organizing; the dashed line represents those focused on interracial political competition.[53]

There were three basic patterns evident in the cyclical changes. First, the two annual trends roughly mirrored one another; the more one frame was invoked in a given month of the cycle, the less the other was invoked. Second, the rhetoric remained ambivalent at all times—at least partially hopeful for the success of interracial organizing, and at the same time reticent about social and political competition. In every month of the calendar cycle, the political competition frame was more prevalent, with the exception of September where the two trends converged.

The third pattern was the most important. The relative level of optimism or reticence was shaped by the election cycle. The proportion of items that were positive about the prospects of interracial organizing gradually increased through the spring and summer as the campaigns heated up and organizing got underway. The peak for these statements was reached in September, just before the fall elections. The proportion then dropped off sharply in October when elections for state-level offices were held, and remained low through the federal election in November and the winter months that followed. By contrast, the relative proportion of statements concerning interracial political competition grew through the spring and summer campaign season, but it reached its peak in October, during and immediately after the first round of elections.

There was also a longer-term trend at work. The experiences of the Georgia Populists in repeated elections—particularly the repeated Democratic attacks on the issue of race—stifled the white Populists' assessment of the coalition strategy. The ambivalent nature of the movement's reaction to blacks always remained, but the relative strength of the different elements of that reaction changed, with the more defensive views increasing in frequency and with new kinds of arguments about political competition emerging over time.

In the wake of the 1892 election, amid reports of Democrats buying black votes for whiskey and cash, a different language began to surface in the discussions of political competition. Watson and other Georgia Populists had always recognized that Democrats were using the charge of "negro domination" against them. Some of the reactions to Democratic pressure were still sympathetic to the idea of interracial coalition. Amid details of extensive election fraud and vote buying, one editorial remarked, "The tenants were threatened that if they voted the People's ticket they would be driven from their homes . . . The colored voter, whose every interest is with that of the laboring white man, was bulldozed, intimidated, driven from the polls, and in some instances shot for attempting to exercise the rights of citizenship and vote as they pleased."[54] Another picked up the same claim. "I heard one negro begging, within five feet of the ballot box, to be allowed to go away without voting, and saying that he did not want to vote, and the fellow that was forcing him told him that if he did not vote he would shoot him. Some of the negroes who did vote the People's party ticket have since been made to leave the houses in which they were living. But our people are giving them houses."[55]

But many other comments betrayed an increasing hostility toward the black voters themselves. It became unclear whether the villains in the eyes of the Populists were the Democratic vote buyers or the black voters who were bought. One author summed up the scene of the election in Augusta this way: "The daily press says that 'enthusiasm reigned,' while any perfectly sober man knows that whisky reigned . . . Possibly twenty-five hundred in line [to vote] . . . one-third negroes—and the only thing democratic about them was the whisky they had imbibed. Money was the black man's consideration."[56] In the Populist reports and testimony on the fraud, "negro" almost always modified "repeater," referring to the practice of sending the same person to vote multiple times under assumed names.

The issue of coerced and bought votes was a particularly salient one that spawned its own subgenre of commentary after the election. Coerced votes were by definition the opposite of independent ones and therefore were in tension with the republican ideal. Bought votes were worse yet, since they implied that independence sold cheap. "Some colored people do not seem to know the sacredness of their votes, for they were bought as low as fifteen cents," claimed one editorial.[57] Black Populist supporters also sometimes condemned the "bought votes," leading to a complex response: "A colored brother, writing us from Zeigler, Georgia, complains that the price of negroes has awfully depreciated within the last forty years. He says that he was put upon the block somewhere in the forties, and was sold for fifteen hundred dollars cash down; but during the late election he saw one fellow bought for a glass of cider, a second for a 'two-for-a-nickel' cigar, and a third for a pint of peanuts. He thinks the 'free nigger' is holding himself entirely too cheap. We are not sure but the prices paid were a fair measure of both buyer and seller."[58] It was a fair measure of worth, in the eyes of Watson and other white Populists, because it suggested that black voters might not be capable of the civic virtue after all. Although trickery or physical force could not be avoided, vote buying suggested that while self-interest always prevails, it might not always do so in the way that Watson thought it would.

A second new rhetorical claim emerged as white Populists began to turn the Democrat's own claims about "Negro domination" back onto them. Watson's editorials began to use the argument as the 1892 campaigns came to a close. "The Crawfordsville Hotel was well supplied with colored people," he pointed out after one Democratic rally, raising implicitly the issue of social equality. "They were in the rooms up-stairs as well as down-stairs. Yet the Democrats raised no row. Why? They were Democratic negroes. That makes all the difference in the world. See?"[59] Another white Populist took up the argument. "Major [Black], why do you ask for the colored vote? I thought you were afraid of negro supremacy."[60]

The argument that it was actually the Democrats who were fostering social equality through social mixing and "Negro domination" through black votes became a common thread through the election season of 1893 and into 1894. Before taunting the Democrats, Watson often declared his belief in white racial superiority. If Democrats believed the same, then how could they be afraid of negro domination, he asked, particularly while using blacks to pad their own electoral victories?[61] In his speeches and editorials, Watson used this point to stress the importance of a "free ballot and a fair count,"[62] as well as to lay bare his opponent's strategies: "To settle this race question by giving the negroes what the law says is theirs is to settle it right, and I believe that is the only way to settle any question whatsoever . . . You say to me 'you want the negro vote.' I say, 'Yes, I do, don't you?' [Laughter and applause.] If you do, quit abusing me about it. If you don't, tell the negroes so. [Laughter.] Just pay your money and take your choice. [Laugher and applause]."[63]

Although Watson's campaign speeches continued to ask for black votes the claim about "negro domination" cut both ways. It was used to ridicule the Democrats for violating their own standard, but it also implicitly supported that standard. The increasingly open message was that the Populists did better at enforcing the color line than did the Democrats. Watson and the *People's Party Paper* even began charging that Grover Cleveland was a promoter of social equality for his act of hosting Frederick Douglass and his family at the White House, for appointing blacks to his cabinet as foreign ambassadors,[64] and for establishing mixed-race schools while he was in the post of governor of New York—"wherein the colored child and the white child would drink

FIGURE 6. Georgia Populists view the "Democratic negro." Caption: "The Jackson Argus says: 'A piano party is a party of the blackeys and the whitekeys.' Here's a State Democratic Executive Committee piano party. Steve Clay and Mr. Ross, of New York, discussing the situation as to election managers. Mr. Ross, of New York, tells how he did it in Alabama." (*People's Party Paper,* September 21, 1894)

from the same dipper, set on the same bench . . . [and] get whipped with the same switch."[65]

The Populist language also began to employ the term "Democratic negro" as a common epithet—referring to those blacks who, in the eyes of white Populists, could not see that their long-term interests were with the third party. Often represented as a slick city politician in search of an easy life of political patronage, the Populists painted the Democratic negro as lazy and insolent.[66] The "Democratic negro" became personified in "Mr. Ross, of New York" an "imported negro hireling" brought to Georgia by the state Democratic committee as an advisor in the election and evidently as editor of a Democrat-friendly newspaper.

Whatever the rancor of the elections of 1892 and 1893, they were dwarfed by the hostility that arose from the challenge of 1894 and its aftermath. As in earlier years, the Georgia Populists began their campaigns in earnest during the spring and summer months. The Populists placed James K. Hines in the race for governor, and again featured Watson against J. C. C. Black in the tenth district congressional campaign. The Populists campaigned for black support during the election, but only half-heartedly. On the eve of the election, several white and black Populist supporters alike voiced their belief that a victory was still possible and that biracial support could be mustered, but these appeals did not rise to the same heights of optimism that they had previously.[67]

The Populists actually fared better in 1894 than in 1892, and there was far less violence in the elections despite election fraud on a massive scale. In the state election, the Populists now controlled forty-one seats in the House and six in the Senate, as compared with fifteen and one in 1892. The race for governor was close, but the official tally was in favor of Atkinson, the Democrat. In the congressional races, the Populists lost in every district (Shaw 1984: 115–17; Woodward 1963: 269–70). The most devastating loss was that of Watson. Black had won only two counties in the district, but he had polled most of the votes. Black alone received nearly 14,000 votes in the key county of Richmond, nearly 2,000 more than the total number of registered voters (Woodward 1963: 270).

Despite the improved outcome (Shaw has remarked that "the third party emerged from the struggle robust and upbeat" [1984: 118]), the possibility of forging an interracial voting bloc for reform became more remote than ever. One election report from Cherokee County in the Ninth district typified the change in the tone. "The evening before the train brought up all the Negro filth of Woodstock and Lickskillit districts. Accommodations and whisky were furnished Tuesday night by 'the men who control' in Canton. Their supposed friends around Canton were invited to come Tuesday night and help manage them and give them whisky."[68] While the report went on to praise the "honest colored voters" who "voted with the people," the image of black votes bought cheap for the Democrats with half-dollars and whisky became far more common than that of the upstanding black Populist voter.

## CONCLUSION

The prospects for Georgia Populism revived after 1894 and the movement continued, but its promise of interracial coalition did not. In this chapter I have examined the making and unmaking of the Populist movement as an interracial coalition in Georgia. Given the space of opportunity open to the movement, deriving from the social and economic conditions in Georgia and from the movement's narratives, the question is how it developed over time. This chapter has thus focused on the internal issues of the negotiation of race and political interest. Georgia is often considered to be one of the movement's most successful sites and, largely due to Watson's influence, one of the most racially progressive. In the pages above, however, I have pointed to a more complex picture.

The shift into politics brought many of the racial issues to the fore, as a comparison of the positions of Tom Watson and Leonidas Livingston shows. Despite their common backgrounds, the two had very different positions on racial matters. Watson brought to the Georgia Populists a more racially egalitarian message, but the tenor of the Populist appeal to black voters changed over time. Although the demand for political equality for blacks remained in place ("a free ballot and a fair count" was the motto), the movement's understanding of race became more centered on interracial political and status competition. The experience of repeated losses in the course of organizing gradually changed the Populists' construction of racial interests.

Watson's own take on racial matters was somewhat more complex than either his admirers or his detractors have realized. His message on the question of racial equality was relatively consistent during his years as a Populist candidate: "yes" on political and economic matters, but "no" on social equality. In other words, while the rhetoric of the Georgia populists sometimes suggested that the movement could overcome racial divisions, Watson always recognized race as an important factor in the practical consciousness of Georgians, his own included. While this message remained consistent, Watson's emphasis changed during the years that the Populists challenged Democratic control in Georgia. This change was not a rediscovery of suppressed racism on Watson's part; rather, it was merely a shift in emphasis from one side of the formula to the other. In the early years of the challenge, the Georgia Populists emphasized "yes on political and economic equality." As white farmers in Georgia became less secure about their future, the white farmers could at least potentially see themselves in the same economic position as black tenants and even farmhands. As the Democratic charges of "negro supremacy" took hold, the emphasis shifted to "no on social equality."

There are a few general but speculative points that emerge from these conclusions. First, if coalition politics were the most direct route to a truly interracial route for Populism (a claim that I will consider in more detail in the next chapter), a strong movement was not necessarily a benefit. To state this as a general hypothesis: the stronger the movement in a given locale the lower the importance that its leaders and members place on coalition-building. A second and related point is that alternatives matter. In Georgia, black voters had a choice between the Democrats and the Populists; they did not have a viable Republican Party structure and therefore had little bargaining power. Historical alternatives matter as well. In the absence of history of serious political coalitions, and given a relatively strong base for the third party statewide, the Georgia Populists expected that black voters would go along with them. When this supposedly "natural" alignment of interests turned out to be less direct than the white Populists initially thought, it was not treated as a failure of coalition (as it was in Virginia) but as a moral failure of the black voters themselves.

CHAPTER 7

# RACE AND THE AGRARIAN REVOLT IN VIRGINIA

The Populists cannot carry Virginia without the aid of the [black] Republicans. It is useless to deny that fact.
—JOHN MITCHELL JR.

In March 1890 a white Virginia farmer and Alliance leader named James Bradshaw Beverley wrote to the *Journal of United Labor* to express his support for the growing ties between the Farmers' Alliance and the Knights of Labor. Beverley made it clear that he favored the Alliance's early expressions of political neutrality. Like most white Populists at this time, Beverley saw himself primarily as a Democrat and did not want to break with the party completely. But like many others, he also saw the need to make the movement's support for the Democrats conditional. "I believe in the resolutions of the St. Louis Convention of the Farmer's Alliance," he said, "Let us follow out the ideas of that convention and join forces against our mutual enemy—the financial policy of the government—and after we have settled that[,] *then* let us settle our own differences between us. . . . We have too much sense to think of a third party; two are bad enough." He counseled that farmers and laborers should become "independent of party, and both parties will come to us."

Then he repeated a joke that he had heard from John Jasper, a black Richmond preacher who had become famous in the region for his traveling sermons.

> I had a dream the other night. I dreamed I went to heaven and knocked at de door, and St. Peter said, "Who's dar?" Says I, "John Jasper." Says he, "Is you mounted?" Says I, "No." Den he 'lows "Yer can't come in here 'les you are mounted." I walked along back and presen'ly I met General Mahone a-walkin' up de hill. I say, "General, where you gwine?" "Gwine up to heaven." Say I, "You can't get in dar 'les yer mounted—I just tried." He scratched his head a minute, den he says, "John, I jus' thought how we can both get in. You get down on all fours and I'll ride yer right in." So I got down and de General a-straddled me, and up we went. I felt so good I fairly cantered. We got dar and de General he rapped. Says St. Peter, "Is yer mounted?" General he says, "Yes" "Well," 'lows St. Peter, "tie yer horse to de fence and come on in!"[1]

Although on the surface this joke seems fatalistic, its use on the lecture circuit and in a letter to a progressive journal suggests that it was meant as a call to action. The different facets of the joke give an indication of the political discontent felt by both black Republicans and white Alliancemen. In 1890, Beverley used the joke to illustrate his feeling that the major party candidates were using the farmers and laborers as vehicles. Working people provided the electoral muscle to get the candidates into office, but then they were forgotten about soon after.

The same logic that drove Beverley to appeal to the Knights of Labor for a united political movement would soon drive Virigina's white Populists to appeal to black Republicans, who had their own reasons for seeing promise in such a coalition. From the point of view of the preacher John Jasper, the joke originally summed up the bitter feelings of many blacks toward William Mahone, the white leader of Virginia's Readjuster movement. In the early 1880s, Mahone's Readjusters were carried into office by a combination of black and white voters. Mahone later became the unofficial leader of the Republican Party, which remained relatively vital in a cluster of majority black counties. Mahone was a convenient but incidental butt of the joke for Beverley, but for Jasper and other black Virginians he was the whole point. Although Mahone had produced some benefits for black voters, many felt that he and other white Republicans took them for granted, since they had nowhere else to turn for representation.

In 1890, the joke thus resonated with different groups unhappy with existing political conditions. For a time, both sides saw the Populist Party as a workable solution. White Populists and black Republicans alike initially saw Virginia's history of previous interracial alliances—under the Readjusters as well as the Knights of Labor—as an indication that interracial coalition was viable. In the course of organizing the Populist electoral challenge, both sides came to see things differently. Three years later, the joke would have resonated just as well for both sides, if for different reasons. By then, Beverley himself was the Populist nominee for lieutenant governor of Virginia, and the movement had stopped seeking black support. White Populists felt that black voters were still being duped into carrying opposing candidates to victory. According to the Populists, black votes were being "bought" by white Democrats seeking to destroy the movement. Black voters, for their part, felt that the reform movement had used their support but forgotten about their interests. To them, Beverley had become the same as Mahone.

In this chapter I examine the shifting calculations of interest about interracial coalition under the Populist movement in Virginia. Virginia is important as a "failed" site for the movement—the conventional wisdom is that electoral Populism was never viable in the state because the political interests of black Republicans and white Populists did not coincide. While Populist candidates were never able to capture statewide support, they were initially a powerful force in a cluster of majority-black counties. By forging a strategic alliance there, the Populists became a serious threat to the Democrats in state and congressional elections. The failure of the interracial movement in Virginia was the result of changing assessments of interest by the potential allies in the coalition.

In the first section of this chapter I deal with the economic and social conditions that shaped the expressions of interest that emerged in the state. In the rest of the chapter I consider how the construction of interest changed among both white and black reformers with the development of events in the movement. Although I describe the emergence of the white and black Alliance organizations, my analytical focus is on the political development of the movement because it was there that the changing assessment of interests occurred.

### RACE AND THE ALLIANCE APPEAL

As in the case of Georgia, the economic and social conditions in Virginia provided both opportunities and limits for the emergence of an interracial movement. Virginia is a fascinating case for the study of the agrarian revolt since it is generally considered to be a site in which the interracial coalition was destined to fail. Two factors are commonly cited as reasons for this failure. The first was the particular structure of the state's agricultural economy; the second was the weakness of the Alliance there. As a result, Virginia is seriously neglected in the literature on Populism. On both fronts, conditions were actually more favorable to the movement than they have seemed to later observers.

One important factor that set Virginia apart from many other states in the South was that it did not experience the same economic changes that were overwhelming the cotton-producing states. Studies of the agrarian movements have typically pointed to falling prices for cash crops, increasing farm debt, and the expansion of tenant farming as grievances that drove masses of farmers into the Alliance and provided a platform for the People's Party (see Hicks 1961; Schwartz 1976; Goodwyn 1976). An important component in the mobilization of the movements and in the emergence of an interracial appeal was the degree to which these economic changes threatened small independent farmers and tenants. Compared with many cotton-dependent states, Virginia's agricultural production was more diverse and therefore far less reliant on a single cash crop (see Sheldon 1935).

The depression of the 1890s insured that farmers were not doing well anywhere, but there was no large-scale change in Virginia's agrarian structure. Virginia's counties actually changed very little from 1880 to 1890.[2] This was the case both in counties dominated by large plantations and those with predominantly small farms. Across Virginia's counties, the average size of farms actually decreased by nearly twenty acres over that decade. Nor were there growing masses of tenant farmers. The fact that the average tenancy rate was only 25 percent by 1890, and that this number was actually slightly lower than a decade before, meant that fears of falling had little purchase among Virginia's independent farmers. The Alliance's analysis of mortgages leading to a concentration of land ownership under the control of the Eastern or European "money kings" simply did not fit the evidence that most Virginia farmers saw before them every day.

Of course, tenancy was associated with blacks in Virginia, just as it was elsewhere. Yet the relationship was not terribly strong. The average county in Virginia had a substantial black population of around 40 percent, although as in Georgia the actual number varied tremendously from the mostly white

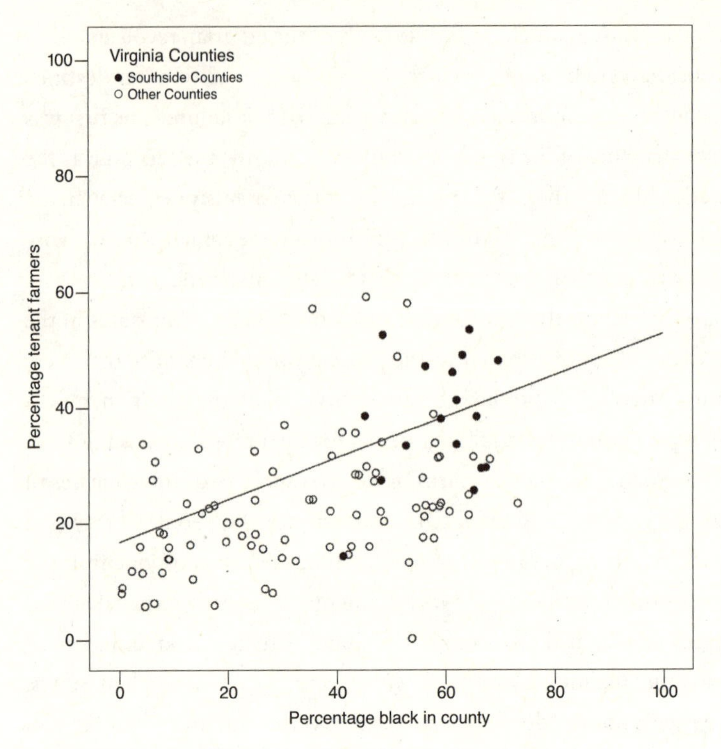


FIGURE 7. Race and Tenant Farming in Virginia Counties, 1890.

western hill counties to the majority-black tidewater and piedmont counties in the east and southeast. Even in the counties that were nearly 70 percent black, the rate generally ranged between 10 percent and 40 percent.

This general trend did not hold for all of the counties, however. Some Virginia counties approximated the conditions in the cotton-producing states. This was particularly true in a cluster of southeastern counties known collectively as the "Southside" region.[3] In these counties, shown shaded on figure 7, the movement narratives of race and class fit reasonably well with local conditions. Relative to the rest of the state the Southside counties were far more reliant on a few cash crops, tobacco in particular (Sheldon 1935: 8–9). They averaged 59 percent black, compared with a statewide average of 34 percent, and they had the state's highest rates of tenancy.[4] Although some organization occurred statewide, the Southside region became central to both the Alliance and the People's Party, and it was in this region that the movement's interracial strategy was meaningful and potentially transformative.

The second reason that Virginia Populism is often overlooked has to do with a perception by scholars that the Alliance was relatively weak, leading to a lack of carryover support for the People's Party. Robert McMath (1975: 20) notes that the Virginia Alliance was organized at a relatively late date, and that it never attained the size or influence that it did in other southern states. Lawrence Goodwyn's assessment also rests on organizational weakness. The Virginia Alliance had a "loosely organized state structure, a thin lecturing system, and an absence of thrust among the leadership." Lacking a solid Alliance base, "the third party simply failed to achieve a genuine statewide political presence" (1976: 340–41). This argument also underestimates the movement's potential in Virginia.

While the membership of the Alliance was appreciably smaller in Virginia than in many other states, it was far from anemic. The first white sub-alliance was organized in Rockingham County in September 1887, and a county alliance followed two months later (Dunning 1975 [1891]: 248). Rockingham was a mostly white mountain county bordering West Virginia in the north-central part of the state. From that point, the movement spread quickly. Five counties reported some organization by 1888, and thirty-five reported by the following year. By 1890, there was some Alliance presence in all but four of Virginia's one hundred counties. The movement's membership was listed as 33,406 in 1891, by which date the movement had lecturers at work in each of the state's congressional districts.[5]

Virginia's white Alliance managed to organize a number of cooperative stores as well as a few cooperative manufacturing and tobacco warehousing facilities (McMath 1975: 120). The manufacturing establishments included a fertilizer factory and a cooperative foundry making farm equipment. These establishments were generally unprofitable, but they showed that Virginia shared in the sense of visionary potential that permeated the movement. The case of the "Farmers Alliance Cooperative Manufacturing Co."—a producer of farm implements—aptly demonstrates this point. The cooperative was organized in 1889 and was reorganized the following year with an operating capital of $30,000, raised from stock bought by Alliancemen. On four acres in Allegheny County, the company planned a foundry, a machine shop, an assembly and painting shop, and a woodworking shop. The company's prospectus gives a sense of its idealism. After finding that "the leading manufacturers of agricultural implements refused to sell to the alliances except through their agents, and at retail prices," the Alliance decided to build for itself instead. The company produced plows, land rollers, threshing machines, and other tools, and they planned to sell them below prevailing prices.[6]

The membership of the Colored Farmers' Alliance was also smaller in Virginia than in most southern states, and the seminal study of the farmers' movements in Virginia concluded that it had only "minor significance" (Sheldon 1935: 35). But even here, Virginia was better organized than it might appear. The State Colored Alliance meeting in fall 1890 represented thirteen counties. Humphrey claimed that there were fifty thousand members in Virginia as of December 1890, but more trustworthy were the statistics that came from within the state. J. J. Rogers, the state CFA leader, placed the number more realistically at eight thousand, concentrated in the black belt counties.[7] Of the state's nineteen delegates to the national CFA meeting the next year, nine were from Southside and the rest were from one or two counties away. The sole exception was a delegate from a coastal county northeast of the region.[8]

Like the white Alliance, the CFA maintained its own cooperative enterprises. State Superintendent Rogers, a white man and a friend of Humphrey's, served as the manager of the CFA exchange in Norfolk. The Norfolk Exchange actually preceded the official organization of the state CFA in Virginia. At the founding meeting of the state Alliance in summer 1890, in the Henrico County Courthouse in Richmond, Rogers was thanked for his work on the exchange and was elected president of the state body with a "storm of unanimity."[9] By 1891, the Norfolk Exchange was in trouble; the CFA delegates to the state meeting expressed "grave doubts" about the management of the exchange, and they appointed a committee to go to Norfolk for the purpose of reviewing the accounting books and making a report.

The cooperative spirit of the organization was not completely dampened, and it began to seek ties to other black enterprises. At the 1891 meeting, the CFA delegates received the president of the black Virginia Industrial, Mercantile, and Building Association, who spoke to the assembly. The speaker, George Williams, recognized the failure of several previous efforts at black economic organization in Virginia (including the Freedmen's Savings bank), but suggested that the two organizations work together to build cooperative stores "and other business enterprises."[10] Even after the decline of the Norfolk Exchange, other black cooperative ventures were organized to fill its place. There was, for instance, a report of the organization of the Virginia Co-operative Business Association, a black wholesale and retail grocery in Norfolk.[11]

The controversy that began over Rogers's management of the Norfolk Exchange also provided evidence of the autonomy and relatively outspoken nature of the Virginia CFA's black leadership. The delegates at the meeting had elected a black state lecturer and organizer named W. H. Warwick to replace J. J. Rogers as state superintendent. Warwick was a rising star in the organization, having been elected as a representative of the Virginia Exchange to the national meeting in 1890.[12] It was Warwick who had risen to challenge Rogers's stewardship of the CFA exchange at Norfolk, and it was he who was later elected at the multiorganizational St. Louis meeting of 1892 to the position of assistant secretary for the meeting, the only black delegate so honored.[13] Rogers and Humphrey declared the vote to appoint Warwick as lecturer to be null and void, and they stated that no dues, reports, or fees should be sent to him. The Colored Alliance of Cumberland County promptly issued its own response to the matter, referring to Rogers and Humphrey as "avaricious and malevolent men" and accusing them of voiding Warwick's election "so that they may run the Order according to their own sweet wills." The Cumberland Alliance resolved to direct all of their official business to Warwick, and they asked other Alliances to do the same: "This alliance would remind Mssrs. Humphrey and Rogers, that they do not constitute the Va. Alliance, and that they are the hirelings and not the masters of the Va. Alliance; and it is for the people to decide who shall be their officers."[14]

One reason that to later observers the movement has appeared so anemic was that there was little contact between the white and black Alliances even by 1891. White Alliance leaders did admit to having some interest in organizing the black farmers and farmhands, and their organization would benefit if the CFA were to succeed. The Petersburg *Rural Messenger* remarked that the way to boost Alliance support in tidewater counties was to reach out to the large number of black farmers. "If there were colored Alliances here nine-tenths of the farmers of the section would soon be within the pale of the Alliance. This is an additional argument for allowing them to organize." In reprinting this statement, the *National Economist* advised the white farmers to get in touch with Humphrey to find CFA organizers.[15] The high point of interorganizational relations occurred when the white Alliance's state legislative council passed in spring 1892 the resolution that the district-based lecturers for the Alliance should be authorized to lecture for CFA audiences to whatever degree "they in their judgement think best, within the line of their duty to their own order."[16] Despite this, most white Alliancemen never had personal contact with the CFA. "It is not generally known that there is a Colored Farmers' Alliance in Virginia," the state's white Alliance journal admitted, before quoting some official statistics on the movement.[17]

Another important aspect of the local context was the legacy of previous interracial coalitions in the state. At the local level, the Knights of Labor had been successful in Richmond politics during the 1880s. At the state level, Mahone's Readjusters lasted from 1879 to 1883. As a coalition of disaffected Republicans, Democrats, and independents, the Readjusters had broken with conservative "funders" over the issue of state war debt. Mahone, himself a former slaveholder and Confederate officer, created an interracial coalition by emphasizing poll taxes and school funding—issues that had been central to black voters (Wynes 1961; Moore 1975; Morton 1918; Dailey 2000: 33–45). The movement's strength was in urban areas and in two key Republican strongholds—the predominantly white western mountain areas and the majority-black southeastern counties (Dailey 2000: 33, 34 map 2). Despite this regional constraint, the Readjusters gained control of the state legislature in 1879 by virtue of coalition with Republicans. The coalition then won the gubernatorial election of 1881, and Mahone himself was appointed to the U.S. Senate in the same year (Moore 1975: 178–9; Dailey 2000: 55). The Readjusters' success continued in 1882, but increasingly heated campaigns began to take their toll on the coalition. The 1883 campaign was a turning point. Mahone campaigned openly for black support while the Democrats emphasized racial solidarity, essentially charging that Readjuster control meant black domination in politics.[18] The Readjusters lost the election by a wide margin, although several counties in the Southside's fourth district retained their black representatives. Although Mahone continued to coordinate state campaigns under the Republican banner in 1885 and beyond, retrenchment continued amid allegations of Democratic election fraud (Morton 1918: 121–22, 122 n.41, 124–25; Wynes 1961: 28–31).

Conditions in Virginia thus allowed for the possibility of a viable interracial coalition. The core of the potential coalition was limited in scope to the Southside district and surrounding counties, where economic and social conditions most closely matched the movement narratives and where there were both white and black Alliance structures from which to build. The previous interracial political coalitions provided another important factor. Although the Populists rarely mentioned them explicitly, Beverley's joke suggests that they were certainly present in the minds of both white and black voters. This history provided distinctly ambiguous lessons, however; when observed from different vantage points and at different moments in time, both cases of political coalition-building suggest how such coalitions could work, or how they could be undone.

To say whether or not such a coalition was in the interest of these groups presumes a priori what should be the question—whether and to what degree both sides came to see coalition as in their interest. Moreover, it misses the fact that arguments about interest are shaped over the course of interaction. In the rest of this chapter I examine the changing interest claims of the two groups. Evidence is drawn primarily from two newspapers where the arguments about interest took shape—the *Virginia Sun* and the Richmond *Planet*. These papers are considered influential voices rather than strictly representative ones. The *Virginia Sun* (earlier known as the *Exchange Reporter*) was the central Populist paper in the state. A number of different individuals contributed to the ongoing discussion of interest in its pages, but its overall editorial voice flowed far more from the leadership than from the rank-and-file members. The Richmond *Planet*, under the direction of John Mitchell Jr., was the most established public voice of Virginia's black voters, most of whom remained Republicans. Although the editorial voice of the *Planet* was effectively Mitchell's alone, that voice carried a great deal of weight among black Republicans statewide. Significantly, the Virginia CFA chose the paper as its outlet for announcements and for news about the movement for members and other interested black readers statewide.

### CONVERGING INTERESTS, 1891–1892

As in other states, the Alliance began to pressure Democrats in 1890, but it was not until the following year that the challenge began in earnest. The political strategy emerged as the Alliance's economic efforts began to run aground. One problem was organized opposition, as wholesalers boycotted many Alliance cooperatives, while state-run railroads refused to grant them the bulk discounts that they made available to other businesses (see Schwartz 1976: 210). Additionally, poor management and a lack of capital plagued the Alliance businesses. By 1891, the Virginia Alliance began to reorganize its cooperative enterprises in response to these problems. The reorganization gave some new life to the cooperatives by instituting retail prices for goods and by eliminating credit accounts. This had the effect of guaranteeing that the income met the outlays, since credit was no longer extended to the local cooperatives and their members. But it also meant that the benefits were restricted to the relatively well-off farmers who could pay cash for their goods and afford to purchase a share in the enterprise (see McMath 1975: 120; Goodwyn 1978: 198).[19]

At the same time, the Alliance made its way into politics. On the strength of its membership, the Virginia Alliance was able to pledge all of the state's Democratic congressmen to the "Alliance yardstick" in 1890 (Sheldon 1935: 64). So long as most white Alliancemen remained Democrats and most Democrats were pledged to the Alliance, no interracial political coalition seemed necessary to the Populists. After the official organization of the People's Party in May 1891, Virginia's Alliance paper, the *Exchange Reporter*, announced to its readers that the Alliance and the new party would remain strictly separate. "It should never be forgotten that the Alliance is nonpartisan," the editorial stated. "The very fact that our membership is restricted to one class of citizens shows the absurdity of any claim on our part to become a political party."[20] At the same time, the Alliance paper made it plain that the People's Party, not yet endorsed by the Alliance, could provide additional political leverage: "We are proud and thankful that the People's Party has incorporated our demands in its platform, and we advise the Republicans and the Democrats to do the same, if they wish to have an equal claim on our regard. If the mountain will not come to Mahomet, then Mahomet must come to the mountain."[21]

By "one class of citizens" the paper's editors meant farmers, but they could as easily have been talking about race. Two developments during the year nudged the white Alliance toward a more direct challenge of Democratic control, and toward a more serious consideration of coalition with black Republicans. The first was what the Alliance considered a failed meeting between the chairman of the Democratic State Committee, M. Taylor Ellyson, and a representative of the Virginia Farmers' Alliance, A. R. Venable Jr. The Alliance expected that the Democrats would bend to accommodate Alliance demands. Instead, Ellyson warned Venable to back away from using support for a railroad reform bill as a local Alliance "yardstick" for measuring candidates in the upcoming fall election: "If the Democratic party wished to secure the support of the Alliance, the Democratic press must cease its unfriendly policy of never losing an opportunity of slapping at it . . . That was all the deal that was made [with Ellyson], and we are ready to make the same deal with the Republicans."[22]

The second factor was the Democratic fraud and race-baiting that occurred in the course of the 1891 state elections. Alliance attention was drawn to two majority-black southern counties in particular. In Norfolk, the Alliance charged that the regular Democrats, who controlled the election process, had thrown out the votes for one precinct where the Alliance-backed Democratic candidate had won heavily in an otherwise close election.[23] In Mecklenburg, the racial dimension of the political tension became clear. The Alliance-backed candidate, J. Thomas Goode, won a seat in the General Assembly, but was opposed when he attempted to join the Democratic caucus. In an open letter, Goode was accused of secretly accepting black Republican support. The Democratic charge was that Goode had clandestinely accepted the Republican nomination. The secretary of the county Alliance wrote in to the *Exchange Reporter* to rebut the charges. To the accusation that a black organizer and "white man-hater" led Goode's campaign, the secretary admitted that Ross Hamilton, a black Republican, had indeed spoken for Goode at almost a third of the candidate's appointments in the county. But he argued that the regular Democrats opposing Goode in the race also "carried around" a black Republican.[24]

Until this point, the Alliance had been very quiet about race. The discussion in the Alliance paper made it clear that most Alliancemen were not willing to endorse social equality, but also that strategic alliances were being seriously considered. Until the 1891 election, however, only hints of the broader discussion were visible in the paper. In August the *Exchange Reporter* ran a story on the strength of the Virginia CFA, in which was stated: "We regard this movement with great interest, because it seems to us to offer us a promising solution of the 'negro problem' . . . White Alliancemen should do all in their power to help the colored brother towards his real emancipation—an emancipation from ignorance, laziness, vice and general unthrift—a knocking off the shackles of political bummery."[25] The Mecklenburg controversy became one site where the Alliance's calculations of interest came to the surface. A coalition between the white Alliance and black Republicans began to be considered seriously, although the *Exchange Reporter* was also clear that strict quid pro quo arrangements had been rejected: "It was well known that the colored Republican leaders had offered to the Alliance that if the Alliance would make no nomination for the two commissioners of revenue (two offices that have been filled by negroes for the past eight or ten years) they would give the Alliance all the other county offices. This proposition was thoroughly considered in open Alliance and at first accepted, but the idea of nominating two negroes was never considered by the Alliance nor advocated by Colonel Goode."[26] Between Democratic claims and Alliance counterclaims the facts of the 1891 arrangement are unclear, but the racial strategy of the Alliance at least became obvious. They were willing to seek black Republican support but were not willing to formally fuse.

The results of the election might have been seen as a victory for the Alliance. Between Alliance-pledged Democrats, Alliance-backed independents, and sympathetic Republicans, the Alliance could reasonably claim influence over a majority of the legislature (Sheldon 1935: 70). Significantly, the Alliance did not see it that way. In the early months of 1892, the political discussions in the pages of the *Exchange Reporter* were shaped by the disappointments of the 1891 elections. The Mecklenburg issue became the central point for an editorial titled "Partyism Run Mad," in which the Democratic Party in general was accused of protecting the party "bosses" at the expense of the rank and file.[27] The issue was divisive, however. A sub-alliance president from western Virginia thought that "Colonel Goode was treated exactly right by the [Democratic] caucus, and we advise him to remember what happens when pitch is touched." The president did not think that the time was right to abandon the Democrats, "as it is [a year for a] national election." But even he conceded that "it begins to look like a third party would soon become a necessity."[28]

By March, the Alliance's break with the Democrats was apparent and a third party challenge was being planned. The movement paper (now renamed the *Virginia Sun* and serving as the voice of the People's Party) listed the members of the General Assembly, grouping them as "friend," "enemy," or "dodger."[29] Twenty counties were reportedly organized by late May, and it was announced that a statewide convention of the People's Party would be organized for June.[30] The number of counties reported to be "in line"—that is, at least temporarily organized and expected to be represented at the state convention—expanded quickly. The number stood at thirty-one in the first

FIGURE 8. Bowing down to the Farmers' Alliance. Caption: "It seems the Democratic Party is bowing down to the Farmers' Alliance. The farmers regard with amusement its attitude, while the Colored man awaits the result of the meeting." (Richmond *Planet*, July 18, 1891)

week in June, including fifteen of the seventeen Southside counties. The number grew to forty in the second week and forty-six in the third week.

During this time, the Richmond *Planet* was optimistic and vocal about the changes that might come about as a result of the white Alliance's pressure on the Democratic Party. The well-reported meeting between Venable and Ellyson was a case in point. The white Alliance complained that it did not get the concessions it hoped from the old party. For the editor John Mitchell, however, the meeting itself was a sign of the Alliance's potential. The *Planet*, with obvious glee, quoted the Democratic *Richmond Dispatch* about the meeting: "The Alliance is a power in Virginia, and as the Dispatch has frequently asserted, the Democratic party is in full sympathy with most of the objects sought to be accomplished by the organization."[31] Below the quote appeared a cartoon drawn by Mitchell himself in which a well-dressed Democrat with hat in hand sits astride a kneeling donkey marked "Democratic Party." He faces a stout white farmer marked "Farmer's Alliance of Va." In the distance, a black farmer "awaits the result of the meeting."[32]

The point of the cartoon was that the Alliance was unlikely to be a savoir of the race, but it might be a worthy vehicle for reform. Even as the Alliance denied that the meeting resulted in any kind of favorable deal from the Democrats, the *Planet* remarked: "Colored men, the Farmers' Alliance is looming up in the distance. Let us watch and wait."[33] Although the *Planet* did not approve of the Alliance's economic demands, many of which ran counter to those of the national Republican platform, Mitchell was pleased by the fact that the Democrats were being put to the test. "The fight which seems imminent between the Farmers' Alliance and the Democratic Party, places the Afro-American in a position to take sides," he observed. Mitchell realized that it was unclear whether the Democrats would pledge themselves to the Alliance demands, and he thought it better for black Republicans if they did not.

> We shall see what we shall see, but if the Democratic Senators or Congressmen sign pledges in accordance with the above demands, there will be no Alliance political party in the state. If not, its efforts will be felt from one section of this commonwealth to the other.
>
> We see the indications, and in all probability the next legislature in Virginia will be composed of farmers or those who represent their principles.
>
> There will be wholesale "cussing" in the Democratic camp, but what cares the farmer?[34]

A second *Planet* cartoon again featured the stout white farmer representing the Farmers' Alliance, this time standing at a blackboard and presenting the Alliance demands to a donkey-headed man (the Democratic Party) who was scratching his head in bewilderment. The party was clearly failing at the Alliance's "Political College." The implication was that this was good for the goals of the white farmers (not all of which Mitchell endorsed) but that it would also give black voters a decisive role in the political contest.[35]

Mitchell's view of the Alliance's political activity thus moved from guarded optimism ("let us wait and see") to enthusiasm as the Alliance break with the Democrats became increasingly decisive. Virginia's most outspoken black paper had seen the political organization of the white farmers' movement in Virginia as a promising development: "The farmers may have hay-seed in their hair, but they have what they want in their minds. Their next move is to engraft it upon the statute books of this country, both state and national. And what man can hinder?"[36]

FIGURE 9. Balked on the first question. Caption: "The Democratic Party attempted to pass the examination for admission to the Farmers' Alliance Political College, but balked on the first question." (Richmond *Planet,* August 29, 1892)

But Mitchell's position was illustrative in another way as well. Mitchell never argued that black voters should give up the Republican Party, which remained relatively strong in Virginia's black belt counties. Instead, he thought that the split in the Democratic camp would lead to gains for black Republicans as the earlier interracial coalitions had done. The *Planet* reprinted an editorial from the New York *Mail and Express* to the effect that the Republican Party was gaining sway in the Alliance: "Of course the Farmers' Alliance votes will go with the Republicans from the moment they see this great truth . . . Heaven is on the side of peace and plenty, and the Republican Party is the agent for disseminating these benefits to the farmers."[37]

The *Planet* also concurred that the Democrats were stirring up racial troubles. Mitchell remarked that Democratic plans would separate white and black school funding revenues,[38] institute Jim Crow cars on the railroads, and restrict the franchise. In doing so, the party "would thereby arouse the worst prejudices, array one race against the other and afford a feast which unscrupulous politicians would enjoy." As for the interests of black Republicans,

"[Democrats] have already excluded colored men from their primary elections. They have bodily passed laws intended to defraud us of the right to vote, and have caused thousands of us to be denied the rights to exercise the elective franchise. In view of this condition of affairs, it behooves us to leave no stone unturned to encompass the defeat of that party, causing them to realize that we will do all we can to overthrow those who oppress us."[39]

## DIVERGING INTERESTS, 1892–1893

The Virginia People's Party was officially launched in the Southside's Amelia County.[40] The report of the meeting was as interesting for what it did not say as for what it did say about the launch. In a majority-black county, the new party had to hope for black Republican support. Yet there was no mention of any black involvement in the meeting, and no mention of a "fusion" strategy with the Republicans. Subsequent discussions of the third party began to make the appeal more explicit, although it remained subdued. This was soon dropped in favor of a more open discussion of common interest. The *Virginia Sun* expressed the hope that black voters would support the People's Party "as faithfully as they have followed the Republicans heretofore, seeing they, being by a vast majority laborers, are naturally drawn by their interests to that party."[41] At some moments, the paper proposed an even grander vision of the outcome: "As long as there are only the two old parties, the colored brother will keep on voting the Republican ticket, though he is even more disgusted with his party than we are with ours. But now that there is a Third party where the reformers of both colors can meet on common ground for the common good, the colored people will flock to it, and the color line will be eliminated from politics."[42]

Following these claims, some organizing in the Southside began to target black voters directly. An indication that this often happened through the remaining Alliance organizations is provided in a letter from a Mecklenburg county organizer. "By request I addressed a colored Alliance in this county on Saturday," he wrote on July 13, 1892. "They seemed deeply interested and paid close attention throughout[;] and at the close, without any suggestion from the speaker, a member moved that they endorse the St. Louis platform, and everyone voted in the affirmative, and stated that no one could get their votes who did not stand by the St. Louis platform."[43] From Loudoun County in the extreme north of the state, a Populist wrote to the *Virginia Sun* about the necessity of appealing to black voters, and he pinned his hopes on the work of W. H. Warwick, the CFA leader who was squarely behind the People's Party. "As most of them cannot read, they must be talked to, which talk, to have any effect, must be done by one of their own color. He therefore hopes that Bro. W. H. Warwick . . . will visit his section and give the colored brethren the light they so much need."[44] In central Virginia's Orange County, a white Populist supporter wrote to say that he had organized a black Populist club with thirty-six members and he hoped to organize more before the election. The state chairman's assessment was that "the colored people are . . . pledging their allegiance to the party of reform."[45]

Thus, at the beginning of the election campaign of 1892, white and black Populist supporters held out hope for the emergence of an interracial voting bloc. In tension with this hope was the increasing use of charges of "negro supremacy." As the Democrats accused the Populists of promoting social equality and negro supremacy, the white Populists turned the charges back upon the Democrats in the same way that the Georgia Populists had done. One man wrote to report that his Democratic friend had gone to a political rally only to find that at the dinner "whites and negroes were all invited to the same table at the same time, and ate side by side, shoulder to shoulder." The man then reported that the experience had so disgusted his Democratic friend that he now planned to vote for the People's Party.[46] An editorial in the *Virginia Sun* carried the allegations further: "It is time the Democrats ceased abusing the People's Party as a negro party. Democratic returns from Alabama, Arkansas, Florida and Georgia show that they carried those states by colored votes . . . The first negro office-holder in Virginia was appointed by a Democratic legislature, and a negro [Fredrick Douglass] was the honored guest of Mr. and Mrs. Cleveland at their wedding reception. It begins to look as though the Democratic Party is to be the party of the negro, and the People's Party the white man's party."[47]

The outcome of the election of 1892 did nothing to change the minds of the Populists on this point. The Populist presidential ticket did poorly throughout the state, but the Populist congressional candidates in the Southside region had been expected to win. The Populists claimed that fraudulent vote counts kept them from victories in four election districts. Most disappointing was the defeat of J. Thomas Goode in the fourth congressional district, which contained most of the Southside counties. Mecklenburg Populists charged that the Democratic election board threw out returns from Goode's strongest precincts. Similar tactics were reported in Prince George County, while supporters in Amelia reported that money was "used lavishly to buy votes."[48] As in Georgia, the "bought" votes by and large were black ones. The post-election report of the state chairman shifted the identity boundaries of the movement: "It must be remembered that these 10,000 votes [counted for the Populist presidential candidate] are the votes of white men, the colored vote either going for Harrison or bought for Cleveland. These white men stood their ground in the face of calumny, vindictive abuse, intimidation, and social ostracism dictated by bitter [party] prejudice and venomous passion."[49]

After this point, the inclusion of black voters into the Populist rhetoric and organizing efforts was sporadic and tepid. Objecting to Democratic calls for a restriction of the franchise, a Populist editorial recognized that its "undisguised object is to restrict negro suffrage." Rather than mount a defense of black voting rights, the editorial asked instead what such a measure could accomplish that Virginia election laws did not already grant in practice: "We still cannot see how a constitutional restriction of the suffrage can benefit the party very much, unless it be that it is cheaper to keep the negro from the polls altogether than to buy him after he gets there."[50] Another editorial listed charges of election fraud in several counties, and then argued that it was leading to *white* disfranchisement: "It is no use to say that these iniquities are practised to 'preserve white civilization' . . . It was white men who were robbed of their votes, and white men who were defrauded of the offices to which they were elected."[51] Even when the party rhetoric demanded "honest elections and fair counts" for all, the leadership realized that the black vote in Virginia was not as easily swayed to the Populists as earlier rosy pronouncements had assumed: "No one dares to assert that the negro will control this country or even a small portion of it. It is false to nature for a superior race to be governed by an inferior. All the negro desires is justice at the hands of those in authority, and political suffrage. The grasp of the Republican party is gradually loosening its hold upon him. Its promises have never been fulfilled. Silently the negro looks on to see what inducements the new party offers."[52] Such a state of affairs did not bode well for the state elections in November 1893. The Populists nominated Edmund Cocke for governor and James Bradshaw Beverley for lieutenant governor, both of whom were Alliance men. Although the Populists' strongholds of support continued to be the majority-black counties in the south, race was never mentioned in the platform.[53]

The candidates for statewide office were hampered by the fact that their basis of support was concentrated in one area of the state. Still, the Populists had some hope for victory. Cocke, a descendent of a former Democratic governor, was one of the wealthiest farmers in the area. The Virginia Populists hoped that his prominence would lend him an air of legitimacy. The Democrats nominated a congressman, Charles T. O'Ferrall, as their candidate with Robert C. Kent for lieutenant governor. Kent had also been a prominent Allianceman,[54] and he provided the Democratic ticket with a claim to legitimacy on the question of monetary reform—one area where the third party's platform proved widely popular (Sheldon 1935: 97–98).

Even though the Republicans did not run their own candidates in the state elections, the Populists did not reach out to black voters in 1893. Cocke won 81,000 votes by the official count, mostly in the Southside, but lost the election.[55] The Populists did, however, elect ten members to the state assembly from the region. The party continued with minor victories in the legislature over the following three years, but they did not again become a realistic vehicle for interracial coalition. By the time that Mahone worked with the Populists on the issue of election reform in 1895, the chances for such a coalition had passed. Though Sheldon (1935: 111) argues that cooperation with Mahone left the Populists open to the charge that they had been swallowed up by the Republicans, they had stopped actively seeking black support. After 1894, Populists in Virginia had reconsidered the entire strategy of coalition, as they had in Georgia. They began to argue, too, that the Democrats easily manipulated black votes. A cartoon in Georgia's *People's Party Paper* bitterly adopted Jasper's joke by showing a "colored Democratic voter" with a "Democratic Office Seeker" on his back. A fat character (identified as the "Democratic Party") says, "Good Morning, Neighbor; I'm Glad to See You; Just Hitch Your Horse and Come In."[56]

The campaign of 1892 was thus a crucial turning point for the white Populists, but it was also a turning point for black Republicans. The decisive political break with the Democrats that brought the Alliance Democrats to the People's Party left Mitchell again optimistic about the possibilities of such a coalition at the state level, even though he continued to support the Republicans for the national ticket. "When the laboring white men of the South sink their prejudices, look at facts and realize that their interests and those of the Negro are identical, then the condition of both will be improved," he argued, echoing Populist language.[57] Still, Mitchell and other black Republi-

FIGURE 10. Democratic Party hitching post. Caption: "Democratic Party: 'Good Morning, Neighbor. I'm Glad to See You; Just Hitch Your Horse and Come Right In.'" (*People's Party Paper,* August 24, 1894)

cans throughout the state continued to qualify their support on the basis of Populist-Republican coalition. "The People's party will need the solid Republican support to win. The disintegration of the Democratic party will hardly be widespread enough to accomplish the result," Mitchell wrote.[58] Like the Alliance, Mitchell remained interested in the coalition even as he realized that fraud was likely. In commenting on the loss of Alabama's Populist Reuben Kolb, Mitchell noted that "except in cases where there is an overwhelming revolution in the ranks of the Democratic Party[,] a fair count is out of the question."[59]

In general, the *Planet* was quieter about the potential coalition in 1892 than it previously had been, apart from the scattered mentions throughout August. A statement in September confirmed that this relative silence corresponded to a general reconsideration of interests by Mitchell. Charlotte Smith, the suffragist and head of the Women's National Industrial League of America, wrote to the paper to inquire about political strategy, among other issues. As she wrote: "I am more than surprised at the indifference manifested in your paper . . . and am surprised to think you do not more closely watch your own interest, and the interest of the colored women. I consider that the time has about arrived when the Negro should by all means ally with the People's Party, and be of the people."[60] Mitchell's response provided an important window onto his evolving thoughts regarding political interest. After considering the shortcomings of the Republican Party, he turned to the issue of coalition. Mitchell's comments focused on the presidential ballot, since within the state Mahone threw Republican support to the Populists. His comments spoke to a general strategy, however:

> You urge us to ally ourselves with the People's Party. What are we to expect or hope from such an alliance? In the doubtful states such a movement would prove disastrous to the race at large. And why?
>
> It would draw from the Republican Party that element so essential to its success and according to facts not to be ignored, [and] would not result in the elevation of the candidates of the People's Party to the Presidency and Vice-Presidency of the United States.
>
> The logical outcome then is and would be that in voting the national ticket of the People's Party, we indirectly assist in the election of the Democratic nominees.
>
> It is hardly necessary to argue whether or not we could afford to do this or discuss the probable result of the complete possession of the government by the Democrats.[61]

Although it was "hardly necessary," Mitchell did go on to discuss the consequences in the next section of the letter. He mentioned in particular the restrictions on black voting rights and the emergence of Jim Crow railroad cars, which "causes uneasiness whenever the elevation of the Democratic Party to unlimited power is imminent." What is important here is that the changing assessment was at least partly driven by the same problem faced by the white Populists. As Mitchell put it, "When the Democrats of the South have no other issue upon which to rally the white laboring element, they yell 'Nigger.' "[62]

By the end of the following election cycle, the paper had soured on the movement. Mitchell was sure that the Populists would not help them and might in fact hinder the progress of the Republican Party. The Populists were themselves less enthusiastic about black support at this point, but equally important was the fact that the Republican hopes for a meaningful fusion were also gone. Working for a fusion of black Republicans and white Populists would have been a good strategy if the Populists were willing to make concessions, and if they were in a position to win. By the end of the 1893 campaign, this strategy began to look like a mistake to Mitchell. The Republican Party had atrophied when the Populists became the major alternative to the Democrats, and the Republicans had not even nominated a state ticket. The Populists were unwilling to make concessions, and could count on significant vote fraud to limit their impact. Mitchell's views in all likelihood reflected those of many black Republicans in the Southside, who were left with an unappealing choice. "This necessarily gives the colored man the alternative of three things: vote the Populists ticket, the Prohibition ticket, or remain at work and give politics the 'go-by' this year. We as a people are at the parting of the road. Which way shall we go?"[63]

Mitchell left the question unanswered, but it was clear that he viewed the Prohibition ticket as a losing cause, and the other two options as equally dismal. His post-election summary is worth quoting, as it marked the end of any hopes for a fruitful union between black Republicans and the mostly white Populists. "The result of the election in Virginia last week was no surprise to us," Mitchell wrote. "There was no Republican ticket in the field and the Populist campaign was managed just as though there were no colored voters in the state, so far as our observation goes . . . The Democratic Party of the state had too much at stake to yield easily and members of it would not have stopped short of murder but what a Democratic legislature should be returned."[64]

### CONCLUSION

The scope of the farmers' movements was limited in Virginia. Contrary to many existing accounts, the basic factor limiting the impact of the movements on the statewide level was not any inherent organizational weakness. Indeed, where the movements gained a foothold, they were quite well organized. Instead, the interesting story really lies in the way that calculations of interest first enabled a potential political allegiance between black and white agrarians in Virginia, and then shifted in the course of organizing. From the early electoral work of the Farmers' Alliance in 1891 to the Populist campaign of 1892, white Populists and black Republicans saw their interests in cooperation, even though both sides expressed some reservations. From the end of the campaign of 1892 through the state elections of 1893, these relations soured as both sides came to view the potential coalition with suspicion. The critical breaking point in the development of both interest claims was the election season of 1892 and its aftermath.

The *Virginia Sun* was initially quiet on the matter of interracial coalition, unwilling to risk internal dissent and external race baiting. As the Populists began to move away from the Democrats and toward an independent political challenge, the developing discussion of interest changed from one reticent and wary of coalition to one willing to use black support in the Southside to further its own ends while feeling relatively positive about the prospects of such a coalition. Although never in favor of "social equality" and always based in strategic reasoning, the Populist claims began to express an interest in allying with black Republicans as farmers and as people not well served under the existing political system. Although the black Republican claims were expressed differently, their trajectory was strikingly similar. The Richmond *Planet* moved from initial reticence to an eagerness to use the Populists to its own ends. It, too, was enthusiastic about the prospects of coalition. While never in favor of abandoning the Republican Party altogether, the *Planet* began to express an interest in allying with the Populists as representatives of working people and as people not well served under the existing political system.

It is worth underlining the fact that both sides supported the coalition for strategic rather than altruistic reasons. The interest claims among white Populists initially supported the coalition not to promote "political equality" for blacks—although Populist narratives did generally support this—but to improve their own chances of winning in the majority-black counties where the movement was most viable. Black supporters, coming to the political movement from the increasingly beleaguered Republican Party, supported the coalition for the same reasons. Equally important was the fact that both sides began to recognize and anticipate the difficulties that would arise in a coalition pursuing a third-party strategy. Most of the problems that the Populists faced in 1892, such as the fraudulent vote counts and the Democratic race baiting, had also occurred in Virginia's interracial coalitions of the 1880s. Both the *Virginia Sun* and the Richmond *Planet* saw these as obstacles. But in 1891 both saw the earlier coalitions as reason to work together. The lesson of the earlier coalitions at this point was that the Democrats were not invincible and that such a strategy could work.

The 1892 election was a bruising one, and the hopes of the Populists were dashed. But even before the election, the Virginia Populists began to reconsider their interests. On the one hand, the Populists continued to work toward a coalition and to do so more or less in good faith. On the other hand, they began to adopt a defensive claim about the Democrats promoting "negro supremacy," a discourse essentially about interracial political competition. In short, the black Republicans became both the solution and the problem in the Populist discussions. Something similar occurred in the interest claims produced by the *Planet.* Although the People's Party continued to be identified as a potential ally, the result was seen as ambiguous at best. Fraud would continue to "count out" the Populist votes, and even success might spell the end of the Republican Party as a viable entity in Virginia. Part of this shift had to do with a different understanding of the lessons of the 1880s. After 1892, the Populists recalled the defeat of Mahone's Readjusters under the same charges of "negro supremacy" that the Democrats were beginning to use against them. Black Republicans came to view their role in the Populist movement as equivalent to that of Mahone's horse—a convenient vehicle for their success, but one that would be left outside when the rider arrived.

CHAPTER 8

# CLASS, STATUS, POWER, AND THE INTERRACIAL PROJECT

Despite the incomplete project of the Reconstruction and the continued existence of old racial hierarchies, the 1880s and 1890s presented "forgotten alternatives" for race relations, as C. Vann Woodward wrote so eloquently in 1955 in *The Strange Career of Jim Crow.* Relationships between black and white southerners were being renegotiated in social life, and for a moment new arrangements seemed possible. The same decades presented alternatives for class formation, and a powerful and widespread critique of capitalism and wage labor captured the public imagination across the country. The Knights of Labor and the Southern Populists were at once the most important class movements of the Gilded Age and the era's most important vehicles for interracial organizing. As these movements waned, so did the possibility of the broad realignment of the joint boundaries of race and class that they symbolized. Did these movements provide real alternatives to the dominant structure of race/class relations, or were they simply curious exceptions that proved the general rule?

Analysts looking back on the legacy of the Populists and the Knights could easily see the collapse of the coalitions as predetermined by the seemingly inevitable divisions of interest and identity that separated white and black "producers." The Knights and the Populists looking back on their own defeats could easily see the same thing. Getting closer to the actual narratives and processes reveals much more complexity, however. During the giddy heyday of the movements, the Populists and the Knights of Labor felt that everything was possible—even overcoming the "color line" once and for all. Not knowing what the outcome would be, both sides began to try to work out their interests, revising as they went along.[1] Yet despite the complex and dynamic nature of this radical moment, it did not lead to transformative social change. The most important effect of the movements' collapse was the way that both black and white southerners re-read the meaning of past attempts to transcend the color line and the prospects of future efforts: the lesson came to be that such coalitions were fruitless. In the early years of the twentieth century, a union movement like the booming American Federation of Labor could conclude that organizing southern blacks was not worth the trouble. After all, look where it got the Knights of Labor. By the same token, a figure like Tom Watson, previously outspoken in his demand for political equality, became a defender of political disfranchisement.

But the importance of what the movements accomplished is not precluded by the closure that happened afterward; it is instead highlighted by it. While the Populists and the Knights were replaced by supposedly more practical and hard-headed trade unionism and Progressive-era politics, it was a very long time before any class movement managed to match their level of commitment and potential in organizing across the color line. In 1968, the machinist, editor, and socialist radical Julius Jacobson edited a volume titled *The Negro and the American Labor Movement*. The central theme of his introduction was the continued failure of the then-dominant AFL-CIO to come to grips with its own exclusive boundaries. "On paper and in resolutions, the AFL-CIO is committed to racial equality in a most general way," he wrote. "But what happens to the Negro-labor alliance when, in the course of the struggle for jobs and economic betterment, it is brought home to the Negro masses that major obstacles to their acquiring skills and entering the job market have been set up and defended by powerfully entrenched sections of the same union movement that is the presumable ally of Negro organizations and an advocate of civil rights legislation?" (1968: 13, 23–4).

By that same standard, the Knights and the Populists might well also be found wanting. In the essays in Jacobson's volume, however, the movements were seen as the institutional embodiment of the sort of radical possibility that Woodward described. For Ray Marshall, the era represented a moment when "Southern Negro and white workers and farmers might be welded together politically and economically in the Populist movement and the Knights of Labor" (1968: 130–31). The leftist historians August Meier and Elliott Rudwick noted that it was a transformative era for white leaders "who were more inclined toward economic solidarity among the laboring classes than toward economic solidarity within the race" (1968: 32–33).

Interracial organizing did not come to a complete halt after the decline of the Knights and the Populists, of course. In the early decades of the twentieth century, industrial and agrarian organizations attempted to revive the promise of the Gilded Age movements. David Roediger (1994) has explored a similar orientation for the southern Wobblies; and the Depression-era interracialism of the socialist-led Southern Tenant Farmers Union also compares with that of the Knights and the Populists in fascinating ways (see Kester 1997 [1936]). So too does the Alabama Communist organizing that Robin D. G. Kelley (1990) has explored. In these cases, a more explicitly revolutionary ideology nevertheless drew from some of the same cultural currents that sustained the earlier movements. Some of the same egalitarian spirit also remained in organizations such as the United Mine Workers. These later movements did not, however, attain the same level of national prominence or political clout as did the Knights and the Populists. The organizational message had changed, of course, but not nearly so much as had the historical moment. The organization of American working people across the racial divide had not become an impossible task, but it had again become practically unthinkable.

The moment of possibility for a broad and meaningfully interracial coalition of American working people that seemed so ripe in 1885 thus seemed like a distant utopian dream by 1900. In the half century since Woodward outlined the possibilities and paradoxes of this moment of southern history, scholars have come to terms with the radical class potential of the republican movements. Despite their eventual collapse, the legacy of that potential lived on and provided a bridge to later forms of mobilization. As yet, there has been no similar consensus about the racial legacy of the movements. My aim in this book has been to provide a more satisfying set of answers that recognize both the sources and the limits of the possibilities they offered.

I have argued that the confusion over the racial legacy of the movements has been largely a function of the way in which the alternatives have been posed; indeed, Eric Arnesen nailed this problem when he labeled it the "how racist/racially egalitarian were they" question (1998: 156). Far more satisfying answers emerge when we can admit that the opposition is a false one. The boundaries of the movements were both inclusive and exclusive in equal measure. The Knights and the Populists were both racist and sincere in their efforts to build coalitions across the color line. In order to make sense of this, I have focused on the subjective side of interests—the "complex of meaning" within which class and race were understood by those involved—as well as on the more grounded process in which interests developed over time and in particular locations.

Richard Oestreicher (1986) has pointed out that solidarity and fragmentation went hand in hand for the Knights of Labor, and the same can be said of Populism. Solidarity was never an accomplished fact for either movement. It did not simply exist; it was, rather, always a project under construction. Its making rested upon what the sociologist Anthony Giddens has called the "grey areas of practical consciousness" (1979: 57–58). By emphasizing the construction and maintenance of class and race as social boundaries, I have pointed out the underlying reason for this dialectic of solidarity and fragmentation. Boundaries are always inclusive and exclusive at the same time. In asking the question "Who is with us?" the movements also necessarily asked "Who is not?" The stronger the bonds of solidarity, the stronger are the resulting exclusions. This dialectic played out at two levels.

At one level, I have examined the connection between race and class boundaries in the movement narratives. Of particular importance within the movement narratives were the broad boundaries of the producerist class identity and the importance of civic virtue as a central resource for the class movements. This republican class framework has received very different scholarly receptions over the years. Some of the foundational work on the labor movement saw it as an impediment—as a "backward-looking" or "middle-class" idiom standing in the way of a more radical ideology. Most prominently, Selig Perlman (1928) identified producerism as one of the main reasons why class consciousness did not advance in America.[2] This idiom, Perlman felt, blunted the radical potential of the working class in America and led to what he thought was a soft anti-monopoly populism instead of true class consciousness.

More recent work has tended to view class as a malleable boundary that has taken different forms in different eras. Accordingly, this work has come to a new appreciation of the radical potential of producerism and its broader republican framework for class formation in the eighteenth and nineteenth centuries. This cultural expression of class constrained the way that class was understood but also enabled new social critiques and forms of opposition.

The republican class language so deeply knit into these movements had implications for race as well. While earlier manifestations of the republican idiom had been mobilized for the defense of a white republic, the same language suggested broader possibilities at a later moment.[3] The narratives did not extend to everyone equally, however, and this explains in large part the historical puzzle posed by the Knights and the Populists—they were at the same time among the most racially open movements of their age and the most vehemently exclusionary. Moreover, the movements justified both inclusion and exclusion on the basis of material and political interest. For the Knights, one cultural narrative linked black workers to an "interracial organizing" frame and in doing so largely presumed common class position and common cause between white and black working people. Another tied new immigrants to a very different frame about competition. These seemingly disparate narratives were driven by a consistent underlying emphasis on civic virtue as a central resource at stake in the class struggle. The Chinese, Italian, and Hungarian immigrant workers that the Knights rejected so vehemently were all undeniably workers and "wage slaves" just as were whites. But to the Knights, they did not appear capable of upholding the civic duties of republican citizenship. The immigrants seemed instead to be competing with white workers by undermining their capacity to support the communities and civic institutions that helped to maintain the independence and autonomy of independent democratic citizens. Black workers appeared at least potentially able to do so, however. In sharp contrast with the earlier republican reactions to black workers as anti-citizens, the same underlying schema afforded a very different view after Reconstruction.

In the Alliance and the People's Party, a similar republican orientation drove a parallel analysis of the logic of interracial organizing. When it came to black farmers and voters, the Populist narratives were split—they were both class equals worth organizing and potential competitors of whom to be wary. Also like the Knights, the Populist narratives linked discussions of material competition to a set of ethnic or national "others" rather than to American blacks. For the Populists, the foreigners were threats from "above" rather than from "below." In particular, the English banker was a target of Populist abuse, but the national label also became racialized—the English banker became the Jewish usurer.

The boundaries drawn in the movement narratives were thus inclusive and exclusive at the same time. The narratives did not operate independently but rather were mediated through actors' practical consciousness in particular local settings, which provided the second level of analysis I address in this book. At the local level, the development of interests was a more varied and open-ended process. The conditions in different local contexts mattered a great deal for the development of the interracial project. Interracial organizing was most successful and sustained where there was a close connection between the movement claims and local economic and political conditions, and where there were preexisting organizational and political resources to draw upon. This was the case in Richmond, where there was an established history of such coalitions within the labor movement and where the black community was both spatially cohesive and civically rooted. Interracial organizing faltered for the Knights in Atlanta, however. The two cities were similar in some ways—for example, both were about the same size and had roughly similar proportions of black residents. But Atlanta was a much newer city, and it had neither a history of interracial labor organizing nor an organized and autonomous black community that could sustain its own local assemblies in the face of hostility. By contrast, the Populists were much stronger in Georgia than in Virginia. This difference was due, in part, to the very different economic patterns of the two states. In Georgia, relatively high rates of tenancy and a dependence on cotton farming statewide meant that the movement's claims matched rather well with local conditions. In Virginia, a lower tenancy rate and a more diverse agrarian economy made it hard for the Populists to organize statewide. In the state's "Southside" district, however, economic conditions were more like those of Georgia, and so was the movement's strength.

The simultaneously inclusive and exclusive tendencies of the interracial project emerged at the local level as well. Black members and potential supporters of the movements generally had fewer resources to draw upon, but established black civic and political organizations, leaders, and communities all helped to sustain interracial organizing. Such resources made it possible for black members to retain a degree of autonomy from white control, and a long history of such organization meant that some black involvement was taken for granted by white organizers. Where there was no such history, blacks often appeared to white Knights and Populists as the Chinese did—an unorganized mass that did not seem to fit the civic goals of the movements. As the comparison between Richmond and Atlanta showed, it was often paradoxically a degree of segregation (in communities, in civic organizations, and within the movement itself) that sustained interracial organizing for the Knights. Moreover, the inclusive and exclusive tendencies were continually in flux at the local level as interests were worked out over time. While the analyses of the movement-level narratives explored the role of the republican class language in the formation of the movements' racial boundaries, the local-level analyses explored the temporally dynamic nature of the process. As the chapter on Virginia Populism showed most clearly, different lessons could be read from the same historical precedents at different points in time.

The interracial project had different implications when measured in different ways, however. Max Weber famously distinguished between three kinds of resources upon which claims to social position can be made: class, status, and political power. The three dimensions are never truly separate in lived experience, and while this book has focused on the connection between class and the color line, political and civic considerations were never far from view. Yet it is worth returning here to the other dimensions. By providing different metrics against which racial boundaries and their meanings and costs were understood, considerations of politics and social status were sometimes at odds with class concerns.

Electoral politics proved to be thorny territory in many respects, but the movements knew as much long before they tested the waters. The "political question" was a major point of internal debate for the Knights and the Alliance well in advance of their decisions to campaign. The movements' ambivalence about partisan involvement was in fact one of the central paradoxes of their republican legacy. While they saw politics as an important and necessary part of their reform agenda, many also saw partisan politics as inherently corrupt. In general, electoral politics was a mixed bag for the movements—some stunning successes were matched by some striking losses—but at least the political arena allowed the Knights and the Populists to capture the spotlight for their causes.

More to the point, political organizing provided its own paradoxes when it came to the interracial project. The party is a looser organizational form than is the fraternal brotherhood, and so equal membership was less threatening. At least formally, for example, the Populists became more clearly interracial when they shifted from the Alliance to the People's Party as a central vehicle for protest. At the same time, established political identities and interests proved hard to overcome, even when both sides saw the logic of coalition. Because white and black supporters were drawn to the third parties from different political backgrounds, movement success meant something different for each side, despite the common appeal that the third party movement held for both. For whites, successful third party activity meant that the dominant Democratic Party would be pressured into living up to its Jacksonian legacy. Most white supporters and many of the leaders of the Populists, for example, were quite plain in stating that they would support the Democratic Party if the party would support them. For potential black supporters, the third party was an important vehicle for gaining some influence and concessions in post-Reconstruction politics. This was particularly true while the Populists were openly pursuing fusion tickets with Republicans. Yet it also meant potentially putting the last nail in the coffin of the Republican party. Even though it was struggling in many places throughout the South, deeper black involvement with the Populist movement meant relinquishing some control over the one political institution that still responded to black votes and elected black leaders, however tenuously.

The problem of status distinctions—often expressed by the movements as a concern over "social equality"—has been a consistent theme woven throughout this book, but it deserves some explicit consideration here as well. At least since E. P. Thompson, scholars have emphasized that the expression of class is not cleanly distinct from status concerns, and of course racial distinctions are similarly entangled with status distinctions. Social status—that is, claims to social honor or prestige—is difficult to measure directly because it is an inherently social good. It does not exist if it is not recognized and accepted by others. Status claims were, however, at the heart of the concerns of the Knights and of the Populists. The post–Civil War era was a crucial period in the history of American class formation in large part because the mass mobilization of the workers and farmers marked a struggle over the place of working people as "honorable" producers. This status struggle was waged around race and class simultaneously.

Adolph Reed Jr. has pointed out that the academic debate about how race and class are connected has misrepresented both dimensions by portraying them as ontologically and empirically distinct elements rather than as dual parts of a single system of social power. In his view, race represents "a social category that has evolved to denote an especially durable kind of ascriptive civic status in the context of American capitalism and the political and ideological structures through which it is reproduced as a social order" (2002: 266). This point is an important one. The central place accorded to the independent artisans and yeomen in the romantic ideal of the Knights and of the Populists was not simply because of their autonomous class position or because of the political resources that they controlled; rather, it was because these were linked to the social status that the independent producers held in the republic. Similarly, the claim that the producers of the late nineteenth century were becoming "wage slaves" and "party slaves" was at the same time about the loss of economic and political standing and about their fears over losing civic status as well. In claiming that labor was "noble and holy" the Knights and the Populists were saying that laborers should be respectable and respected.[4] But of course this republican class language initially rested on a set of clear status distinctions marked by race.

One of the toughest ironies involved in making sense of the connection between class and the color line for these movements is that the status dimension was at the same time both a source of and a limitation for the interracial project. In fact a major point of division for the movements came in trying to separate notions of class equality and political equality from what they called "social equality." The logic of interracial organizing for class goals was widely accepted even among white members, and at times the logic of political equality gained acceptance as well. This did not extend to what white members termed "social equality," however. The Knights of Labor struggled with the issue continually in the relationship between white and black local assemblies, but it became particularly salient in the crossfire of opinions concerning the 1886 General Assembly in Richmond. The dilemma bedeviled the Populists too. The Democratic opponents of the Populists used internal tension over the question of social equality as leverage for its attacks, thus leading to an important shift in the way that white Populists evaluated their defeats. Their early optimistic assessments of their initial efforts, centering on the demand for political equality, turned gradually into bitter charges that it was the Democrats themselves who were fostering social equality.

At the movement level, the class narratives that were so rooted in civic ideals pushed the organizations toward a recognition of black "producers" as class equals worthy of a place in the great reform movement. At the same time, the narratives set up a sort of test of republican worthiness based on this civic model. This was a test that the new immigrants failed, but so too did black workers and farmers in many places. The difference between Powderly's impression of black Richmond and Atlanta residents illustrates this. Given a coherent community life and a long history of self-organization, Powderly thought Richmond's black residents stood in line with the movement's aims. In Atlanta, he saw a civically unorganized mass—and thus a stumbling block. In the course of local organizing, the concern with status led the movements to demand democratic equality in economic and political matters. Initially, the demand was about equality for the white workers and farmers, relative to the power of the "trusts and combinations" and the "bourbons and plutocrats." By extension it became a demand for equality between the races—the equal status of all "producers." Yet status concerns also pressed white Southerners to cling to social distinctions. Social equality was widely rejected because it was associated with a loss of status in the personal, local interactions that mattered to white Knights and Populists.

# APPENDIX

*Data Collection, Sources, and Methods*

In writing this book, I have drawn upon a number of different data sources. Sometimes, my use of these sources has been transparent; at other times, I have built my arguments upon one or another data source without discussing it explicitly. Throughout the book I have tried to place the substantive arguments, rather than the underlying data, on the center stage. In doing so I hoped to make the book palatable to a broad audience. However, the value of a study like this is inherently tied to the quality of the data and its use.

Because different chapters of the book relied on different kinds of data, it may be hard for readers to get an overall sense of the data from reading the book chapter by chapter. My first goal in writing this appendix is therefore to simply outline all of the major primary and secondary data sources that I rely on. My second goal is to supply details about the data collection, coding, and analysis procedures for each type of data. Some of the data sources that I rely upon are well known, while others are not. Even in the case of some of the well-known primary sources, my methods of data collection and analysis are sometimes quite different from those of other authors. Most of this appendix addresses my treatment of the primary data sources. My use of secondary data sources is more standard, and so I treat these together in the last section.

## RACE/CLASS COMMUNICATIONS FROM MOVEMENT JOURNALS

Chapters 2 and 5 of this book center on one question: How did the Knights of Labor and the Populists understand the connection between class and race? As I argue in earlier chapters, answering this question involves moving past the statements of individuals to address the broader movement-level narratives that linked race and class. My goal in these chapters is to identify and then interpret the narratives in order to understand the role of a relatively long-term and deep-seated cultural understanding of class for the way that the movements approached the "color line."

Movement journals were the arenas for the most "public" discussions of class and race interests, aimed as they were at the movement supporters generally. For this reason, I use the journals as a source of systematic data on the narratives linking race and class. First, the analytic variables that I discuss below allow me to empirically identify the movement narratives. While a lot of talk goes on in all movements, not all of it coheres into anything meaningful. This procedure allows me to outline, and thus focus on, the central ways that the movement connected race and class. Second, I use the data as the basis for the more interpretive analysis of the meanings embedded in the narratives.

The *Journal of United Labor* and the *National Economist* were the official papers of the Knights of Labor and the Farmers' Alliance, respectively. The People's Party was a much more decentralized movement, and it did not have a single official newspaper. Instead, it had a large number of regional and local papers produced by committed but often ill-financed Populists. I use the *People's Party Paper* both because of my own focus on Georgia as one important site for movement activism and because that paper, produced by Tom Watson, was widely recognized as setting an agenda for the movement as a whole on racial issues. All of the journals I examined were in their standard microfilm editions.

I read every available issue of these papers published during the periods that the organizations were most active. For the *Journal of United Labor* the relevant period was from the paper's founding in May 1880 through December 1890.[1] For the *National Economist*, the period was from the paper's founding in March 1889 through March 1893. I examined issues of the *People's Party Paper* published from its founding in November 1891 through October 1894. After that point most issues of the paper were lost, but I examined the scattered issues that were available from fall 1895 and 1896 (see table 17).[2]

I collected every item published in the specified time frames that made reference to both class and race. The items were then coded into computer databases. An "item" was defined as a topically discrete block of printed text. Each edition of the paper was thus composed of many items in the form of letters, editorials, notices, reports of local events, and general interest items. Generally, each item appeared under a separate heading, with the exception of notices, which were often grouped together under headings such as "General Industrial News" (see table 18).

A "reference" to class was defined operationally as the use of specific labels for individual or collective positions (e.g., "laborers," "producers," "workingman," "capitalist")

**TABLE 17** Characteristics of paper source

| Characteristic | *Journal of United Labor* | *National Economist* | *People's Party Paper* |
|---|---|---|---|
| Editor and location | Charles H. Lichman, Marblehead Ma.; Robert D. Layton, Pittsburgh, Pa.; Frederick Turner, Charles Litchman, Adelbert M. Dewey, and Board of Trustees, Philadelphia, Pa. | Charles W. Macune, Washington, D.C. | Thomas E. Watson, Atlanta, Ga. |
| Frequency | Monthly to mid-1884, biweekly through 1885 and weekly thereafter | Weekly | Weekly |
| Cost | $1/year | $1/year | $0.50/year |
| Period of examination | 1880–1890 | 1889–1893 | 1891–1894; scattered in 1895 and 1896 |
| Issues with items meeting criteria | 157 | 164 | 154 |

or a substantive discussion of interests or positions in the absence of such explicit labels. Because the movements themselves saw political action as an outgrowth of class interests, political identities and labels (e.g., "plutocrat") are included here too. Because political action was much more pronounced for the Populists than for the Knights, I often refer to class and politics together in the chapters on the Populists.

Similarly, items were included as having made a reference to race if they mentioned specific racial or ethnic/national labels (e.g., "colored," "Chinamen," "Poles," "white"), or if they included a discussion of racial issues or statuses (e.g., a mention of the "race problem" or a comparison of the position of workers to that of chattel slaves).[3]

This process yielded a set of 1,083 communications from the three papers. These were drawn from 475 separate issues of the journals published over the course of sixteen newspaper-years of publication. Two items drawn from the *Journal of United Labor* data can serve as examples to illustrate my handling of the communications. These represent more or less typical communications in the journal. The first example is drawn from a letter printed in the edition of August 6, 1887, and signed collectively by LA 8413 of Graniteville, South Carolina. This communication is coded as record 59 in my database. The entire body of the letter is reproduced here. The second example, record 240, is from an editorial of July 3, 1890, by John W. Hayes, the general secretary-treasurer of the

TABLE 18 Characteristics of newspaper data

| Characteristic | *Journal of United Labor* | *National Economist* | *People's Party Paper* |
|---|---|---|---|
| Editorials and features | 116 (44.6%) | 282 (75.2%) | 326 (72.8%) |
| Letters and reports | 104 (40.0%) | 61 (16.3%) | 103 (23.0%) |
| Other | 40 (15.4%) | 32 (8.5%) | 19 (4.2%) |
| Total | 260 (100.0%) | 375 (100.0%) | 448 (100.0%) |

Knights of Labor. Because this communication is very long, only the most relevant passage is reproduced below.

*Example 1*

I guess you would like to hear from this part of the South. We are about to have some trouble here with the trustees of the Masonic hall, owned by the Masons and Odd Fellows. The trustees said we could not have the hall any more if we permitted the negroes to meet there with us. That is their excuse, but I know better. I see through their little game—they want to break up the Knights of Labor here, but we intend to have the Knights of Labor in spite of all opposition, for we know our noble Order is right, and when we are right God is on our side, and when He is on our side I don't care a straw hat who is against us. You will see what kind of people we are here. We are going to carry on our work without the fear or favor of any one.

*Example 2*

The General Master Workman and the members of the General Executive Board [of the Knights of Labor] visited the Barge Office in New York City on June 21 for the purpose of making a thorough inspection of the system adopted under the management of the national government relative to the landing of immigrants and the enforcement of the contract labor law . . . There is on record in the office a report of the landing, during the past few months, of 1,700 Italians, fourteen of them women, and but twenty-eight pieces of baggage among the entire lot . . . If these people would but make good citizens and live like human beings, there would and could not be so much objection to them; but as they are quartered in the ship coming over so do they continue to live here, grouped dozens in a space that an American would consider too small for one. Their low standard of living makes them formidable competitors in the field of labor, bringing closely home the truth of the iron law of wages. A large number of them are reported on their way South, and it is quite probable that their advent here will give rise to new and serious social complications.

We are threatened with a further human plague in the shape of a large influx of immigrants from Western Asia, mostly Arabs. Fifty thousand are reported on their way hither, these forming merely the advance guard. What with the difficulties

> attending the assimilation of the laboring poor of Southern Europe, the problem becomes more complex when we come to take into consideration what is to be done with the shiftless people from Arabia, unused to habits of thrift and the methods of industry. With but few exceptions, all who have hitherto found their way to this country have not been able to rise any higher above mendicancy than to become petty itinerant merchants . . . Our much vaunted protective system should assuredly afford this, the humblest and neediest of our own citizens, the fullest measure of protection against unfair, excessive, foreign competition.

From these communications I recorded several types of information into the computer database records. Contextual variables included the date the item was published, its form (letter, editorial, notice, report, other), and the author's name and affiliation when it was listed. I also coded several analytic variables. For the purposes of this book, the important analytic variables are the racial or ethnic/national "others" listed in the communications and the movement frames of interest that connected race and class. Both of these variables were coded inductively. Rather than defining the relevant categories a priori, my goal was to capture the way that the movements themselves defined the categories in practice. Finally, I recorded relevant passages of the communications into the database records to facilitate the interpretive work of chapters 2 and 5.

The first analytic variable was the racial and ethnic "others" listed in the communications. The terms used by the movements were recorded verbatim into the computer records. For the first example above, the term "negroes" was recorded; for the second, "Italians" and "Arabs." Terms that referred to a single racial or ethnic category were then grouped together for analytic purposes. When only one racial or ethnic term was used in a given communication, this was counted as a single reference to that group. When multiple terms were used for the same "other" in a single communication (e.g., "Negro" and "colored"), this was counted as one reference, although I recorded both. When different groups were named in the same communication (e.g., "Italians" and "Arabs"), this was counted as two separate references. Finally, when a communication included a general discussion of race without naming any particular group, the value of the variable was "none." In most of these cases, the item either engaged the question of slavery or discussed the "race" problem in general terms.

The second analytic variable was the frames of interest that tied race and class together. Conceptually and methodologically, my coding of this variable followed other recent work on movement "frames" and "discourses." Frames of interest are defined as the "relatively bounded sets of arguments organized around a specific diagnosis or solution to some social problem" (Ellingson 1995: 107).[4] Rather than focus on movement frames of interest broadly, this variable codes only those frames of interest that were invoked in the communications to link race and class. This could be done through moral, political, social, or economic justifications (see Steinberg 1999:754). Following standard practice, I built the categories of this variable inductively by organizing them around the natural clusters that occurred in the movement discussions (see Gamson

1992: 24; Babb 1996:1036). New categories were introduced during the course of the coding when a statement about interest did not fit easily within any previous category. After each item had been coded from a particular source, I refined the categories and combined closely related ones. This method insured that the coding scheme was consistent across the cases without being too rigid to capture subtle meanings presented by the items.

Like all movement frames, those used by these organizations reflected the internal process of contention through which interests were worked out in the course of organizing.[5] The authors of the items in these papers typically signaled one of a number of standard frames of interest and then took a position on it. Because of this, I recorded both the general frame that each statement adopted and the more specific position that the author took relative to that frame.

In the first example above, the general frame was recorded as "interracial organizing" since, like many of the Knights of Labor communications, the link between race and class was the need to continue organizing black workers—"We are going to carry on our work without the fear or favor of any one." The more specific position was "positive"—that is, unlike many of the communications, the author did not simply report neutrally on such organizing but instead gave an active, positive evaluation of it. In the second example, the general frame is coded as "material/political interests." Unlike the first example, organizing is not the relevant issue in this communication. Instead, the link between class and race in this item was the question of whether or not different groups had similar or competing interests. Here the more specific frame is "competing interests" since the item proposes that Italians and Arabs are competitors with native-born workers.

### LETTERS FROM THE TERENCE VINCENT POWDERLY PAPERS

The movement journals described above were relatively democratic forums, including as they did many letters from all over the country and exhibiting a sometimes surprising amount of openness about internal disagreements over fundamental questions. There is always the danger that there is a gap between elite and non-elite voices in the movement (perhaps especially on racial matters), and that this gap is not represented in the data collected from the official movement journals. In the case of the Knights of Labor, an important supplementary source of "discursive" data is in the letters sent from movement members and followers to Terence V. Powderly. Unfortunately, there is no similar source for the Farmers' Alliance or for the People's Party.

My source was the correspondence records in the Terence Vincent Powderly Papers collection. Powderly's correspondence files for the time of his tenure at the head of the Knights from 1879 to 1893 take up fifty-eight microfilm reels. Letters flooded in to Powderly's office from across the country. Many were from movement leaders and were focused on official business. Many others were decidedly not from movement elites—these missives were barely legible, written with a shaky hand and phonetic spelling on available scraps of paper. Such letters also were often remarkably personal, asking for help with troubled local assemblies or telling of desperate conditions that the authors hoped Powderly could fix.

The data-collection strategy that I used for this source was different from the method I used for the movement newspapers. Rather than attempt to gather only the relevant documents, I sampled from all documents addressed from southern states between 1880 and 1890. In doing this, I was able to get a sense of how much the issue of race came up in the course of Southern correspondence relative to other issues. I sampled only those letters addressed in alternate months—January, March, May, July, September, and November. The result is an additional database that codes 847 letters to Powderly from individuals in the South. I coded these in much the same way as the newspaper data in order to allow comparison across the sources.

Data from this source was used in a relatively formal way in chapter 2 to provide a check on the data from the *Journal of United Labor* and to provide a more interpretive analysis of the view of black and white Knights in the South. The letters are also cited, although more informally, in chapters 3 and 4. Perhaps most important, my close reading of the correspondence from Southern states allowed me to gain a sense of the many issues that the Knights were dealing with in the course of their organizing, and to gain some confidence in my own interpretations of the secondary literature on the movement and on later organizing under the Alliance and the People's Party.

### CITY DIRECTORIES

The third major kind of primary data that I gathered comes from city directories. Chapters 3 and 4 discuss the Knights of Labor and its struggles over interracial organizing in the local contexts of Richmond and Atlanta, respectively. I use the city directory data to assess the structure of class and race in those cities. This assessment is invaluable in interpreting both the differences in the histories of labor organizing before the Knights of Labor and that organization's own interaction with the color line.

There are two major reasons for using city directories rather than census data for this purpose. The first reason is that the aggregate census figures do not include adequate information on the population at the level of wards, which were the primary political and social unit of many cities at the time. The published census reports do list the population of Richmond and Atlanta wards by race, but they do not include any more detailed information on residence, occupation, or gender. Theoretically, it would be possible to reconstruct this information from the manuscript census records. In practical terms, however, this would require sampling, which would not allow the fine-grained analyses of block-level data that I make use of here. Second, the census records only report the racial makeup of the wards in 1890, when the Knights' strength had waned.

As a resource, the city directories are not perfect. Compared with the census, they undercount the black population in most wards. One of the reasons for this is that the city directories capture the head of household, and thus they are likely to miss children as well as boarders and guests. Due to limited means, black households were more likely to have such informal residents, and this may account for much of the discrepancy. Still, breakdowns of the overall class distribution by race from the city directories compare very closely with the census figures, suggesting that the undercount does not result in any systematic bias in the data.[6] If anything, the estimates of residential segregation based on the directories are likely to be conservative ones.

The city directories of the time typically comprised three parts. The "street directory" gave a block-by-block census of residences, listing the addresses and adult residents. Typically, Southern city directories would also indicate race by adding a mark next to the names of black residents (an asterisk or a small letter "c" for "colored"). The "names directory" listed the same information organized by name rather than address, but included occupations as well. Finally, the directories included a section listing organizations, clubs, and societies.

I use city directory information from Richmond and Atlanta for three different purposes. First, I use the street directory information to analyze the spatial distribution of population. The standard approach is to use aggregated ward-level data to analyze citywide distributions. By contrast, I use the directory information to construct finer-grained block-level data. This allows me to analyze the citywide distribution as well as within-ward distributions.[7] Because this was a large undertaking, I coded only the 1885 directories for both Atlanta and Richmond.[8] This date had the advantage of being the most crucial expansion period for the Knights of Labor in the South. It was also conveniently mid-decade, and thus midway between the 1880 and 1890 census data for these cities, which I refer to extensively in these chapters.

I recorded the number of white and black residents for each block within the city boundaries of Richmond (1,039 blocks) and Atlanta (921 blocks). Because cross-streets were included in the directories, it was possible to then code each of the blocks to one of the six wards of each city. This was done by cross-referencing each block listed in the directory with a city map showing ward boundaries. Blocks that were divided in half by ward boundaries were treated in one of two ways. Blocks that were divided by an east/west boundary (i.e., a boundary dividing a northern ward from its southern neighbor) were coded to the southern ward. Blocks divided by a north/south boundary were treated as members of the eastern ward.

From this information, I was able to calculate and map the racial distributions of the city wards. I was also able to map each of the "black" blocks (i.e., those blocks with black populations of 90 percent or greater) in order to assess spatial clustering. Finally, this coding allowed me to calculate block-level measures of segregation and cross-race contact for each ward of Atlanta and Richmond.

I use standard measures for segregation and cross-race contact. My segregation measure is the index of dissimilarity ($D$), which measures the difference between the population of white and black residents in a given spatial area relative to their overall population. The higher the index, the more that the interracial contact measure ($P^*$) is a proxy measure for the likelihood of day-to-day contact between black and white residents in their neighborhoods. As I calculate it, $P^*$ measures the likelihood for black residents coming into contact with white residents. These measures are calculated as follows:[9]

$$Dwb = .5 \sum \left| (w_i/W) - (b_i/B) \right.$$

$$bP^*w = \sum (b_i/B) * (w_i/t_i)$$

Where $w_i$ and $b_i$ are, respectively, the numbers of black and white residents in local area $i$, $W$ and $B$ are the area-wide totals for the groups, and $t_i$ is the total population of local area $i$. Using these measures, I calculated citywide measures (using wards and citywide totals) and within-ward measures (using blocks and ward totals).

Second, I use the names directory information to assess the black and white class composition of each ward. Because I did not need fine-grained data for this task, I used a 1/20 sample of the names in the 1885 directories (1,093 cases in Richmond; 890 cases in Atlanta). In order to calculate class composition, I first assigned occupations to aggregate classes using the same coding scheme as applied to the census occupational data in chapters 3 and 4, and then I coded each person to a ward based on their address.

Third, I collected the organizational information from Richmond and Atlanta directories for 1880, 1885, and 1890.[10] Although I do not discuss the organizational data in any systematic way, I use it extensively in the discussion of Richmond and Atlanta's organizational life. These are a particularly valuable source for my discussion of black churches and other black associations.

### OTHER NEWSPAPER SOURCES

Chapters 6 and 7 examine the Populist negotiation of race and class "on the ground" in Virginia and Georgia. In order to explore the development of those complex relationships, I rely on newspaper data from these sites. In the case of Virginia, I use two papers extensively. The first, the *Exchange Reporter*, was the official paper of Virginia's state Alliance. The paper was later renamed the *Virginia Sun* as the Alliance gave way to the People's Party. This paper is a valuable and largely overlooked source on Populist activity in the state and it provides detail on the changing views of white Populists about the value and expected results of interracial organizing. The *Richmond Planet*, produced by the prominent black editor John Mitchell, provides an important look into the activities and attitudes of Virginia's black Populists and Republicans. Early on, Virginia's relatively outspoken CFA chose the *Planet* to publish its reports and announcements, and the paper continued to follow the movement closely. Mitchell himself was an unapologetic Republican, as were most black potential movement supporters.

I did not code these papers formally in the same manner that I did other movement papers because I did not intend to use them in the same way. Rather, I read these papers carefully over the period of major Populist activity in the state (1890–1894) and then used the information in the more documentary manner of standard narrative history. For Georgia, I rely on reports from the *People's Party Paper*. I have described above how I use the *People's Party Paper* in chapter 5 to discuss the structure of movement narratives of race and class. I use the same source in a different way in chapter 7 to discuss the changing assessment of white populists there.

### SECONDARY DATA SOURCES

Throughout this book, I also rely on a number of secondary data sources. Because these sources are relatively well known and my methods are not obscure, I treat these together in this section. One important source was the census records from the tenth census (1880) and the eleventh census (1890). My most obvious use of the census information comes in chapters 6 and 7, where county-level census records are used to outline the social and economic structure of Virginia and Georgia. Supplementary analyses appear in several other chapters as well. The data for these analyses come from aggregate county-level census records available through the Inter-University Consortium for Political and Social Research (ICPSR). In order to make claims about changes over time, I included 1880 and 1890 social and economic measures for southern states in a single data set. Because some county boundaries changed over that decade I standardized counties using a procedure by James Horan and Peggy Hargis (n.d.), which takes counties that merged or shifted boundaries and combines them into clustered "county units," thereby allowing direct comparison. Over a long period of time this can lead to a large number of very big clusters, but over one decennial period it led to relatively modest changes in most states. Additional census figures drawn from summary reports were used in several chapters to calculate the occupation tables, illiteracy rates, and population characteristics of Richmond and Atlanta wards. The sources for these figures are cited in the text.

A second important source, also held by ICPSR, comes from the Knights of Labor data collected by Jonathan Garlock and N. C. Builder (1973a, 1973b). This data set, the result of a massive undertaking, lists every known Knights of Labor local assembly along with any information known about its location, its birth and death dates, and its racial and gender makeup. The information is culled from the movement newspaper, reports in the General Assembly records, and other information. The structure of this data is somewhat quirky, but because the information is listed by location it was possible for me to link the information on Knights of Labor assemblies with the census records described above. Garlock's (1982) later reference book on local assemblies includes some additional information that I also reference at several points.[11]

# NOTES

## INTRODUCTION

1. In modern sociology, William Julius Wilson has often been cited as a proponent of the first position and Douglas Massey as an advocate of the second, although this in fact says more about the thin terms of the debate than about the positions of these particular authors (see Wilson 1980; Massey and Denton 1993). The debate has long roots and is by no means restricted to sociology. Indeed, the roots of the sociological debate (e.g., Sombart 1976 [1906]; Myrdal 1944; Cox 1948) are in fact also touchstones for a parallel debate in historical scholarship. See Redding (2003) for an overview of the same debate in the context of disfranchisement.
2. Terence Vincent Powderly Papers, letters from T. L. Eastburn, January 19, 1880; February 2, 1880.
3. Terence Vincent Powderly Papers, letters from William Wright, August 21, 1880; September 11, 1880.
4. Terence Vincent Powderly Papers, letter from J. Edward Brown, January 18, 1886.
5. As with racial divisions, class partitioning only occurs in social process, as E. P. Thompson (1966) has famously claimed.
6. One approach has focused primarily on the temporal patterning that is inherent in narrative. This work has generally been packaged in the form of critiques of standard methodological assumptions about temporality and causality in the social sciences (Abbott 1990, 1992; Griffin 1992; Sewell 1996), and a set of techniques for better dealing with these issues (Abell 1987; Griffin 1993; Abbott 1995; Bearman, Faris, and

Moody 1999). A second approach, from which this book takes inspiration, uses narrative as a way to empirically grasp the role of deeper cultural and historical patterns shaping social identity and action (see, e.g., Tilly 2003; Polletta 1998; Joyce 1994; Somers 1992; Bruner 1987).

7. Like almost all work on narrative, historical or sociological, this proceeds from an essentially inductive logic—it yields a simplified model of the movement-level narratives not by starting with a general theory but by starting from the language and claims of the movements. Still, the systematic design is important because it allows for verifiability as well as what Popper (1961: 40–41) termed "falsifiability"—not only can my claims be checked, they can be proved wrong on their own terms. This is unfortunately not the case with much of the current work on narrative.
8. For a theoretically developed account of temporal orientations of action, see Emirbayer and Mische (1998); see also Bourdieu (1992) and Giddens (1979, 1984).

### 1. REPUBLICAN RADICALISM

1. The phrase "citizen-worker" is David Montgomery's (1967, 1993) very apt label for this powerful republican self-image.
2. In the language of explanation, class boundaries have thus moved from "independent variable" to "dependent variable"—that is, from an explanation to a thing to be explained. For recent general discussions of the boundary issue, see Lamont and Molnár (2002); Tilly (2003); Somers (1992, 1994). Bourdieu (1994) and Lamont (1994, 2004) provide influential contemporary studies of class from this perspective. Lamont, significantly, also links class boundaries with race.
3. See Voss (1993); Dawley (1976). Voss in particular compares the pattern of American class formation to the English and French cases. On the French case, see Hanagan (1980); Aminzade (1993).
4. See Woodward (1951). This put farming and manufacture on a more even footing in the South. In 1880 the ratio of the value of farm products to the value of manufactured products stood at 2.3 to 1; by 1890 the ratio was 1.2 to 1—almost parity. The steep price decline of farm products was a major factor in this change, but the figures also indicate that southern cities grew quickly during these years as migrants came from surrounding areas in search of better opportunities in industry.
5. Edward L. Ayers (1992: 9) points out that railroad connections were both a marker and a facilitator of these shifts. By 1890, 90 percent of southern counties had a rail connection.
6. Letter from George A. Williams, March 21, 1887, Terence Vincent Powderly Papers.
7. See also Arnett (1922) for a classic study of the economic context of this system, including the contracting money supply and falling crop prices. Schwartz (1976) provides a more formal analysis of the crop lien system itself.
8. The organized counties were: Parker (8 sub-alliances); Jack (2); and Wise (2). These counties remained the core areas for the Texas Alliance for the next several years.

9. The Knights' membership records actually showed a decline for the year 1881. Ware (1959: 66–67) suggested that the record adjusted for a decline that actually occurred over a period of several years. This seems unlikely, since the number of new local assemblies organized also dropped in that year, but not before or after. It is more likely that the decline was the result of internal struggles, in part over whether to remain a secret organization (see Phelan 2000).
10. The official death of the Knights of Labor was not until 1917, but most observers agree that by the mid-1890s the organization's "importance as an industrial society ceased" (Ware 1959: xi). The factors behind the organization's decline have been more contested than those of its growth. Many older accounts suggest that much of the blame must rest with the weak leadership of Terence V. Powderly, the long-serving and long-suffering general master workman of the Knights of Labor. By most accounts, Powderly was a good orator but a poor strategist and a weak leader—see Ware (1959: xvi); Laurie (1997: 155, 167). From this point of view, Powderly's leadership was not sufficiently radical, and he was far too timid in calling strikes. More recent studies have rightly shifted the emphasis to the important structural and organizational problems that the Knights faced (Phelan 2000; Voss 1993).
11. The southern Knights got started organizing slightly later but also continued longer. Some southern organizing continued after the Knights were virtually extinct nationally: one assembly was chartered in Georgia in 1901 and one in Bethel, North Carolina, in 1914.
12. Some records indicate a fifth assembly (LA 861) founded in 1878, also in Alabama. However, it is not known where in the state the assembly was located, and it is unlikely that it survived for more than a year. In the references that follow, including figures and tables, assemblies without verified records of locations are excluded (see Garlock and Builder 1973a; Garlock 1982). Here and below, my discussion of the assemblies relies on the massive cataloging effort of Jonathan Garlock. Numerical analyses are drawn from a data file I created by merging Garlock's data file with the county-level census records cited above.
13. Two additional mergers were explored but never consummated. The first was with the Farmers' Mutual Benefit Association and the second with the much smaller Northern Alliance. This outline is drawn from both contemporary and later accounts (Dunning 1975 [1891]; Goodwyn 1976; Saloutos 1960).
14. These figures are from the *Southern Mercury*, July 12, 1888, as reported in Saloutos (1960: 76–77). At about the same time that the *Mercury* published these statistics, Macune reported similar rounded figures in his speech to the annual meeting of the Alliance (see Dunning 1975 [1891]: 79). Thus, by 1888 the Alliance was organized in just under half of the counties in the South, but it was quite well organized in those places.
15. As Saloutos notes, the organization was involved in electoral politics after 1890 and had an interest in inflating its membership figures. An equally important reason is that a series of mergers that the organization engineered probably left its

records in a chaotic state. Unlike the Knights of Labor, its inaccuracy was a by-product of its success.

16. Stronger statements from this perspective have simply reversed the traditional materialist emphasis on interests by giving primacy to culture (see Jones 1983). A good overview of the debate is provided in a set of papers and responses in the journal *Social History* (see Mayfield and Thorne 1992, 1993; Lawrence and Taylor 1993; Joyce 1993, 1995) and in a volume on labor history and discourse edited by Lenard Berlanstein (e.g., Sewell 1993; Reid 1993).
17. William Sewell Jr. (1980) contributed one of the most sustained works in this vein by tracing the influence of "corporatist" language in France from the old regime through the revolution of 1848. Richard Biernacki (1995) has contrasted the cultural understandings of class and the patterns of class formation in Germany and Britain (see also Haydu 1997, Fantasia 1995). Ira Katznelson (1986) has famously posited distinct levels of class formation, from the objective structure of resources and relationships through "shared dispositions" and then on to collective action.
18. For a broader theoretical argument about the mutually constitutive relationship between resources and class dispositions (variously termed "schema," "languages," "idioms," or "frames"), see Sewell (1992). Sewell's point is framed as an extension and development of work by Anthony Giddens (1984, 1979) and by Pierre Bourdieu (1992, 1984).
19. This is not to say that later movements conformed to the same "true" interests; the battle between rival visions in the "making" of the union movement in the early twentieth century was often intense (see Kimeldorf 1999).
20. Gregory S. Kealey and Brian D. Palmer (1982: 5–15) provide an excellent if idiosyncratic discussion of this earlier view by tracing it back not just to John R. Commons but also to Friedrich Engels. Engels, in his remarks on the Knights, noted the movement's importance as "the first national organization created by the American working class as a whole" but also that these "modern tendencies" were culturally wrapped together with "the most medieval mummeries" (cited in Kealey and Palmer 1982: 2).
21. It should be noted that this was in part because the movement was largely ignored by the field of labor studies, which was driven by a rather narrow focus on unionism among industrial workers. Populism was commonly treated instead under the heading of economic and political history. See, for example, Arnett (1922); Hicks (1961).
22. In particular, see Phelan (2000); Sanders (1999); Schneirov (1998); Brundage (1994); Voss (1993). This work was prefigured by an extremely influential set of books by Leon Fink (1985) on the Knights and Lawrence Goodwyn (1976) on the Populists.
23. On Powderly and the struggles within the Knights of Labor leadership, see Phelan (2000); Weir (2000). Phelan in particular provides an important reconsideration of Powderly as a practical leader beset by organizational limitations. For a reexamination of Populist leaders, see Goodwyn (1976); Pollack (1987).

24. See Calhoun (1982, 1983) on this concept of a "radicalism of tradition." Regensburger (1987) noted that in a later era the traditional orientation of southern workers similarly offered a basis for radical protest.
25. Letter from A. H. Graham, September 1, 1890, Terence Vincent Powderly Papers.
26. See the discussion of agrarian republicanism in Woods (1991). On the practical links between labor and agrarian republicanism in organizing, see McMath (1993: chapter 2).
27. See Montgomery (1967) on the link between labor republicanism and the Radical Republicans of the 1860s and 1870s.
28. Montgomery (1965) also notes the simultaneously economic and political thrust of republicanism and the fact that the growth of wage labor posed a particular problem for the political use of "free labor" ideals.
29. This intimate connection between politics, class, and community found its classic form in Tocqueville's discussion of the virtue of association and community life (Toqueville 1994). A more recent overview has suggested that the paradox of the republican ideal was that it produced a "rude republic" of egalitarian political and social activism that was nonetheless in pursuit of "upper- and middle-class respectability" (Altschuler and Blumin 2000: 8). These authors insist on the importance of seeing the history of this era within a broader field of institutional reform efforts. In the late decades of the century, this pursuit of respectability took on particular importance in reaction to rapid industrialization and widespread fears of immiseration (Arnesen 1996).
30. The republican and liberal traditions both emphasized the connection between independence and the common good. They divided on the nature of the connection, however. The liberal tradition tended to see the common good arising from impersonal forces (such as the market) supported by individual interests. The republican tradition instead emphasized the duty of free citizens to directly support the institutions of civil society. On this point, see Appleby (1992: especially chapter 1).
31. *Journal of United Labor*, July 5, 1888.
32. The parallel motto for the Knights of Labor was "An Injury to One is the Concern of All."
33. See also Weir (1996); Mitchell (1987). Goodwyn used the term "movement culture" to refer specifically to the Populists, but the culture was shared to a significant degree by both movements. Oestreicher (1986) used the similar term "subculture of opposition."
34. The initiation rituals were the most elaborately scripted. For example, the Alliance ritual included a number of oaths swearing allegiance and secrecy, as well as standard lectures on the principles of fraternity and cooperation. "I will never wrong or defraud a worthy member, but will always assist and protect him and his interests when in my power to do so," the new member would swear upon initiation. After lectures on the nature of brotherhood, the new Allianceman was instructed in the secret signs, passwords, and handshakes (National Farmers' Alliance and Industrial

Union, *Ritual of the Farmers' Alliance*). The ritual of the parallel Colored Alliance was virtually identical (Colored Farmers' National Alliance, *Ritual of the Colored Farmers' National Allinace and Co-operative Union of the United States*). See Weir (1996) for a detailed discussion of the rituals and elaborate symbolic imagery of the Knights of Labor.

35. In 1881, the Knights dropped their policy of secrecy and made the name of the order public for the first time (Foner 1955: 47). Religious titles and oaths were also generally dropped in 1882 in response to pressure from the church. Robert E. Weir (1996: chapter 2) stresses the continued connections between the republicanism and religion for the Knights, yet it was by this point a loose cultural connection rather than a direct source of movement affinity.
36. To take but one example, in 1889 the Atlanta city directory listed six Knights of Labor assemblies. These groups were placed, literally and figuratively, between broader fraternal benevolent associations and secret societies (among them the Odd Fellows, Knights of Honor, and several orders of Masonic and Knights Templar lodges) and narrower trade unions such as the Brotherhood of Locomotive Engineers, Brotherhood of Locomotive Firemen, the Order of Railway Conductors, and the Atlanta Typographical Union. *Atlanta City Directory*, 1890. See Mary Ann Clawson's (1989) excellent analysis of fraternalism for a developed argument about the connections between republicanism and the fraternal form including the Masons' valorization of artisan production.
37. McMath (1993: chapter 2) provides an excellent overview of the Populist roots in the republican mentality, and of the larger possibility for a farmer/labor alliance and its limits. An important part of the literature on the Populist movement is devoted to linking the economic and civic claims of the movement in what might be termed its moral economy. See Pollack (1987); Palmer (1980); Clanton (1991, 1998); McMath (1975). For earlier roots of the same agrarian republican orientation, see Woods (1991).
38. Here I have drawn explicitly from William Gamson's (1992) discussion of the cognitive elements necessary for social protest, particularly what he terms identity frames, enemy frames, and action frames.
39. Eligible members included all workers over the age of eighteen, except lawyers, doctors, bankers, liquor salesmen, and Chinese workers (Foner 1974: 47). In keeping with Knights' philosophy, lawyers, doctors, and bankers were excluded not because they were "middle class" but because they were not "producers" of wealth. The exclusion of liquor salesmen reflects the Knights' affinity for the cause of temperance. The exclusion of Chinese workers, from the perspective of this study, is much more interesting.
40. The southern Tenant Farmers' Union, for example, was in many ways a legacy of the Alliance, but it spoke for a much narrower band of southern farmers (see Kester 1997).
41. Hanagan (1980: 211) suggested that the artisans advocated class interests over craft interests partly for self-preservation. Voss (1993: 160–61, 164–72) claimed that while

craft workers may have helped the organization of less-skilled workers in the community generally, they may have discouraged such organization in their own industries in order to protect their privileges.

42. The orthodox version of the Knights' take on the "labor question" can be found in a set of essays that ran on the front page of the *Journal of United Labor* from late 1883 through 1885.
43. *Journal of United Labor*, October 10, 1884. The issue of September 25, 1884, also has a long treatment of "the land question" that is valuable for an understanding of the Knights' connection to the Alliance on this issue.
44. Knights of Labor, *Record of the Proceedings of the General Assembly*, 1880. The Knights set up a number of producers' cooperatives, with several in the southern states. The report of the 1887 General Assembly in Minneapolis includes mention of a number of these efforts (Knights of Labor, *Record of the Proceedings of the General Assembly*, 1887).
45. Powderly provided his own take on the cooperative crusade in his 1890 book, *Thirty Years of Labor* (1967 [1890]). While he was never deeply versed in the ideals of cooperation, the notion of a more equitable and democratic system remained part of Powderly's understanding of the legacy of the Knights (Powderly 1940: chapters 23–24).
46. The Alliance also generally avoided strikes and boycotts. The one major exception was the jute boycott (Holmes 1994; Schwartz 1976: 235–46). Cotton farmers of the South traditionally used the strong, breathable material to cover bales of cotton before they were sent to the market. A sharp rise in the cost of the jute baling material in 1888, combined with falling cotton prices, pushed southern farmers to complain that the jute manufacturers were squeezing the already hard-pressed farmers. The boycott unraveled, but the Alliance could at least claim a partial victory as the price of jute dropped again after 1890.
47. Other bulk buying plans emerged as well. The Tennessee, Arkansas, and North Carolina state Alliances each appointed a state business agent to coordinate purchases and to distribute the goods to the sub-Alliances. See Dunning (1975 [1891]: 356–57); Schwartz (1976: 203–5); Saloutos (1960: 89–94).
48. Like the cooperative efforts of the Knights, the Alliance efforts eventually failed. The Texas Exchange was all but defunct by 1889, and none of the Exchanges were successful after 1890. One reason was the poor business practices brought on by the tendency of the managers of the Exchange to grant credit too freely to insolvent farmers (Saloutos 1960). An equally important reason was that the Alliance business efforts brought an organized response from merchants, manufacturers, and local banks (Schwartz 1976).
49. See also Arnett (1922) for a classic discussion of economic and monetary policy and its relation to the farmers' movement and Carruthers and Babb (1996) and Babb (1996) for analyses of the monetary proposals of the Populists and the question of whether these were really in the economic interests of the farmers.
50. Goodwyn (1976: 218, 595) points out that key members of the Alliance had a direct

connection to the Greenback movement, but also that the Greenback philosophy suffused the movement for more pragmatic reasons as well.

51. This would free the farmer from reliance on high-interest loans from merchants against the next years' crop. It would also protect farmers from dependence on the market price of the crop at the time of harvest. Farmers could redeem the crop when the market price suited them and therefore insure themselves the best return for their years' labor.
52. On the issue of liberalism and republicanism, see Schneirov (1998); Sanders (1999); c.f. Appleby (1992). Elisabeth Clemens (1997) provides one of the most thorough discussions of the rise of the "people's lobby" of the Progressive Era. On the connection between the state and the battle for workplace democracy in a later period see Haydu (1997).
53. *Journal of United Labor,* December 15, 1880.
54. Ibid., March 25, 1885.
55. Even at this point, the issue was hotly debated within the Knights. A view from "The Other Side" invoked the cautions of Powderly and the antipartisan language of the Preamble and declared that Beaumont and others "had no right to use the positions they occupy in the Order to denigrate the Knights of Labor to the slums of partisanism" (*Journal of United Labor,* June 20, 1889).
56. At each major convention of the Alliance, a "platform" of demands, akin to the platforms of the political parties, was set out. Alliance platforms paralleled the issues central to the Knights of Labor, especially the issues of monetary reform and state ownership of railroads. After the 1890 convention, the sub-treasury plan was added to the platform. The movements diverged over the issues of tax policy and protectionism, however.
57. On the 1890 Alliance gains, see Ayers (1992: 246); Saloutos (1960: 109–11); Woodward (1971: 235–39); McMath (1993: 130).
58. In fact, some significant Jim Crow legislation came from the Alliance legislatures (Ayers 1992: 246–47; Woodward 1951: 236–39).
59. The success of the party varied greatly across the different states, however. In several states, the 1892 election was virtually the last gasp for the Populists. Arkansas, Tennessee, and Florida had some early Populist victories, but went Democratic in 1892. In South Carolina, the Democrat Ben Tillman kept the support of most white farmers and won an easy victory. In Mississippi the Democrats won every race, despite a few close calls. In several other states the Populists maintained some hope despite losses. In Louisiana and Virginia, Populist support was present but contained to specific regions. Populist candidates for governor narrowly lost in Alabama and Texas. The gubernatorial race in Georgia went solidly to the Democrat, but the Populist congressman, Tom Watson, was only narrowly beaten. There were reports of significant election fraud in all three states. The North Carolina Populists suffered a disappointing gubernatorial loss but managed to send eleven new representatives to the legislature (Ayers 1992: 247; Woodward 1951: 236–39).

60. Three of the congressional seats were won after appeal and investigation. See Woodward (1951: 277–78)
61. In many ways, Bryan's nomination indeed marked a moment of acceptance of labor demands by the Democratic Party, particularly on monetary reform and protectionism. It nevertheless proved disastrous for the independent aims of the Populists.
62. Much of the modern work traces back to Hubert Blalock's 1967 study on race relations. Various strains of the model have remained central to the race relations literature (see, e.g., Tomaskovic-Devey and Roscigno 1996; Olzak, Shanahan, and McEneaney 1996).
63. See also Bonacich (1972, 1976). It should be said that there has also been some divergence in the literature over the question of whether white working people or elites stand to gain the most from the racial barriers that are imposed as a result of such conflict. See Tomaskovic-Devey and Roscigno (1996) for an excellent review and assessment of this question.
64. For example, see Nagel (1986); Nielsen (1986); Olzak (1990, 1983). Blalock (1967: 29–39, 150–54) noted that economic and political threats are at least analytically distinct and may have different functional forms, although they are mutually implicated in practice and are in any case driven by the same structural variables in his model—particularly the proportional size of the minority population in a given area. It has proven very difficult to distinguish between them empirically, although there have been attempts to do so (Corzine, Creech, and Corzine 1983; Tolnay, Beck, and Massey 1989; see also Tolnay and Beck 1992).
65. For more on the Chinese labor issue, see Saxton (1971); Boswell (1986); see also Olzak (1989).
66. Letter from D. H. Black, May 22, 1886, Terence Vincent Powderly Papers; see also letter from Duncan Planton, March 9, 1886.
67. Gaither (1977) and Kousser (1974) provide the classic historical discussions of the complex link between Populism and disfranchisement efforts. For more contemporary sociological treatments, see Soule (1992) and Redding (2003).
68. It should be said that even Blalock (1967: 166, n.26) recognized some role for cognition when he admitted that competition only matters when it is perceived. Still, he generally treated "ideological factors" as byproducts of the competition produced by objective interests. At most he considered them as variables entirely exogenous to the production of such interests.
69. Recent benchmark work in this vein can be found in Goldberg (1993); Takaki (2000); Gilroy (1993); Lowe (1998). On the inseparability of race and class in the American context, see Griffin (1995). See Banton (1998) for an overview of the changing ways that race has been viewed within the framework of Western science.
70. See also Saxton (1990) for a more detailed treatment of the political context of this connection of class and race in the nineteenth century.
71. Letwin (1998: 77) points out that the distinction between insiders and outsiders in

the mining districts was not made on strictly racial grounds, and yet "the juxtaposition of black workers and organized labor . . . shaped the thinking of the white Knights themselves. Even those most receptive to black members tended to view them as outsiders, or allies (real or potential), as opposed to fellow *subjects* of the Order" (80).

72. The other part of Roediger's argument, less relevant for the present discussion, was that whites constructed an image of blacks informed by what they were both fearful of and drawn to—a kind of cultural and sexual freedom and carelessness. For a later version of the point about the "wages" of whiteness, see Lipsitz (1998). For a critique of the use of "whiteness" as a historical concept, see Arnesen (2001).
73. Eric Arnesen (1998: 155) has referred to this particular tendency to treat movements as either heroes or failures as the question of "how racist/racially egalitarian were they?" While he was specifically referring to discussions of the CIO, the critique has a broader bite. Examples of the more nuanced kind of scholarship that Arnesen argues for can be found in Rachleff (1984); Honey (1993); Kelley (1990); McKiven (1995); Letwin (1998); Kelly (2001); as well as in the work of Arnesen himself (2000, 1993).
74. Saxton (1971: 1) also noted this two-sided nature of white workers' position both as exploiters and exploited. Yet for this author, "racial identification cut at right angles to class consiousness"—a claim that pushed him closer to the competition model, despite an otherwise more culturally sensitive framework.
75. See also Ayers (1992: chapter 6) for details on this topic.
76. Cecelia O'Leary (1999) provides a fascinating discussion of this cultural adoption.
77. Letter from William Wright, September 11, 1880, Terence Vincent Powderly Papers.
78. On this issue of the shifting racial and civic status of the immigrants, see Higham (1955); Gleason (1980); Gerstle (2001). For a theoretical treatment of the issue, see Stoller (1997).
79. On the racial balance, while the average for the region was roughly 30 percent black, the variance was dramatic across counties, even within the same state. Upland counties often had virtually no black residents, while coastal and cotton plantation regions typically had large black majorities. The massive migration of blacks from the South to the North did not begin in earnest until around 1930 (see Hamilton 1964).
80. Goodwyn (1976) provides a relatively positive account, while Gaither (1977) is more leery of the movement's racial legacy; see also Holmes (1973, 1975).
81. The document for the acts of incorporation was more direct. After listing several general goals of the organization, the document stated that the organization existed "to form for these purposes a more close union among all white persons who may be eligible to membership in this Association" (Dunning 1975 [1891]: 63).
82. *National Economist,* March 14, 1889.
83. Humphrey's own short history of the organization lists sixteen black delegates to

the original meeting of the Colored Farmers' Alliance, including the black president and secretary.

84. To my knowledge, no copies of the paper are still in existence. Frequent excerpts from the paper were reprinted in the *National Economist,* however, and the Richmond *Planet* became a semi-official outlet for announcements by the Colored Farmers' Alliance.

85. By this claim 750,000 of the members were adult males, 300,000 were women, and 150,000 were males under twenty-one. The membership of the Colored Alliance in the various states, also inflated, was reported as follows: Alabama, 100,000 members; South Carolina, 90,000; Mississippi, 90,000; Texas, 90,000; Georgia, 84,000; Tennessee, 60,000; North Carolina, 55,000; Louisiana, 50,000; Virginia, 50,000. Arkansas and Kentucky were reported to have 20,000 and 25,000 members, respectively, although neither state had a chartered state Alliance. Other states were reported to be partly organized (Saloutos 1960: 80–81).

86. Like the white movement, the black organization grew through mergers within a field of similar organizations. For example, Saloutos (1960) claims that the Colored Alliance in South Carolina followed from the organizing attempts of Hiram F. Hoover, a white organizer who attempted to build what he called the "Cooperative Workers of America." Actually, Hoover's organization was likely an unauthorized version of the Knights of Labor (see Baker 1999). The Colored Farmers' Alliance did, however, pick up where the Knights left off by organizing the South Carolina piedmont in 1888 and 1889 (Saloutos 1960: 80).

87. *National Economist,* October 5, 1889.

88. The black members of the Wheel were formally organized only in Tennessee, where there was a separate state Wheel (the Tennessee Colored Agricultural Wheel), with roughly 3,500 members (Saloutos 1960: 64).

89. *National Economist,* February 22, 1890; see also Holmes (1975: 188); Saloutos (1960: 80).

90. During the exchange of delegates, Humphrey introduced a motion to promote financial cooperation between the two organizations. The motion adopted by the white Alliance's Committee on Co-operation, and reported proudly in the Alliance paper, read in part: "Be it Resolved, That it is detrimental to both white and colored to allow conditions to exist that forces our colored farmers to sell their products for less and pay more for supplies than the markets justify" (*National Economist,* March 14, 1889). Relations between the orders were close enough that Humphrey presided at one session of the 1891 white Alliance meeting in Waco, Texas (*National Economist,* May 16 1891). Even before the 1891 Waco meeting, the two groups publicly presented their interests as linked. In 1890, Macune addressed the House Committee on Ways and Means regarding proposed legislation. He was accompanied by two leaders of the southern Alliance and by Humphrey and J. J. Rogers, the superintendent of the Colored Alliance in Virginia and North Carolina (*National Economist,* May 24, 1890). Humphrey later testified before the Senate in support of

the sub-treasury plan, then under debate in the form of a bill (*National Economist,* June 7, 1890).

91. *National Economist,* August 16, 1890. See also National Farmers' Alliance and Industrial Union, *Ritual of the Farmers' Alliance*; *National Economist,* February 14, 1891. The report of this meeting is also reprinted in Dunning (1975 [1891]).
92. The exchanges were in Houston, New Orleans, Mobile, Charleston, and Norfolk.
93. Richmond *Planet,* October 17, 1891. The white Alliance barely mentioned the strike at all. The sole statement in the white Alliance journal, the *National Economist,* was that the strike "is now the subject of much comment. The *Economist* has no reliable data as to whether such a move was made or not; but one thing seems certain, if a strike was ordered it has proved a failure, as it certainly deserved to be" (*National Economist,* September 26, 1891).
94. Circular reprinted in *National Economist,* February 14, 1891.
95. *National Economist,* January 2, 1892. The Colored Alliance had less than half as many seats as the Southern Alliance but more than any other organization, including the Knights of Labor. The distribution of seats for the major organizations at the St. Louis convention were as follows: National Farmers' Alliance and Industrial Union, 246; Colored Farmers Alliance and Cooperative Union, 97; Knights of Labor, 82; Patrons of Husbandry, 75; Farmers' Mutual Benefit Association, 53; National Farmers' Alliance (commonly known as the "Northern Alliance"), 49.
96. See Abramowitz (1950, 1953) for succinct discussions of black involvement in the Alliance and the People's Party. In particular, racial tension erupted over the "force bill." This bill, also known as the Lodge Election Bill after its sponsor, Henry Cabot Lodge, was designed to shore up black voting rights in the South and to increase the federal oversight of elections (Gaither 1977: 29). Despite the complaint of the white Populists that election fraud diminished their strength, the movement was steadfastly against the bill (see Holmes 1975; Abramowitz 1950, 1953). The public argument, at least, was that while black voting rights should be supported, a "more efficient" plan was needed (*National Economist,* January 10, 1891; January 17, 1891). The Colored Farmers' Alliance announced itself in favor of the legislation, however.
97. *National Economist,* December 27, 1890.
98. Ibid., August 2, 1890.

**2. RACE, CLASS, REPUBLICAN VIRTUE IN THE KNIGHTS**

1. An exception here is Olzak (1989), who quotes from one of Powderly's anti-Hungarian rants.
2. Recent scholarship, particularly on "whiteness," has recognized that the distinction was in flux during this period. See Ignatiev (1995) and Jacobson (1998) for two well-known recent treatments of the emergence of "whiteness" among what are now considered white ethnic groups. Stoller (1997); Gleason (1980); and Foley (1997) provide important discussions of whiteness and migration. The 1880s was a par-

ticularly important moment of this transformation; while earlier immigrant groups (particularly the Irish) had been contesting the boundary for decades, more recent immigrants were considered at best not quite white. Arneson (2001) maintains that the term "whiteness" may be too fuzzy to capture this process, although it was clearly an issue of boundary-making (see Gerteis and Goolsby 2005).

3. For discussions on the use of narratives in the social sciences, see Franzosi (1998); Steimetz (1992); Somers (1994). The methods used in this chapter and in chapter 5 to capture the movement-level narratives are discussed in detail in the appendix on data sources and methods; the approach here was developed from similar recent treatments of social movement "frames" (e.g., Polletta 1997; Johnston 1995; Gamson 1992; see also Goffman 1974), although my approach draws upon the relational connections between actors, events, and meanings that are inherent in narrative (see also Franzosi 1994). For an early analysis of the rhetoric of the Knights of Labor, see Sisco (1966).
4. As some authors have pointed out, collective narratives such as these have to be considered as emergent properties. The narratives reconstructed here and in chapter 5 are not those of individuals but of the movements as a whole. See Steinmetz (1992: 490) and Somers (1994: 618–19).
5. The classic discussion of the relational composition of narrative is provided by Burke (1969).
6. The literature on social movement "frames" is well developed. For Snow and Benford, movement frames refer to the set of "interpretive schemata that simplifies and condenses the 'world out there' by selectively punctuating and encoding" situations, ideas, and events. Movemenet frames thus interpret and legitimate activism (Snow and Benford 1992: 136–37). Johnston (1995) has noted the connection between this term and more culturally attuned terms such as "discourse," or the "relatively bounded sets of arguments organized around a specific diagnosis or solution to some social problem" (Ellingson 1995: 107). I adopt the latter definition, though I use the term "frame" throughout this book for clarity.
7. As late as 1890, the General Master Workman recommended increasing both the subscription rate and the practice of soliciting many different authors to provide editorial essays for the paper (Knights of Labor, *Record of the Proceedings of the General Assembly*, 1890).
8. See the appendix for details on data collection and coding.
9. Letters and notices sent in from around the country provided a large proportion of the communications (35.8 percent and 11.2 percent respectively). Editorials comprised 40 percent, but only about half of these were written by the editorial staff of the paper or by national leaders of the movement. More than twenty different authors submitted the rest, and a few were reprinted from other publications.
10. Perhaps not surprisingly, the terms used to designate racial and ethnic identity (the "we" terms) were more restricted than were the racial "others" that the Knights discussed. When specific terms were given for racial and ethnic identities, the term

"white" was dominant. By contrast, there were many different designations of racial/ethnic "others."

11. Like all movement frames, these were not completely unified. Instead, they reflected the internal process of contention through which interests were worked out in the course of organizing (see Steinberg 1999: 745; McLean 1998: 55; Ellingson 1995: 107–8). The items in the *Journal of United Labor* typically signaled one of a standard number of frames of interest and then took a position within it. Because of this, table 3 presents both the general frame that each statement adopted and the more specific position taken relative to that frame.
12. Opposition is more visible when the "backstage" statements of southern members (rather than the "official" discussions of the national organization) are examined. This point is discussed at greater length below.
13. Table 3 also includes a residual category composed of other statements of interest that did not coalesce into a meaningful discourse. Most interesting were the few examples of racial humor. Two of these communications cartooned the speech of uneducated blacks; one was simultaneously a jab at the social position of black workers and Irish aspirations to a protected racial status ("[Housekeeper:] 'Well, I suppose you at least know how to wash dishes?' [Applicant:] 'Indade, mum, if it's a common dish-washer ye want ye better be after hirin' a nager. Good day, mum.'" *Journal of United Labor*, April 23, 1887).
14. Both Lambda and the Uncertainty Coefficient indicate the proportional reduction in error of predicting the "other" in question when the discourse is known compared with when it is not known. In both cases, the reduction in error is large (43 and 28 percent, respectively) and significant.
15. Additional checks on the data reveal that the narratives were quite robust. When broken down by temporal period, the three narratives outlined above appeared in each. The changes in relative prevalence that did occur across time are shown in the text below.
16. One could argue that a fourth narrative appears here—one that connects whites to interracial organizing. I have not claimed this as a separate narrative, due to the small number of cases and to the fact that this was simply a mirror of the first narrative as produced by black members. In the text below I discuss this in conjunction with the first narrative.
17. Of course, as Gutman (1987) points out it is easy to overplay the degree of social "breakdown" among immigrants. Even when formal organization is rare, there is often a more coherent community than natives might see. Moreover, oppressed groups have the capacity for "hidden resistance" (Scott 1990). My point here is not that the assessment made by the Knights of Labor was right but that it mattered and had consequences. Viewed through the class culture of the Knights, the civic disorganization of new immigrant groups marked them as competitors rather than allies.
18. *Journal of United Labor*, June 15, 1881.

19. Ibid., June 12, 1890.
20. Ibid., February 18, 1888.
21. Ibid., August 6, 1887.
22. Ibid., July 9, 1887.
23. Ibid., August 15, 1880.
24. Ibid., October 15, 1887.
25. Ibid., August 15, 1880.
26. Ibid., October 1, 1886.
27. Ibid., January 17, 1889.
28. Ibid., November 26, 1887.
29. Ibid., June 20, 1888.
30. Ibid., March 21, 1889.
31. Ibid., April 16, 1890.
32. Ibid., November 4, 1888.
33. Ibid., February 15, 1883. This item develops the corporate metaphor directly: "Chinese cheap labor is the worm that destroys all the chance for free labor." The article did not blame the Chinese alone for this state of affairs, but also pointed to the "cunning agents of corporations" who were willing to erode the position of white workers as "free citizens"—that is, as a central part of the body of the republic. This argument about "enslavement" overlapped to some degree with the third Knights of Labor narrative discussed below.
34. *Journal of United Labor,* January 25, 1886.
35. See Takaki (2000: 217–19) for a brief discussion of some of the mechanisms of Chinese importation, as well as a longer discussion of the American image of the Chinese immigrants.
36. *Journal of United Labor,* October 1, 1887.
37. Ibid., February 15, 1884.
38. Ibid., September 20, 1888.
39. Ibid., April 16, 1890.
40. Ibid., July 24, 1890.
41. Ibid., May 15, 1883.
42. Ibid., August 15, 1880.
43. Ibid., Aug. 16, 1887.
44. Ibid., October 11, 1888.
45. See Steinfeld (2001: 253–54). The labor contracts common before the mid-nineteenth century were not unlike earlier forms of indentured servitude. Importantly, they were also similar to the later contracts to which Chinese workers were bound.
46. Ibid., August 15, 1883.
47. Ibid., October 22, 1888.
48. Ibid., August 29, 1889.
49. Ibid., August 22, 1889.

50. Ibid., August 6, 1887. While the conditions of white indentured servants were indeed harsh, what is interesting here is that those workers themselves chafed under their servile status in an effort to distance themselves from the permanently bound black workers. See Jones (1998).
51. *Journal of United Labor,* April 17, 1890.
52. This rests on a different methodology than the analysis of the items in the movement newspaper. Here, letters from southern states dated in odd-numbered months between 1880 and 1890 were collected without regard to content. Overall, 847 communications were included in the sample. Roughly 10 percent of these communications (84) made an explicit mention of race. Of these, most references were to blacks ("negro," "negroes," "colored"). Most of the rest referred to whites, though a few scattered references were made to another racial/ethnic group, or simply to "race." See the appendix for data collection details.
53. From Fort Worth, Texas, one member wrote that "the company proceeded in getting colored men to take the longshoremen's places at 40 and 60 cents per hour. The men then offered to take their places back at the company's terms. But the company replied that they had pledged themselves to give the colored men the work as long as they proved satisfactory to the company" (Letter from D. H. Black, May 22, 1886, Terence Vincent Powderly Papers). Other situations were more complex. One letter from Wilmington, North Carolina, reported that two black men were sending out to other locales for black stevedores. White Knights, eager to keep their jobs, had to pool their resources to send the men back home. The author wanted Powderly to issue a circular to warn against such recruiting. (Letter from James M. McGowan, November 24, 1886, in Terence Vincent Powderly Papers.)
54. In one important essay on the topic, David Roediger (1994) has pointed out that the distinction between "stomach equality" and "social equality" was useful in convincing reluctant whites in the Industrial Workers of the World to join an organization that included blacks. While whites were not willing to support social equality, they could support the more narrow class-based logic that better conditions for some meant better conditions for all.
55. Letter from T. L. Eastburn, January 19, 1883, Terence Vincent Powderly Papers. It is worth noting that this passage from the District Master Workman was within an otherwise routine letter reporting on the state of local organizing.
56. Letter from Alexander Walker, May 18, 1886, Terence Vincent Powderly Papers.
57. See Gaither (1977) and Redding (2003). This was a serious issue even before the Populist political uprisings of the later 1890s seriously threatened the white Democratic vote, since many counties had large black majorities, and blacks were roughly 30 percent of the population of the South as a whole in the 1880s.
58. Letter from Dan Frazer Tomson, January 24, 1887, Terence Vincent Powderly Papers.
59. Letter from Thomas Vaughan, July 18, 1889, Terence Vincent Powderly Papers.

## 3. KNIGHTS OF LABOR IN RICHMOND, VIRGINIA

1. Terence Vincent Powderly Papers, May 7, 1885.
2. U.S. Bureau of the Census, *Tenth Census of the United States*, vol. 19, 1880, 85.
3. Tables are calculated from U.S. Bureau of the Census, *Eleventh Census of the United States*, vol. 1. Table 7 contains a small number of Chinese who were included with blacks in the census category "colored." The 1880 census reported occupational breakdowns for several Southern cities but did not include information on race.
4. A variant of this first pattern was that some shops would buy slaves directly. Large industrial firms, like the Tredegar Iron plant in Richmond, provided company housing for the slaves, as they did for white workers. In small shops, slaves were treated more or less as apprentices, with the exception that their position was not transitional but permanent.
5. For one thing, the system led to self-organization on the shop floor. Large shops in particular introduced quota systems with "overwork" incentives (see O'Brien 1990: 23; Tyler-McGraw and Kimball 1988: 64). In such arrangements, a quota was set for a full day's work, with standard workdays ranging between ten and fourteen hours, and usually six days a week. If production exceeded the quota, then bonuses would be paid directly to the slaves. Such systems led to a measure of self-organization on the shop floor. As workplace ethnographies of more recent contexts have shown, quota systems tend to produce informal but elaborate contracts among coworkers in order to regulate the level of base production, thus making incentive rewards predictable (see Burawoy 1979). In other words, the mastery of clock time in the industrial day (Thompson 1967) could benefit workers as well as the factory. In Richmond shops, black laborers often regulated the pace of work through the use of songs and chants. Such regulation paid off for black workers in the antebellum period, as bonuses were often a significant part of their income. The system of industrial slavery thus significantly blurred the boundary between the large number of slaves and the much smaller number of free blacks by granting the slaves a level of economic self-determination even while they remained formally bonded. See Tyler-McGraw and Kimball (1988: 23); Rachleff (1984: 6–7); O'Brien (1990: 23). For a few, the industrial system could provide the route from slavery to freedom—while it was by no means common, some slaves were able to save enough money through overwork and thrifty living to be able to purchase their own freedom from their masters, or to purchase the freedom of spouses or children. O'Brien (1990: 27–28) reports that records from Virginia show that more than two hundred Richmond slaves purchased their freedom between 1830 and 1865.
6. There were only fifteen black churches listed in the Richmond city directory of 1885; eleven were Baptist, three Methodist (AME), and one Episcopal (*Chataigne's Directory of Richmond, Va.*, 1885).
7. See Rabinowitz (1978) for an analysis of the spatial organization of the color line in Southern cities during this era. On the importance of the spatial organization of

race and a longer-range analysis of several American cities including Richmond, see Massey and Denton (1993).

8. I have coded information from the directory of 1885, when the Knights were at the peak of their strength. Data are from *Chataigne's Directory of Richmond, Va.*, 1885. I used this resource first to create a 1/20 sample of adult residents, grouped by ward, and then to create a block-by-block database containing an aggregate count of all black and white residents in each. See the appendix for details of data collection and coding.
9. See Massey and Denton (1987). For both the dissimilarity and contact measures, wards are commonly the unit of analysis (Massey and Denton 1993). My analysis calculates both ward-level and block-level measures, which allow for different conclusions. A discussion of the calculation of the measures is located in the appendix.
10. Here, blocks are the units of observation but the ward (rather than the city as a whole) is the unit of analysis.
11. Blau (1977) and Blau and Schwartz (1984) develop the simple but powerful insight from Simmel (1971 [1908]) that interaction across a social boundary such as race diminishes the salience of the boundary, and they point out that the effect is always greater for the minority group than for the majority.
12. See Tyler-McGraw (1994: 173–74). Data are calculated from *Chataigne's Directory of Richmond, Va.*, 1885 (see appendix for details).
13. In fact, calculations from Richmond city directories from 1880 and 1890 show that segregation increased over the decade in each of the wards. Within wards, block-level segregation increased. Across wards, Jackson got "blacker" even while the black population increased in proportion in other wards as well.
14. The area has remained the center of black Richmond. A book about Richmond's historic neighborhoods, published in 1975, notes that the terms "Jackson Ward" and "the ward" were still popularly used to designate the black section of town, despite the fact that the political division ceased to exist in 1905 (Scott 1975: 223).
15. The "resource mobilization" literature is vast; see Jenkins (1983) for an overview and an account of the emergence of the paradigm. Later studies, especially Morris (1981) and McAdam (1982) have directly discussed the importance of institutions in the black community as resources.
16. On this point, my thinking has been directly influenced by several excellent sources. It is a central argument in Peter Rachleff's *Black Labor in the South* (1984). Rachleff particularly emphasizes the web of fraternal and labor societies that emerged in Richmond's black community in the 1870s, and shows how these provided a platform for Knights of Labor organizing. Rabinowitz (1978) focuses on churches and other public organizations in his comparative study of southern cities.
17. For an example of sociological work linking strikebreaking and racial hostility, see Bonacich (1976).
18. Local assembly data are calculated from Garlock (1973). Ten assemblies were

founded by the Knights of Labor in Danville, sixteen in Lynchburg, and twenty-five in Petersburg.

19. Interracial activity was also crosscut by gender. The records from the Knights indicate that there were nine assemblies of women workers, seven of which were white and two black.
20. Terence Vincent Powderly Papers, March 1, 1886.
21. See Fink (1985: 154–55) on the speed of black organizing.
22. On the class side, Rachleff calculates that two thirds of black tobacco workers in Richmond were organized under DA 92 by 1886. On the civic side, he notes that the leaders of DA 92 were closely tied to the web of associational life in the city.
23. Terence Vincent Powderly Papers, October 26, 1885.
24. Ibid., March 7, 1887.
25. Ibid., July 17, 1886.
26. Ibid., November 8, 1886.
27. Ibid., May 28, 1888.
28. *Journal of United Labor*, January 8, 1887.
29. Knights of Labor, *Record of the Proceedings of the General Assembly,* 1885. The General Assembly report listed the names, addresses, and occupations of the official delegates. See Rachleff (1984: 87) on Powderly's reception of Johnson.
30. *Journal of United Labor*, October 25, 1885.
31. *Richmond Dispatch*, October 6, 1886, reprinted in Foner and Lewis (1978). District Assembly 49 was also the site of a later movement to oust Powderly as the head of the Knights of Labor.
32. Knights of Labor, *Record of the Proceedings of the General Assembly,* 1886, 7–8.
33. Ibid., 12.
34. Ibid.
35. *Richmond Dispatch*, October 6, 1886, and October 7, 1886, reprinted in Foner and Lewis (1978); Rachleff (1984: 174).
36. *Chicago Herald*, October 7, 1886, reprinted in Terence Vincent Powderly Papers.
37. *Richmond Dispatch*, October 6, 1886, and *New York Times*, October 7, 1886, reprinted in Foner and Lewis (1978: 109–10).
38. Terence Vincent Powderly Papers, January 22, 1887; May 28, 1888; January 7, 1889; March 3, 1890.
39. Ibid., July 17, 1888.
40. Ibid., March 23, 1888.
41. Ibid., March 8, 1888.

## 4. KNIGHTS OF LABOR IN ATLANTA, GEORGIA

1. U.S. Bureau of the Census, *Tenth Census of the United States,* 1880, vol. 1.
2. Ibid., vol. 19, 157–58; Taylor (1973: 2).
3. U.S. Bureau of the Census, *Tenth Census of the United States,* 1880, vol. 19, 158.
4. Ibid., 157–58.

5. U.S. Bureau of the Census, *Eleventh Census of the United States*, 1890, vol. 1, lxvii.
6. See McLeod (1989) for an excellent overview of the economic organization of Atlanta during this period.
7. These tables are calculated from the occupational categories reported in U.S. Bureau of the Census, *Eleventh Census of the United States*, 1890, vol. 2. As in chapter 3, the 1890 census figures are used because the 1880 figures did not report occupational breakdowns by race. Table 10 contains a very small number of Chinese residents who were calculated with blacks in the census category "colored."
8. Ten of these were Baptist, nine AME, two Presbyterian, and one Congregational. *Weatherbe's Atlanta, Ga., Duplex City Directory*, 1885.
9. Taylor (1973: 214–15); *Weatherbe's Atlanta, Ga., Duplex City Directory*, 1885.
10. Calculated from Garlock (1973). The assemblies were not evenly spread over Georgia's counties, however. Only thirty-three of the state's one hundred county clusters had some Knights of Labor presence.
11. In 1885, total membership in Atlanta was 258; the figures stood at 2,551 in 1886, 1,282 in 1887, and 365 in 1888 (Knights of Labor, *Record of the Proceedings of the General Assembly*, 1884–1888). The information on specific assembly organizing here and elsewhere comes from Knights of Labor, *Record of the Proceedings of the General Assembly* (1880–1888) and from the data compiled by Jonathan Garlock (1982; 1973).
12. Terence Vincent Powderly Papers, January 13, 1886.
13. Ibid., March 11, 1884.
14. Terence Vincent Powderly Papers, November 11, 1884.
15. Ibid.
16. This is an extremely valuable source on Atlanta's industrial growth and history of labor organization, though limited in scope. This section relies heavily on McLeod's account, and the information here on Atlanta's industrial and labor history is drawn from it unless otherwise noted.
17. The strike was settled, but the black workers never had a chance to learn the trade. A mysterious fire burned the mill soon after.
18. Terence Vincent Powderly Papers, June 13, 1886.
19. Ibid., December 14, 1885.
20. Ibid., May 20, 1886; McLaurin (1978: 64); Davis (1990: 186–87).
21. Ibid., March 7, 1888.
22. No other black candidates won a seat in the city council until nearly a century later.
23. The terms "kid gloves" and "wool hat" were used to label class-based factions, but "wool hat" always carried racial implications as well, indicating the *white* working class (Huber 1992).
24. When black candidates were represented, black votes were generally strongly behind them, but in other elections there was not a coordinated black voting trend; see Thornbery (1977: 245); Watts (1974: 275).
25. Black votes were particularly important in the elections of 1870, 1877, 1878, and 1884; see Watts (1974: 272).

26. Terence Vincent Powderly Papers, July 19, 1886.
27. The division of the Republican committee on what to do at this point was telling: one-third favored sticking to a Republican ballot, one-third favored the conservatives, and one-third favored the anti-Conservative People's Ticket (Watts 1974: 280–81)
28. Terence Vincent Powderly Papers, November 17, 1889.
29. Ibid., November 18, 1889.

## 5. RACE AND THE POPULIST "HAYSEED REVOLUTION"

1. The Alliance data include 375 communications, and the Populist data are comprised of 448 items.
2. A decentralized organizational structure meant that the People's Party did not have an official journal, unlike the Knights of Labor and the Alliance. Instead, there were hundreds of local and regional Populist papers. Two of these were broadly influential enough to demand consideration for use in this study: the *Southern Mercury* of Texas, and Georgia's *People's Party Paper.* I use the latter paper for two reasons. First, while it had less regional coverage, it attained somewhat higher status in the movement. Second, under Watson's editorship the paper attempted to establish a general voice for the movement on racial matters. In the words of the historian Gerald Gaither: "It was Tom Watson who served as the official racial interpreter of the order" (1977: 80).
3. Specifically, the *National Economist* communications were collected and coded from the issue of March 30, 1889, through the March 1, 1893, issue. Each issue of the *People's Party Paper* between November 26, 1891, and October 10, 1894, was included. After this point, the paper has not been preserved intact. Issues from May, September, October, and December 1895 were used, as well as issues from March, July, August, September, and October 1896. I chose to include these data rather than cut off the collection after 1894 because these dates reflect the later, less optimistic period of Populism. They also cover the election seasons of 1895 and 1896.
4. See the appendix for a full discussion of the data and methods used.
5. *National Economist,* January 3, 1891. Like all such papers, the *National Economist* also included advertisements that say a great deal about the movement and its members. Alliance material was prominent among these—e.g., notices for the "National Economist Hand-Book" and several Alliance songbooks—as well as ads for grinding mills, harnesses and buggies, shotguns, and entertainment ("ATTENTION! Officers and Secretaries of Alliances: Every Lodge should get up a club for FARM FUN: The Rural Satirist").
6. The racial identity terms used were somewhat more elaborated than they were in the Knights of Labor discussions. As with the Knights, "white" was by far the identity term most often used in the Alliance and Populist communications. In several instances, "Anglo-Saxon," "Saxon," or "Caucasian" was used in place of "white."

7. Here is one example of this ironic use of the term: "The [Democratic] committee spent many hours in anxious consultation and finally came to the conclusion to try to put a cheerful face on the matter and appear not to be too badly scared and to get their biggest men into the field at once, cry 'nigger supremacy,' and try and rally their failing fortunes" (*People's Party Paper,* April 28, 1892).
8. For example, the term "nigger in the woodpile" meant the heart of a problem (see *People's Party Paper,* June 9, 1893). The use of such phrases is interesting in papers that were among the most self-consciously egalitarian in the South. Just as otherwise gender-conscious men at the dawn of the twenty-first century may sometimes catch themselves making sexist assumptions, racially biased terms often slipped by the Southern whites of the 1890s. These moments suggest that much of southern race relations remained below the surface of conscious calculation for many white Populists.
9. Statements urging political coalition between whites and blacks in the Populist data were coded "interracial organizing—positive." In practice, the central opposition in the Populist communications was between such statements and others that were coded "political competition." Statements about political competition were different from those that could be construed as negative terms about interracial organizing. Statements coded "interracial organizing—negative" argued that interracial alliances should not be sought. The "political competition" category reported that competition was eroding or was preventing such alliances.
10. The relationship between these two elements was statistically significant as indicated by the Lambda and Uncertainty coefficients. Both statistics measure the proportionate reduction in error in estimating the racial "other" that an item will address when the interest frame is known compared with when it is not known. It should be noted, though, that the relationship was stronger for the Alliance discussions than it was for the People's Party.
11. *National Economist,* April 6, 1889.
12. For example, the following was typical of this claim: "For a number of years past railroad, mining and other corporations have been importing into this country ship-load after ship-load of foreign pauper laborers to compete with the honest American laborer . . . How long before our English lords will turn their mercenary Hessians loose upon our tenant farmers? Stop and think" (*National Economist,* February 16, 1890). Note here that the threat is to industrial workers rather than to farmers. Note also that the villain is here seen not as the "mercenary Hessians" themselves but the "English lords."
13. *National Economist,* October 8, 1892.
14. Ibid., July 20, 1889.
15. Ibid., December 6, 1890.
16. Ibid., December 6, 1890.
17. Ibid., August 22, 1891.
18. Some typical examples can be found in the editions of the *National Economist* from June 15, 1889, and June 14, 1890.

19. *National Economist,* October 10, 1891.
20. For a theoretically oriented discussion of the origins of this racial mythology and its ties to nationalism, see Arendt (1958), particularly part 1. David Peal (1989) has pointed out that this trope was not only important for the later Nazi movement in Germany, but also centrally for an analogous contemporary movement of German agrarians. While Peal misses the anti-Semitism of the Populists and focuses instead on the electoral and economic similarities of the movements, his discussion of the anti-Semitism of Böckel and other German movement leaders suggests a more direct link between the image of Jewish parasitic usurers as the opposite of the "sturdy yeoman" in this "anti-commercial idiom" (345).
21. *People's Party Paper,* May 12, 1893.
22. *National Economist,* May 18, 1889.
23. Ibid., August 31, 1889. It should be noted in passing that this is a remarkable perspective, in some ways not far from what a sociologist or a historian of today might claim. This was in fact not completely out of the ordinary, as part of the educational campaign of the movement often involved history lessons about social structures and power in past societies, coupled with geography or math problems. It should also be noted, however, that the editorial did not think that "the dignity of our race" was something to be abandoned; rather, it was something to be claimed.
24. *National Economist,* March 22, 1890.
25. These particular terms were rarely used in the movement communications. I have employed them to give a sense of the way that the general trope of slavery was used in relation to two distinct problems that the movements faced.
26. *National Economist,* October 4, 1890.
27. Ibid., May 6, 1889.
28. Ibid., November 8, 1890.
29. Ibid., September 13, 1890.
30. Ibid., January 23, 1892.
31. Ibid., July 9, 1892.
32. *People's Party Paper,* December 31, 1891.
33. Ibid., January 3, 1892.
34. Ibid., April 7, 1892.
35. "$50,000,000 Bonds" on the figure's whip and cattle prod was a reference to a failed attempt by President Grover Cleveland to issue bonds to shore up the gold reserves and ease the money supply; banks instead kept the money supply tight by drawing down the reserves.
36. It should be clearly stated that not all of the Populist communications adopted this narrative. Some in fact claimed that black workers and farmers might be direct competitors to whites. One notice asked all white workers and contractors to boycott an Atlanta firm that replaced whites with black workers (*People's Party Paper*, February 25, 1892). Another reported wage reductions in a coal-mining region and linked the discussion to competition between black and white working people. "It seems to me also that the white people of the South and North who can

look with complacency upon this spectacle of a race of former slaves but recently liberated being forced into a state of want and hunger that makes them willing to work for any wages that will keep out starvation and then given the option to accept such wages or none, must surely be unmindful of their own welfare and that of their children, who may at some future time be forced to become wage workers" (*People's Party Paper,* March 24, 1892). These and other statements adopted a different position than that of the present narrative, but they were driven by the same issue, namely the white farmers' fears of their declining economic and social status.

37. *National Economist,* January 7, 1893.
38. Ibid., January 25, 1890.
39. Ibid., March 8, 1890.
40. Ibid., March 8, 1890.
41. Ibid., May 9 1891.
42. Ibid., June 7, 1890.
43. Ibid., July 4, 1891.
44. Ibid., July 12, 1890.
45. Ibid., May 17, 1890.
46. Ibid., September 13, 1890.
47. Ibid., April 11, 1891.
48. *People's Party Paper,* March 28, 1892.
49. Ibid., March 31, 1892.
50. Ibid., June 3, 1892.
51. Ibid., August 26, 1892.
52. *National Economist,* March 16, 1890.
53. Ibid., July 25, 1891.
54. *People's Party Paper,* May 13, 1892.
55. Ibid., June 17, 1892. The item then suggested that in order to avoid jeopardizing white control in politics, Democrats should switch their votes to the People's Party.
56. *People's Party Paper,* July 29, 1892.
57. Ibid., June 24, 1892.
58. Ibid., July 27, 1894.
59. Ibid., October 12, 1894.

### 6. RACE AND THE AGRARIAN REVOLT IN GEORGIA

1. Although very different in other ways, well-known treatments of Populism converge on the economic factors behind the movement's success (Schwartz 1976; Woodward 1951; Gaither 1977; Goodwyn 1978). On the case of Georgia specifically, Arnett's classic book from 1922 makes the same point.
2. The data here and below are calculated from county census records from 1880 and 1890 (ICPSR 1984). All statistics are from 1890 unless otherwise specified.
3. In terms of race, the counties ranged from 0.8 percent black to 84.2 percent black. Tenancy rates ranged from 5.2 percent to 89.8 percent across counties. The correla-

tion between the two is strong and statistically significant (Pearson correlation is .57; significant at the .001 level, one-tailed test).

4. The counties that did not follow the general trend are the low outliers on figure 4 that had relatively large black populations, but low concentrations of tenant farms (the average tenancy rate was 26 percent in the outliers as opposed to 56 percent for the rest). These counties were of two types. First were the southeastern counties that were still dominated by large plantations and used hired farm labor rather than tenants. Second were the few counties with significant urban and industrial populations.
5. It is important to note here that two major studies of Georgia Populism point to the fact that the movement drew much of its support from independent farmers, structurally between tenants and sharecroppers on the one hand and planters on the other (despite the fact that many of the movement leaders were planters). These studies also point to the fact that this position was culturally significant because of the resonance of republican independence and self-sufficiency for the yeomen. After the Civil War, the rise of rail transportation through the South and the growth of the cotton economy changed much of that traditional independence. See Shaw (1984, esp. chapter 1) on Georgia Populism generally and Hahn (1983) on upcountry Populism.
6. *National Economist,* August 22, 1891. The letter was signed by D. N. Sanders of Lyneville (in the tenth district's Taliaferro County).
7. *National Economist,* May 31, 1890.
8. *Southern Alliance Farmer,* quoted in the *National Economist,* April 25, 1891.
9. *National Economist,* November 1, 1890.
10. Arnett (1922: 83) makes this same point with regard to the St. Louis meeting of 1889, where the issue of race came to the surface much more clearly as the order began to debate a program for political action.
11. See Hahn (1983) on upcountry rebellion in Georgia and its ties to Populism. Hyman (1990) provides a broader view of the "Anti-Redeemer" revolt in the upcountry South generally. Hyman labels the rebels "Anti-Redeemers" to point out that the movement was driven by a common reaction to the consolidation of political control under the "Redeemer" Democrats and their successors.
12. See Hahn (1983: 272–74). Hahn reports that the membership in this area was centered on small independent farmers rather than on larger landholders or tenants.
13. Ward (1943) details the largely behind-the-scenes interactions between the Independent Democrats and the remains of Georgia's Republican Party, which by the late 1870s was disorganized and internally divided.
14. Hahn (1983) emphasizes economic factors behind upcountry Populist voting, while the analysis by Kantor (1995) suggests that political self-determination was the more basic issue.
15. The tenth district averaged 51.6 percent black, and 56.4 percent of farms were worked by tenants in 1890 (compared with 42.8 percent black and 48.7 percent

tenants for the rest of the state). The correlation between the two variables was also higher in the tenth district than in the rest of the state (r = .881 in the tenth compared with r = .537; both one-tailed tests were significant at the .001 level). There was variation within the district—Johnson County was low on both measures while Glassock, Richmond, and Jefferson counties were about average for the state. The rest of the counties of the tenth district—Burke, Columbia, Washington, Taliaferro, Warren, Lincoln, and McDuffie—had large black majorities and were dominated by tenant farmers, however. Parsons, Dubin, and Parsons (1990: 17–22) provide a very useful overview of Georgia's congressional districts during this period, including maps of changing district boundaries.

16. This distinction was most clearly associated with the Populists, but it also found a more general resonance. Roediger (1994) describes a very similar distinction between social equality and "stomach equality" that emerged in the IWW organization of workers in the southern pinewoods after 1900.
17. *Southern Alliance Farmer*, quoted in the *National Economist*, April 23, 1890.
18. *National Economist*, March 8, 1890.
19. Atlanta *Constitution*, July 4, 1890, quoted in Arnett 1922: 107.
20. *National Economist*, August 19, 1891.
21. Whether he cast only one vote or votes for all eleven seats reserved for Georgia delegates of the Colored Farmers' Alliance is an unresolved question (cf. Holmes 1975 [1891]: 190; *People's Party Paper*, March 17, 1892). Holmes saw the incident as an indication of the distance between the Colored Farmers' Alliance white superintendent, who inducted Gilmore, and the black membership. In my view, it says far more about the white Populists' behind-the-scenes argument over black involvement in the political phase of the movement.
22. Quoted in the *People's Party Paper*, March 17, 1892.
23. *People's Party Paper*, March 3, 1892.
24. Ibid., March 17, 1892.
25. Ibid., April 21, 1892.
26. *National Economist*, October 1, 1892.
27. Ibid., October 1, 1892.
28. *People's Party Paper*, September 30, 1892.
29. Knights of Labor, *Record of the Proceedings of the General Assembly*, 1889.
30. Watson's formulation was that "self interest *always* controls." He did not mean that the given economic and political conditions would lead whites to dominate blacks, but rather that if presented with economic arguments and solutions, politically and economically disaffected whites and blacks would abandon their ties to the old parties and support the Populist movement.
31. *People's Party Paper*, June 3, 1892; July 8, 1892; August 19, 1892; August 26, 1892.
32. Quoted in the *National Economist*, April 9, 1892.
33. *People's Party Paper*, April 21, 1892.
34. Ibid., July 1, 1891.
35. Due to the tactical blunders of the race in the Fifth Ward, there were actually two

Populist congressional candidates on the ticket, Sam Taliaferro and Sam Small (see Shaw 1984: 66). The district was written off by Watson and other party leaders. On October 28, 1892, the *People's Party Paper* printed the Populist presidential and congressional ticket but left out the fifth district.

36. Commonly referred to by Democrats as the "Peek Slave Bill," this became a minor issue in the 1892 election (see Shaw 1984: 46, 82; Watson 1963: 236).
37. *People's Party Paper,* October 14, 1892; see also September 20, 1895; October 25, 1895; March 13, 1896.
38. *People's Party Paper,* October 28, 1892; Woodward 1963: 239–40. Shaw 1984: 74, 88–89, however, points out that it is likely that many of the armed Populists came because they had heard it was Watson himself who was in danger.
39. *People's Party Paper,* October 28, 1892.
40. Ibid., June 17, 1892; September 15, 1893.
41. Ibid., October 14, 1892.
42. Ibid., March 17, 1892.
43. At one point in a later campaign, Watson argued that the Populist movement was a part of his faith, and he noted that Christ had also sought equal rights for all. Any message of social leveling in Christian teaching was evidently lost, for in the next breath he assured his listeners that he had not asked blacks to sit with him at his table (*People's Party Paper,* November 3, 1893). See Reinhart (1972); Gaither (1977); Shaw (1984) for other views of this inconsistency.
44. *People's Party Paper,* March 13, 1896. Doyle made these statements in a deposition relating to investigations into election fraud, much of which was reprinted in Watson's paper.
45. See Ward (1943) for an overview of the Republican Party's demise. Wilhoit (1967: 118–19) notes that the 1892 election saw a larger black vote than at any time since Reconstruction; at the same time, he notes that the election also marked the beginning of disfranchisement in Georgia.
46. Optimistic statements printed in the *People's Party Paper* during the summer campaign of 1892 came from Morgan County (July 1, 1892; August 5, 1892), Warren County (July 8, 1892), Hancock County (July 15, 1892), Washington County (July 29, 1892), Macon County (July 29, 1892), Harris County (August 19, 1892), and Monroe County (August 19, 1892).
47. *People's Party Paper,* July 1, 1892.
48. Ibid., August 26, 1892.
49. Ibid., September 9, 1892.
50. Ibid., October 7, 1892.
51. Watson himself did not exactly deny this, but rather scoffed at the pot calling the kettle black, so to speak. On the issue of Democratic threats against Doyle, Watson remarked, "Such are Democratic methods. Yet they talk to colored people of kuklux!" (*People's Party Paper,* October 14, 1892). Woodward (1963) notes the close ties between Watson and the Georgia Klan in Watson's later days.
52. The campaigns of 1892 and 1893 were those in which white Populists were most

engaged with the question of race. They were also the first full years of publication for the *People's Party Paper,* which started during 1891.

53. For clarity, I have here separated those communications that were explicitly about interracial political competition from those that discussed economic competition (i.e., issues of wages or conditions) or status-based competition (i.e., threats to white supremacy in social matters).
54. *People's Party Paper,* October 14, 1892.
55. Ibid.
56. *People's Party Paper,* November 25, 1892. This report went on to claim that "another third in line were boys under age. This leaves only one-third as possible legal voters"—which oddly overlooks the possibility that black votes were also legal votes.
57. *People's Party Paper,* January 13, 1893.
58. Ibid., January 20, 1893; see also March 24, 1893.
59. Ibid., September 9, 1892.
60. Ibid., September 16, 1892.
61. Ibid., July 7, 1893; July 21, 1893.
62. Ibid., September 22, 1893.
63. Ibid., July 13, 1894.
64. Ibid., October 6, 1893; October 13, 1893.
65. Ibid., August 24, 1894; see also September 7, 1894; September 14, 1894; September 21 1894.
66. Ibid., October 20, 1893; November 10, 1893.
67. Ibid., September 7, 1894; September 14, 1894; September 28, 1894; October 12, 1894.
68. Ibid., October 12, 1894.

### 7. RACE AND THE AGRARIAN REVOLT IN VIRGINIA

1. *Journal of United Labor,* March 6, 1890.
2. Economic and social data are from county-level records in the U.S. census (Inter-University Consortium for Political and Social Research [ICPSR], "Historical, Demographic, Economic, and Social Data: The United States, 1790–1970"). All figures are from 1890, unless otherwise specified.
3. The Southside counties were Amelia, Appomattox, Brunswick, Buckingham, Campbell, Charlotte, Chesterfield, Cumberland, Dinwiddie, Greensville, Halifax, Lunenberg, Mecklenberg, Nottoway, Pittsylvania, Powhatan, and Prince Edward (Sheldon 1935: 1, n.1).
4. The Southside counties ranged from 41 percent black to 70 percent black. Tenancy rates for the Southside counties averaged 38 percent (counting both tenant farmers and sharecroppers), compared with 23 percent in non-Southside counties.
5. See Sheldon (1935: 30–33); *Exchange Reporter,* December 12, 1891.
6. Farmers' Alliance Co-operative Manufacturing Co., "Farmers' Alliance Co-operative Manufacturing Co., Iron Gate, Allegheny County, Va."

7. See Saloutos (1960: 81); *National Economist,* May 24, 1890. Rogers also served as the leader of the more populous North Carolina CFA.
8. From the CFA meeting, there were delegates from seven of the Southside counties (two from Dinwiddie and one each from Brunswick, Buckingham, Cumberland, Lunenberg, Mecklenberg, and Powhatan). Other delegates were from nearby counties, including Bedford, Charlotte, Fluvana, Hanover, Henrico, King and Queen, Nelson, Prince George, and Southampton (see Richmond *Planet,* August 15, 1891).
9. Richmond *Planet,* August 30, 1890.
10. Ibid., August 15, 1891.
11. Ibid., August 13, 1892.
12. Ibid., August 30, 1890.
13. Ibid., August 15, 1890; *National Economist,* March 5, 1890.
14. Richmond *Planet,* November 7, 1891.
15. *National Economist*, April 12, 1890.
16. *Virginia Sun,* May 11, 1892.
17. *Exchange Reporter,* August 18, 1891.
18. The strategy worked perhaps better than the Democrats had hoped. Days before the election, a race riot occurred in the black belt city of Danville. The immediate cause of the riot was a fight that broke out after a white man was "jostled" by a black man who refused to step out of his way on the street. This minor incident was given significance by the "Danville circular," an anonymous broadside complaining of "negro domination" in the town (see Wynes 1961: 29–34).
19. The cooperative organizations were originally controlled by a state business agency that sold goods directly to the local exchanges at wholesale prices, saving the cooperatives a good deal of money but also running on a debt (see McMath 1975: 120). The county business agents of Virginia met in Richmond to adopt the "Rochdale" cooperative plan, earlier used by the Grange. Under the new plan, the state agency would procure goods, but the county agents would distribute them to the local exchanges. Instead of selling at wholesale, the goods would be sold at retail prices and the profits distributed at the end of the year among the shareholders. This system allowed the Alliance Exchange at Petersburg to stay in operation until 1895 (Sheldon 1935: 43).
20. *Exchange Reporter,* July 25, 1891.
21. Ibid.
22. Ibid.
23. Ibid., November 14, 1891.
24. Ibid., January 23, 1892; *Virginia Sun,* February 13, 1892.
25. *Exchange Reporter,* August 18, 1891.
26. Ibid., January 23, 1892.
27. Ibid.
28. *Virginia Sun,* February 20, 1892.

29. Ibid., March 5, 1892.
30. Ibid., May 25, 1892.
31. Richmond *Planet,* July 18, 1891.
32. Ibid.
33. Ibid., July 25, 1891.
34. Ibid., August 29, 1891.
35. Ibid.
36. Ibid.
37. Ibid., September 19, 1892.
38. Apparently forgotten for the moment was the fact that at least one county Alliance in Pittsylvania proposed the same measure (Richmond *Planet,* October 24, 1891). The issue of school funding had earlier been a successful campaign issue for the Readjusters.
39. Richmond *Planet,* October 31, 1891.
40. *Virginia Sun,* April 20, 1892.
41. Ibid., April 27, 1892.
42. Ibid., May 25, 1892.
43. Ibid., July 13, 1892.
44. Ibid., July 27, 1892.
45. Ibid., September 14, 1892.
46. Ibid., October 26, 1892.
47. Ibid., October 12, 1892.
48. Ibid., November 16, 1892.
49. *Virginia Sun,* November 16, 1892.
50. Ibid., February 1, 1893.
51. Ibid., June 14, 1893.
52. Ibid., February 15, 1893.
53. Ibid., August 9, 1893.
54. Kent had served as chairman of the Virginia Alliance's Legislative Committee at the same time that Beverley had served as lecturer (*Exchange Reporter,* December 12, 1891).
55. Sheldon's account of the Virginia Populist movement generally discounts the votes of "ignorant" blacks. Of the 1893 vote, Sheldon dismisses Cocke's support: "Probably not 20,000 could be classed as votes of white farmers genuinely interested in the success of Populist principles" (1935: 103). On the other hand, if his claim is correct it would mean that 61,000 votes came from black Republicans and sympathetic white Democrats—the very people that the People's Party needed to win.
56. *People's Party Paper,* August 24, 1894.
57. Richmond *Planet,* October 1, 1892.
58. Ibid., August 19, 1892; August 26, 1892.
59. Ibid., August 13, 1892.
60. *Richmond Planet,* September 10, 1892.

61. Ibid.
62. Ibid., October 1, 1892.
63. Ibid., September 2, 1893.
64. Ibid., November 19, 1893.

## 8. CLASS, STATUS, POWER, AND THE INTERRACIAL PROJECT

1. In other words, it looked like a classic case of what social scientists have called "path dependence," where initially contingent and potentially transformative events are brought into line with durable cultural and material constraints. See Mahoney (2000). The more dynamic view suggests instead what Charles Tilly (2003: v) has called a continual process of error and error correction.
2. See also Grob (1961) for more on this notion.
3. The evocative phrase "white republic" is from Saxton (1990).
4. Patrick Joyce's (1991, 1994) studies of nineteenth-century England make a similar point—there were no clear lines of demarcation between the class, party, and status claims invoked in the democratic constitution of "the people." Although Joyce is not entirely clear on this point, he seems to draw the conclusion that this means that "class" as such was a later construction. My own conclusion is different—much of the thrust of class claims in the nineteenth century had to do with the political and status sides of economic position.

## APPENDIX

1. In late 1889, the paper was renamed the *Journal of the Knights of Labor.* The journal was issued monthly until mid-1884, then biweekly through the end of 1885, and weekly thereafter. There were 318 issues published in the period covered by this study, 5 of which are missing from the collection. Of the 313 issues examined, 157 issues (50.2 percent) contained communications that fit the criteria for inclusion.
2. I include the scattered issues of the *People's Party Paper* in my analyses. This provides some conservative bias—the movement was still independent but it was unraveling as an interracial coalition. For this reason, the statements from the later years were less favorable toward interracial organizing than were those from earlier years. As a result, the first movement narrative from the paper stands out less clearly than it would if I cut off data collection after 1894.
3. Because my interest was in the intersection of class and race within these movements, items that made reference to either class or race but not both were excluded. Although it might be interesting to capture and code items that made reference only to class or political interest, this was not practical since almost every communication would have been included. By contrast, there were only a handful of items in the journals that referenced race but not class.
4. Influential recent work on the concept of movement frames includes Cress and Snow (2000); McLean (1998); Cornfield and Fletcher (1998); Diani (1996); Babb (1996); Benford (1993); Gamson (1992); Gerhards and Rucht (1992); Snow and

Benford (1992); Snow et al. (1986). On the related concept of movement "discourse," see Steinberg (1991, 1999), Jacobs (1996), Ellingson (1995). The concepts of movement "discourses" and movement "frames" have obvious similarities, although their uses have diverged somewhat in recent work. Frames are often portrayed as relatively complete ideological packages that are produced and deployed by social movements, while "discourses" are seen as more deeply tied to underlying historical schemas. As a result, several recent critiques have pointed to the framing of literature's inattention to discursive processes (see Johnston 1995; Polletta 1997). It should be noted that I use the language of "frames" because it is less cumbersome and because it is familiar to most readers. However, my use of the term does not imply strongly instrumentalist assumptions, and it is not incompatible with "discourse." This is more or less how Goffman (1974) originally used the term.

5. Movement frames or discourses always involve some internal contention. What matters in defining a frame is not uniform agreement; rather, it is that all of the statements included adopt the same "frame" of reference in defining the problem. See Steinberg (1999:745); McLean (1998:55); Ellingson (1995:107–8).
6. One possible exception is that the city directory data report fewer black industrial laborers. The difference is most likely due to different categorizations of occupation. In the city directory data, a very large proportion of black men gave their occupation simply as "laborer." In the census data, many of these day laborers were classified by industry (e.g., as tobacco workers or iron workers). While the census thus distinguishes industrial workers from others, the city directory labels capture the essentially unskilled basis of most black men's jobs.
7. See Massey and Denton (1987; 1993) on the construction of ward-level analyses. I do not mean to disparage this approach in general, since it is very well suited to comparative analysis. The finer-grained block level analysis is more appropriate for the kind of historical approach that I take in chapters 3 and 4.
8. Data are from *Chataigne's Directory of Richmond, Va.*, 1885, and *Weatherbe's Atlanta, Ga., Duplex City Directory,* 1885. These and supplemental directories published between 1880 and 1890 were obtained on microfilm from the Library of Congress and from Duke University's Perkins Library.
9. I take these equations from Massey and Denton (1987) directly. My only modification to their calculations is using block-level rather than ward-level data to produce the measures.
10. The Richmond directories were *Chataigne's Richmond City Directory for the Years 1979–80*; and *Chataigne's Directory of Richmond, Va.*, 1885, 1889. Atlanta directories were *Shole's Directory of the City of Atlanta, Ga. for 1880*; *Weatherbe's Atlanta, Ga., Duplex City Directory,* 1885; and *Atlanta City Directory for 1890*.
11. Some of the information was later updated by Garlock (1982), although most modifications were slight.

# REFERENCES


### NEWSPAPERS

*Exchange Reporter* (1891–1892). Richmond. Published by the Farmers Alliance and Hypothecation Warehouse of Virginia. [Microfilm.]

*Journal of United Labor* (1880–1890). Marblehead, Mass.; Pittsburgh and Philadephia, Pa. [Microfilm].

*National Economist* (1889–1893). Washington, D.C. Edited by Charles W. Macune. Published by the National Economist Publishing Co. [Microfilm]

*People's Party Paper* (1891–1896). Atlanta. Edited by T. E. Watson. Published by the People's Party Paper Publishing Co. [Microfilm].

*The Planet* (1890–1894). Richmond. Edited by John Mitchell. Published by the Planet Publishing Co. [Microfilm.]

*Virginia Sun* (1892–1894). Richmond. Published by the Virginia Sun Publishing Co. [Microfilm].

### ARCHIVAL SOURCES AND DOCUMENTS

*Atlanta City Directory for 1890.* Compiled and published by R. L. Polk and Co.

*Chataigne's Richmond City Directory for the Years 1879–80.* Compiled by J. H. Chataigne. Published by Rudolph and English Booksellers.

*Chataigne's Directory of Richmond, Va.*, 1885, 1889. Compiled and published by J. H. Chataigne.

Colored Farmers' National Alliance and Co-operative Union. *Ritual of the Colored Farmers' National Allinace and Co-operative Union of the United States.* Houston: Culmore Bros., n.d.

Farmers' Alliance Co-operative Manufacturing Co. "Farmers' Alliance Co-operative Manufacturing Co., Iron Gate, Allegheny County, Va." New Market, Va.: Henkel and Co.'s Steam Print, n.d.

Inter-University Consortium for Political and Social Research (ICPSR). "Historical, Demographic, Economic, and Social Data: The United States, 1790–1970." [Computer data file.] Ann Arbor, Mich.: Inter-University Consortium for Political and Social Research, 1984.

Knights of Labor, *Record of the Proceedings of the General Assembly*, 1880–1889. In Terence Vincent Powderly Papers 1864–1937 and John William Hayes Papers 1880–1921. Edited by John A. Turchenske Jr. Glen Rock, N.J.: Microfilming Corporation of America.

National Farmers' Alliance and Industrial Union. *Ritual of the Farmers' Alliance*. Dallas: Mercury Job Office, n.d.

*Shole's Directory of the City of Atlanta, Ga., for 1880*. Compiled by A. E. Sholes and C. F. Weatherbe, published by Sholes and Co.

Terence Vincent Powderly Papers 1864–1937 and John William Hayes Papers 1880–1921. Letter file. Edited by John A. Turchenske Jr. Glen Rock, N.J.: Microfilming Corporation of America.

U.S. Bureau of the Census. *Tenth Census of the United States*, 1880, 22 vols.

U.S. Bureau of the Census. *Eleventh Census of the United States*, 1890, 25 vols.

U.S. Commissioner of Labor. "Twenty-first Annual Report of the Commissioner of Labor, 1906. Strikes and Lockouts." Washington, D.C.: Government Printing Office, 1907.

*Weatherbe's Atlanta, Ga., Duplex City Directory*, 1885. Compiled and Published by C. F. Weatherbe.

### BOOKS AND JOURNAL ARTICLES

Abbott, Andrew. 1990. "Conceptions of Time and Events in Social Science Methods." *Historical Methods* 23:140–50.

——. 1992. "From Causes to Events: Notes on Narrative Positivism." *Sociological Methods and Research* 20:428–55.

——. 1995. "Sequence Analysis: New Methods for Old Ideas." *Annual Review of Sociology* 21:93–113.

Abell, Peter. 1987. *The Syntax of Social Life: The Theory and Method of Comparative Narratives*. Oxford: Clarendon Press.

Abramowitz, Jack. 1950. "The Negro in the Agrarian Revolt." *Agricultural History* 24:89–95.

——. 1953. "The Negro in the Populist Movement." *Journal of Negro History* 38:257–89.

Altschuler, Glenn C., and Stuart M. Blumin. 2000. *Rude Republic: Americans and Their Politics in the Nineteenth Century*. Princeton, N.J.: Princeton University Press.

Aminzade, Ronald. 1993. *Ballots and Barricades: Class Formation and Republican Politics in France, 1830–1871*. Princeton, N.J.: Princeton University Press.

Appleby, Joyce. 1992. *Liberalism and Republicanism in the Historical Imagination.* Cambridge, Mass.: Harvard University Press.

Arendt, Hannah. 1958. *The Origins of Totalitarianism.* Cleveland: Meridian Books.

Arnesen, Eric. 1993. "Following the Color Line of Labor: Black Workers and the Labor Movement before 1930." *Radical History Review* 55:53–87.

——. 1996. "American Workers and the Labor Movement in the Late Nineteenth Century." In *The Gilded Age: Essays on the Origins of Modern America,* ed. Charles C. Calhoun. Wilmington, Del.: Scholarly Resources. 39–61.

——. 1998. "Up from Exclusion: Black and White Workers, Race, and the State of Labor History." *Reviews in American History* 26:146–74.

——. 2000. "'Like Banquo's Ghost, It Will Not Down': The Race Question and the American Railroad Brotherhoods, 1880–1920." *American Historical Review* 99:1601–33.

——. 2001. "'Whiteness and the Historians' Imagination." *International Labor and Working Class History* 60:3–32.

Arnett, Alex Mathews. 1922. "The Populist Movement in Georgia: A View of the 'Agrarian Crusade' in the Light of Solid-South Politics." New York: Columbia University.

Ayers, Edward L. 1992. *The Promise of the New South: Life after Reconstruction.* New York: Oxford University Press.

Babb, Sarah. 1996. "'A True American System of Finance': Frame Resonance in the U.S. Labor Movement, 1866 to 1886." *American Sociological Review* 61:1033–52.

Baker, Bruce E. 1999. "The 'Hoover Scare' in South Carolina, 1887." *Labor History* 40:261–82.

Banton, Michael. 1998. *Racial Theories.* Cambridge: Cambridge University Press.

Bearman, Peter, Robert Faris, and James Moody. 1999. "Blocking the Future: New Solutions for Old Problems in Historical Social Science." *Social Science History* 23:501–33.

Beck, E. M., and Stewart E. Tolnay. 1990. "The Killing Fields of the Deep South: The Market for Cotton and the Lynching of Blacks, 1882–1930." *American Sociological Review* 55:526–39.

Bellamy, Edward. 1988 [1888]. *Looking Backward.* New York: Penguin Books.

Benford, Robert D. 1993. "Frame Disputes within the Nuclear Disarmament Movement." *Social Forces* 71:677–701.

Biernacki, Richard. 1995. *The Fabrication of Labor: Germany and Great Britain, 1640–1914.* Cambridge: Cambridge University Press.

Blalock, Hubert M. Jr. 1967. *Toward a Theory of Minority-Group Relations.* New York: Wiley.

Blau, Peter M. 1977. *Inequality and Heterogeneity: A Primitive Theory of Social Structure.* New York: Free Press.

Blau, Peter M., and Joseph E. Schwartz. 1984. *Crosscutting Social Circles: Testing a Macrostructural Theory of Intergroup Relations.* Orlando, Fla.: Academic Press.

Bonacich, Edna. 1972. "A Theory of Ethnic Antagonism: The Split Labor Market." *American Sociological Review* 37:554–59.

——. 1975. "Abolition, the Extension of Slavery, and the Position of Free Blacks: A Study of Split Labor Markets in the United States, 1830–1863." *American Journal of Sociology* 81:601–28.

——. 1976. "Advanced Capitalism and Black/White Race Relations in the United States: A Split Labor Market Interpretation." *American Sociological Review* 41:34–51.

Boswell, Terry E. 1986. "A Split Labor Market Analysis of Discrimination against Chinese Immigrants, 1850–1882." *American Sociological Review* 51:352–71.

Bourdieu, Pierre. 1984. *Distinction: A Social Critique of the Judgement of Taste.* Cambridge, Mass.: Harvard University Press.

——. 1992. *The Logic of Practice.* Stanford, Calif.: Stanford University Press.

Brundage, David. 1994. *The Making of Western Labor Radicalism: Denver's Organized Workers, 1878–1905.* Urbana: University of Illinois Press.

Bruner, Jerome. 1987. "Life as Narrative." *Social Research* 54:11–33.

——. 1990. "Folk Psychology as an Instrument of Culture." In *Acts of Meaning,* ed. Jerome Bruner. Cambridge Mass.: Harvard University Press. 33–65.

Burawoy, Michael. 1979. *Manufacturing Consent.* Chicago: University of Chicago Press.

Burke, Kenneth. 1969. *A Grammar of Motives.* Berkeley: University of California Press.

Calhoun, Craig. 1982. *The Question of Class Struggle: Social Foundations of Popular Radicalism during the Industrial Revolution.* Chicago: University of Chicago Press.

——. 1983. "The Radicalism of Tradition: Community Strength or Venerable Disguise and Borrowed Language?" *American Journal of Sociology* 88:886–914.

——. 1993. "'New Social Movements' of the Early Nineteenth Century." *Social Science History* 17:385–427.

——. 1994. "Social Theory and the Politics of Identity." In *Social Theory and the Politics of Identity,* ed. Craig Calhoun. Cambridge, Mass.: Basil Blackwell. 9–36.

Carruthers, Bruce, and Sarah Babb. 1996. "The Color of Money and the Nature of Value: Greenbacks and Gold in Postbellum America." *American Journal of Sociology* 101: 1556–1591.

Clanton, Gene. 1991. *Populism: The Humane Preference in America, 1890–1900.* Boston: Twayne Publishers.

——. 1998. *Congressional Populism and the Crisis of the 1890s.* Lawrence: University of Kansas Press.

Clawson, Mary Ann. 1989. *Constructing Brotherhood: Class, Gender, and Fraternalism.* Princeton, N.J.: Princeton University Press.

Clemens, Elisabeth S. 1997. *The People's Lobby: Organizational Innovation and the Rise of Interest Group Politics in the United States, 1890–1925.* Chicago: University of Chicago Press.

Conell, Carol, and Kim Voss. 1990. "Formal Organization and the Fate of Social Movements: Craft Association and Class Alliance in the Knights of Labor." *American Sociological Review* 55:255–69.

Cornfield, Daniel B., and Bill Fletcher. 1998. "Institutional Constraints on Social Movement 'Frame Extension': Shifts in the Legislative Agenda of the American Federation of Labor, 1881–1955." *Social Forces* 76:1305–21.

Corzine, Jay, James Creech, and Lin Corzine. 1983. "Black Concentration and Lynchings in the South: Testing Blalock's Power-Threat Hypothesis." *Social Forces* 61:775–96.

Cox, Oliver Cromwell. 1970 [1948]. *Caste, Class, and Race: A Study in Social Dynamics.* New York: Monthly Review Press.

Cress, Daniel M., and David A. Snow. 2000. "The Outcomes of Homeless Mobilization: The Influence of Organization, Disruption, Political Mediation, and Framing." *American Journal of Sociology* 105:1063–104.

Dailey, Jane. 2000. *Before Jim Crow: The Politics of Race in Postemancipation Virginia.* Chapel Hill: University of North Carolina Press.

Danto, Arthur. 1965. *Analytical Philosophy of History*. Cambridge: Cambridge University Press.

Dawley, Alan. 1976. *Class and Community: The Industrial Revolution in Lynn.* Cambridge Mass.: Harvard University Press.

Destler, Chester McArthur. 1965. *American Radicalism, 1865–1901: Essays and Documents.* New York: Octagon Books.

Diani, Mario. 1996. "Linking Mobilization Frames and Political Opportunities: Insights from Regional Populism in Italy." *American Sociological Review* 61:1053–69.

Dunning, Nelson A. 1975 [1891]. *The Farmers' Alliance History and Agricultural Digest.* New York: Arno Press.

Ellingson, Stephen. 1995. "Understanding the Dialectic of Discourse and Collective Action: Public Debate and Rioting in Antebellum Cincinnati." *American Journal of Sociology* 101:100–44.

Emirbayer, Mustafa, and Ann Mische. 1998. "What Is Agency?" *American Journal of Sociology* 103:962–1023.

Fantasia, Rick. 1995. "From Class Consciousness to Culture, Action, and Social Organization." *Annual Review of Sociology* 21:269–87.

Fields, Barbara J. 1982. "Ideology and Race in American History." In *Region, Race, and Reconstruction: Essays in Honor of C. Vann Woodward,* ed. J. Morgan Kousser and James M. McPherson. New York: Oxford University Press. 143–77.

Fink, Leon. 1985. *Workingmen's Democracy: The Knights of Labor and American Politics.* Urbana: University of Illinois Press.

Foley, Neil. 1997. *The White Scourge: Mexicans, Blacks, and Poor Whites in Texas Cotton Culture.* Berkeley: University of California Press.

Foner, Philip. 1955. *History of the Labor Movement in the United States.* New York: International Publishers.

——. 1974. *Organized Labor and the Black Worker, 1619–1973.* New York: Praeger.

Foner, Philip S., and Ronald L. Lewis. 1978. *The Black Worker during the Era of the Knights of Labor.* Philadelphia: Temple University Press.

Franzosi, Roberto. 1994. "From Words to Numbers: A Set Theory Framework for the Collection, Organization, and Analysis of Narrative Data." *Sociological Methodology* 24:105–36.

——. 1998. "Narrative Analysis—Or Why (and How) Sociologists Should Be Interested in Narrative Analysis." *Annual Review of Sociology* 24:517–54.

Gaither, Gerald H. 1977. *Blacks and the Populist Revolt: Ballots and Bigotry in the "New South."* Tuscaloosa: University of Alabama Press.

Gamson, William A. 1992. *Talking Politics.* New York: Cambridge University Press.

Garlock, Jonathan. 1982. *Guide to the Local Assemblies of the Knights of Labor.* Westport, Conn.: Greenwood Press.

Garlock, Jonathan, and N. C. Builder. 1973a. "Knights of Labor Data Bank" [computer data file]. Ann Arbor, Mich.: Inter-University Consortium for Political and Social Research.

——. 1973b. *Knights of Labor Data Bank: User's Manual and Index to Local Assemblies.* Ann Arbor, Mich.: Inter-University Consortium for Political and Social Research.

Gerhards, Jürgen, and Dieter Rucht. 1992. "Mesomobilization: Organizing and Framing Two Protest Campaigns in West Germany." *American Journal of Sociology* 98:555–96.

Gerstle, Gary. 1997. "Liberty, Coercion, and the Making of Americans." *Journal of American History* 84:524–58.

——. 2001. *American Crucible: Race and Nation in the Twentieth Century.* Princeton: Princeton University Press.

Gerteis, Joseph, and Alyssa Goolsby. 2005. "Nationalism in America: The Case of the Populist Movement." *Theory and Society* 34: 197–225.

Giddens, Anthony. 1979. *Central Problems in Social Theory: Action, Structure, and Contradiction in Social Analysis.* London: Macmillan.

——. 1984. *The Constitution of Society: Outline of the Theory of Structuration.* Berkeley: University of California Press.

Gilroy, Paul. 1993. *The Black Atlantic: Modernity and Double Consciousness.* Cambridge, Mass.: Harvard University Press.

Gleason, Philip. 1980. "American Identity and Americanization." In *Harvard Encyclopedia of American Ethnic Groups,* ed. Stephan Thernstrom, Ann Orlov, and Oscar Handlin. Cambridge, Mass.: The Belknap Press of Harvard University Press.

Goffman, Erving. 1974. *Frame Analysis: An Essay on the Organization of Experience.* Cambridge, Mass.: Harvard University Press.

Goldberg, David Theo. 1993. *Racist Culture: Philosophy and the Politics of Meaning.* Oxford: Blackwell.

Goodwyn, Lawrence. 1976. *Democratic Promise: The Populist Moment in America.* New York: Oxford University Press.

——. 1978. *The Populist Moment: A Short History of the Agrarian Revolt in America.* New York: Oxford University Press.

Griffin, Larry J. 1992. "Temporality, Events, and Explanation in Historical Sociology." *Sociological Methods and Research* 20:403–27.

——. 1993. "Narrative, Event-Structure Analysis, and Causal Interpretation in Historical Sociology." *American Journal of Sociology* 98:1094–133.

——. 1995. "How Do We Disentangle Race and Class? Or Should We Even Try?" *Work and Occupations* 22:85–93.

Griffin, Larry J., and Robert R. Korstad. 1995. "Class as Race and Gender: Making and Breaking a Labor Union in the Jim Crow South." *Social Science History* 19:425–54.

Grob, Gerald N. 1961. *Workers and Utopia: A Study of Ideological Conflict in the American Labor Movement, 1865–1900.* Evanston, Ill.: Northwestern University Press.

Gutman, Herbert G. 1987. "A Note on Immigration History, "Breakdown Models," and the Rewriting of the History of Immigrant Working-Class Peoples." In *Power and Culture: Essays on the American Working Class,* ed. Herbert G. Gutman. New York: Pantheon Books. 255–59.

Habermas, Jürgen. 1987. *The Theory of Communicative Action. Volume 2: Lifeworld and System: A Critique of Functionalist Reason.* Boston: Beacon Press.

Hahn, Stephen. 1983. *The Roots of Southern Populism: Yeoman Farmers and the Transformation of the Georgia Upcountry, 1850–1890.* New York: Oxford University Press.

Halpern, Rick. 1994. "Organized Labor, Black Workers and the Twentieth-Century South: The Emerging Revision." *Social History* 19: 359–83.

Hamilton, C. Horace. 1964. "The Negro Leaves the South." *Demography* 1:273–93.

Hanagan, Michael P. 1980. *The Logic of Solidarity: Artisans and Industrial Workers in Three French Towns, 1871–1914.* Urbana: University of Illinois Press.

Haydu, Jeffrey. 1997. *Making American Industry Safe for Democracy: Comparative Perspectives on the State and Employee Representation in the Era of World War I.* Urbana: University of Illinois Press.

Hechter, Michael. 1975. *Internal Colonialism: The Celtic Fringe in British National Development, 1536–1966.* Berkeley: University of California Press.

Hicks, John D. 1961. *The Populist Revolt: A History of the Farmers' Alliance and People's Party.* Lincoln: University of Nebraska Press.

Higham, John. 1955. *Strangers in the Land: Patterns of American Nativism, 1860–1925.* New Brunswick, N.J.: Rutgers University Press.

Hofstadter, Richard. 1956. *The Age of Reform from Bryan to F.D.R.* New York: Knopf.

Holmes, William F. 1973. "The Arkansas Cotton Pickers Strike of 1891 and the Demise of the Colored Farmers's Alliance." *Arkansas Historical Quarterly* 32:107–19.

——. 1975. "The Demise of the Colored Farmers' Alliance." *Journal of Southern History* 41:187–200.

——. 1994. "The Southern Farmers' Alliance and the Jute Cartel." *Journal of Southern History* 60:59–80.

Honey, Michael K. 1993. *Southern Labor and Black Civil Rights: Organizing Memphis Workers.* Urbana: University of Illinois Press.

Horan, Patrick M., and Peggy G. Hargis. n.d. "Documentation for the 'County Longitudinal Template.'" Unpublished report.

Humphrey, R. M. 1975 [1891]. "History of the Colored Farmers' National Alliance and

Co-operative Union." In *The Farmers' Alliance History and Agricultural Digest,* ed. Nelson A. Dunning. New York: Arno Press. 288–92.

Hyman, Michael R. 1990. *The Anti-Redeemers: Hill-Country Political Dissenters in the Lower South from Redemption to Populism.* Baton Rouge: Louisiana State University Press.

Ignatiev, Noel. 1995. *How the Irish Became White.* New York: Routledge.

Jacobs, Ronald N. 1996. "Civil Society in Crisis: Culture, Discourse and the Rodney King Beating." *American Journal of Sociology* 101:1238–272.

Jacobson, Julius. 1968. "Introduction: Union Conservatism: A Barrier to Racial Equality." In *The Negro and the American Labor Movement,* ed. Julius Jacobson. Garden City, N.Y.: Anchor Books.

Jacobson, Matthew Frye. 1998. *Whiteness of a Different Color: European Immigrants and the Alchemy of Race.* Cambridge, Mass.: Harvard University Press.

Jenkins, J. Craig. 1983. "Resource Mobilization Theory and the Study of Social Movements." *Annual Review of Sociology* 9:527–53.

Johnston, Hank. 1995. "A Methodology for Frame Analysis: From Discourse to Cognitive Schemata." In *Social Movements and Culture,* ed. Hank Johnston and Bert Klandermans. Minneapolis: University of Minnesota Press. 217–46.

Jones, Gareth Stedman. 1983. *Languages of Class: Studies in English Working-Class History, 1832–1982.* Cambridge: Cambridge University Press.

Joyce, Patrick. 1991. *Visions of the People: Industrial England and the Question of Class, 1848–1914.* Cambridge: Cambridge University Press.

——. 1993. "The Imaginary Discontents of Social History: A Note of Response to Mayfield and Thorne, and Lawrence and Taylor." *Social History* 18:81–85.

——. 1994. *Democratic Subjects: The Self and the Social in Nineteenth Century England.* Cambridge: Cambridge University Press.

——. 1995. "The End of Social History?" *Social History* 20:73–91.

Kantor, Shawn Everett. 1995. "Supplanting the Roots of Southern Populism: The Contours of Political Protest in the Georgia Hills." *Journal of Economic History* 55:637–46.

Katznelson, Ira. 1986. "Working-Class Formation: Constructing Cases and Comparisons." In *Working-Class Formation: Nineteenth-Century Patterns in Western Europe and the United States,* ed. Ira Katznelson and Aristide R. Zolberg. Princeton, N.J.: Princeton University Press. 3–44.

Kaufman, Jason. 1999. "Three Views of Associationalism in Nineteenth-Century America: An Empirical Examination." *American Journal of Sociology* 104:1296–345.

——. 2002. *For the Common Good? American Civic Life and the Golden Age of Fraternity.* New York: Oxford University Press.

Kealey, Gregory S. and Bryan D. Palmer. 1982. *Dreaming of What Might Be: The Knights of Labor in Ontario, 1880–1900.* Cambridge: Cambridge University Press.

Kelley, Robin D. G. 1990. *Hammer and Hoe: Alabama Communists during the Great Depression.* Chapel Hill: University of North Carolina Press.

Kelly, Brian. 2001. *Race, Class, and Power in the Alabama Coalfields, 1908–1921.* Urbana: University of Illinois Press.

Kester, Howard. 1997 [1936]. *Revolt among the Sharecroppers.* Knoxville: University of Tennessee Press.

Kimeldorf, Howard. 1999. *Battling for American Labor: Wobblies, Craft Workers, and the Making of the Union Movement.* Berkeley: University of California Press.

Kirk, Neville. 1994. "History, Language, Ideas and Post-Modernism: A Materialist View." *Social History* 19:221–40.

Kousser, J. Morgan. 1974. *The Shaping of Southern Politics: Suffrage Restriction and the Establishment of the One-Party South, 1880–1910.* New Haven, Conn.: Yale University Press.

Lamont, Michèle. 1994. *Money, Morals, and Manners: The Culture of the French and American Upper-Middle Class.* Chicago: University of Chicago Press.

———. 2002. *The Dignity of Working Men: Morality and the Boundaries of Race, Class, and Immigration.* Cambridge, Mass.: Harvard University Press.

Lamont, Michèle, and Virág Molnár. 2002. "The Study of Boundaries in the Social Sciences." *Annual Review of Sociology* 28:167–195.

Laurie, Bruce. 1997. *Artisans into Workers: Labor in Nineteenth-Century America.* Urbana: University of Illinois Press.

Lawrence, Jon, and Miles Taylor. 1993. "The Poverty of Protest: Gareth Stedman Jones and the Politics of Language—A Reply." *Social History* 18:1–15.

Letwin, Daniel. 1998. *The Challenge of Interracial Unionism: Alabama Coal Miners, 1878–1921.* Chapel Hill: University of North Carolina Press.

Lipsitz, George. 1998. *The Possessive Investment in Whiteness: How White People Profit from Identity Politics.* Philadephia: Temple University Press.

Lowe, Lisa. 1998. *Immigrant Acts: On Asian American Cultural Politics.* Durham, N.C.: Duke University Press.

Maclachlan, Gretchen Ehrmann. 1992. "Women's Work: Atlanta's Industrialization and Urbanization, 1879–1929." Ph.D. dissertation, Emory University.

Mahoney, James. 2000. "Path Dependence in Historical Sociology." *Theory and Society* 29:507–48.

Marshall, Ray. 1968. "The Negro in Southern Unions." In *The Negro and the American Labor Movement*, ed. Julius Jacobson. Garden City, N.Y.: Anchor Books.

Marx, Karl. 1987 [1896]. *The Eighteenth Brumaire of Louis Bonaparte.* New York: International Publishers.

Massey, Douglas A., and Nancy A. Denton. 1987. "Trends in the Residential Segregation of Blacks, Hispanics and Asians: 1970–1980." *American Sociological Review* 52:802–25.

———. 1993. *American Apartheid: Segregation and the Making of the Underclass.* Cambridge Mass.: Harvard University Press.

Mayfield, David, and Susan Thorne. 1992. "Social History and Its Discontents: Gareth Stedman Jones and the Politics of Language." *Social History* 17:165–88.

——. 1993. "Reply to 'The Poverty of Protest' and 'The Imaginary Discontents.'" *Social History* 18:219–33.

McAdam, Doug. 1982. *Political Process and the Development of Black Insurgency.* Chicago: University of Chicago Press.

McKiven, Henry M. Jr. 1995. *Iron and Steel: Class, Race, and Community in Birmingham, Alabama, 1875–1920.* Chapel Hill: University of North Carolina Press.

McLaurin, Melton A. 1978. *The Knights of Labor in the South.* Westport, Conn.: Greenwood Press.

McLean, Paul D. 1998. "A Frame Analysis of Favor Seeking in the Renaissance: Agency, Networks and Political Culture." *American Journal of Sociology* 104:51–91.

McLeod, Jonathan W. 1989. *Workers and Workplace Dynamics in Reconstruction-Era Atlanta: A Case Study.* Los Angeles: University of California, Center for Afro-American Studies.

McMath, Robert C., Jr. 1975. *Populist Vanguard: A History of the Southern Farmers' Alliance.* Chapel Hill: University of North Carolina Press.

——. 1993. *American Populism: A Social History, 1877–1898.* New York: Hill and Wang.

McNeill, George E. 1887. "Declaration of Principles of the K. of L." In *The Labor Movement: The Problem of To-day,* ed. George E. McNeill. Boston: A. M. Bridgeman and Co.

Meier, August, and Elliott Rudwick. 1968. "Attitudes of Negro Leaders toward the American Labor Movement from the Civil War to World War I." In *The Negro and the American Labor Movement*, ed. Julius Jacobson. Garden City, N.Y.: Anchor Books.

Mitchell, Theodore R. 1987. *Political Education in the Southern Farmers' Alliance, 1887–1900.* Madison: University of Wisconsin Press.

Montgomery, David. 1967. *Beyond Equality: Labor and the Radical Republicans, 1862–1872.* New York: Knopf.

——. 1993. *Citizen Worker: The Experience of Workers in the United States with Democracy and the Free Market during the Nineteenth Century.* New York: Cambridge University Press.

Moore, James T. 1975. "Black Militancy in Readjuster Virginia, 1979–1883." *Journal of Southern History* 41:167–86.

Morris, Aldon. 1981. "Black Southern Student Sit-In Movement: An Analysis of Internal Organization." *American Sociological Review* 46:744–67.

Morton, Richard L. 1918. "The Negro in Virginia Politics, 1865–1902." Ph.D. dissertation, University of Virginia.

Myrdal, Gunnar. 1944. *An American Dilemma: The Negro Problem and Modern Democracy.* New York: Harper.

Nagel, Joane. 1986. "The Political Construction of Ethnicity." In *Competitive Ethnic Relations,* ed. Susan Olzak and Joane Nagel. Orlando, Fla.: Academic Press. 93–112.

Nielsen, François. 1986. "Structural Conduciveness and Ethnic Mobilization: The Flemish Movement in Belgium." In *Competitive Ethnic Relations,* ed. Susan Olzak and Joane Nagel. Orlando, Fla.: Academic Press. 173–98.

O'Brien, John Thomas, Jr. 1990. *From Bondage to Citizenship: The Richmond Black Community, 1865–1867.* New York: Garland Publishing.

Oestreicher, Richard Jules. 1986. *Solidarity and Fragmentation: Working People and Class Consciousness in Detroit, 1875–1900.* Urbana: University of Illinois Press.

O'Leary, Cecelia Elizabeth. 1999. *To Die For: The Paradox of American Patriotism.* Princeton, N.J.: Princeton University Press.

Olzak, Susan. 1983. "Contemporary Ethnic Mobilization." *Annual Review of Sociology* 9:355–74.

——. 1989. "Labor Unrest, Immigration, and Ethnic Conflict in Urban America, 1880–1914." *American Journal of Sociology* 94:1303–333.

——. 1990. "The Political Context of Competition: Lynching and Urban Racial Violence, 1882–1914." *Social Forces* 69:395–421.

——. 1992. *The Dynamics of Ethnic Competition and Conflict.* Stanford, Calif.: Stanford University Press.

Olzak, Susan, Suzanne Shanahan, and Elizabeth H. McEneaney. 1996. "Poverty, Segregation, and Race Riots: 1960 to 1993." *American Sociological Review* 61:590–13.

Omi, Michael, and Howard Winant. 1994. *Racial Formation in the United States: From the 1960s to the 1990s.* New York: Routledge.

Palmer, Bruce. 1980. *"Man Over Money": The Southern Populist Critique of American Capitalism.* Chapel Hill: University of North Carolina Press.

Parkin, Frank. 1979. *Marxism and Class Theory: A Bourgeois Critique.* New York: Columbia University Press.

Parsons, Stanley B., Michael J. Dubin, and Karen Toombs Parsons. 1990. *United States Congressional Districts, 1883–1913.* New York: Greenwood Press.

Parsons, Stanley B., Karen Toombs Parsons, Walter Killilae, and Beverly Borgers. 1983. "The Role of Cooperatives in the Development of the Movement Culture of Populism." *Journal of American History* 69:866–85.

Patterson, Orlando. 1982. *Slavery and Social Death: A Comparative Study.* Cambridge, Mass.: Harvard University Press.

Peal, David. 1989. "The Politics of Populism: Germany and the American South in the 1890s." *Comparative Studies in Society and History* 31:340–62.

Peffer, W. A. 1975 [1891]. "Government Control of Money." In *The Farmers' Alliance History and Agricultural Digest,* ed. Nelson A. Dunning. New York: Arno Press. 262–71.

Perlman, Selig. 1928. *A Theory of the Labor Movement.* New York: A. M. Kelley.

Phelan, Craig. 2000. *Grand Master Workman: Terence Powderly and the Knights of Labor.* Westport, Conn.: Greenwood Press.

Pollack, Norman. 1987. *The Just Polity: Populism, Law, and Human Welfare..* Urbana: University of Illinois Press.

——. 1990. *The Humane Economy: Populism, Capitalism, and Democracy.* New Brunswick, N.J.: Rutgers University Press.

Polletta, Francesca. 1997. "Culture and Its Discontents: Recent Theorizing on the Cultural Dimensions of Protest." *Sociological Inquiry* 67:431–50.

——. 1998. "'It Was Like a Fever . . .': Narrative and Identity in Social Protest." *Social Problems* 45:137–59.

Popper, Karl R. 1961. *The Logic of Scientific Discovery.* New York: Science Editions.

Powderly, Terence V. 1967 [1890]. *Thirty Years of Labor: 1859–1889.* New York: A. M. Kelley.

——. 1940. *The Path I Trod: The Autobiography of Terence V. Powderly.* Edited by Harry J. Carman, Henry David, and Paul N. Guthrie. New York: Columbia University Press.

Rabinowitz, Howard N. 1978. *Race Relations in the Urban South, 1865–1890.* New York: Oxford University Press.

Rachleff, Peter J. 1984. *Black Labor in the South: Richmond, Virginia, 1865–1890.* Philadelphia: Temple University Press.

——. 1989. "Black Richmond and the Knights of Labor." *Research in Urban Sociology* 1:23–52.

Redding, Kent. 2003. *Making Race, Making Power: North Carolina's Road to Disfranchisement.* Urbana: University of Illinois Press.

Reed, Adolph, Jr. 2002. "Unraveling the Relation of Race and Class in American Politics." *Political Power and Social Theory* 15:265–74.

Regensburger, William. 1987. "Worker Insurgency and Southern Working-Class Combativeness: Miners, Sailors, and the Emergence of Industrial Unionism in the South." In Howard Kimeldorf and William Regensburger, *Insurgent Workers: Studies of the Origins of Industrial Unionism on the East and West Coast Docks and in the South During the 1930s,* ed. Maurice Zeitlin. Los Angeles: University of California. 71–159.

Reid, Donald. 1993. "Reflections on Labor History and Language." In *Rethinking Labor History: Essays on Discourse and Class Analysis,* ed. Lenard R. Berlanstein. Urbana: University of Illinios Press. 39–54.

Reinhart, Cornel Justin. 1972. "Populism and the Black: A Study in Ideology and Social Strains." Ph.D. dissertation, University of Oklahoma.

Roediger, David R. 1991. *The Wages of Whiteness: Race and the Making of the American Working Class.* London: Verso.

——. 1994. "Gaining a Hearing for Black-White Unity: Convington Hall and the Complexities of Race, Gender and Class." In *Towards the Abolition of Whiteness: Essays on Race, Politics, and Working Class History,* ed. David R. Roediger. London: Verso.

Rudwick, Elliot M. 1964. *Race Riot at East St. Louis, July 2, 1917.* Carbondale: Southern Illinois University Press.

Russell, James Michael. 1988. *Atlanta, 1847–1890: City Building in the Old South and New.* Baton Rouge: Louisiana State University Press.

Saloutos, Theodore. 1960. *Farmer Movements in the South: 1865–1933.* Berkeley: University of California Press.

Sanders, Elizabeth. 1999. *Roots of Reform: Farmers, Workers, and the American State, 1877–1917.* Chicago: University of Chicago Press.

Saxton, Alexander. 1971. *The Indispensible Enemy: Labor and the Anti-Chinese Movement in California.* Berkeley: University of California Press.

———. 1990. *The Rise and Fall of the White Republic: Class Politics and Mass Culture in Nineteenth-Century America.* London: Verso.
Schlesinger, Arthur M. 1944. "Biography of a Nation of Joiners." *American Historical Review* 50:1–25.
Schneirov, Richard. 1998. *Labor and Urban Politics: Class Conflict and the Origins of Modern Liberalism in Chicago, 1864–1897.* Urbana: University of Illinois Press.
Schultz, Ronald. 1993. *The Republic of Labor: Philadelphia Artisans and the Politics of Class, 1720–1830.* New York: Oxford University Press.
Schwartz, Michael. 1976. *Radical Protest and Social Structure: The Southern Farmers' Alliance and Cotton Tenancy, 1880–1890.* Chicago: University of Chicago Press.
Scott, James C. 1990. *Domination and the Arts of Resistance.* New Haven, Conn.: Yale University Press.
Scott, Mary Wingfield. 1975. *Old Richmond Neighborhoods.* Richmond, Va.: Valentine Museum.
Sewell, William H. Jr. 1980. *Work and Revolution in France: The Language of Labor from the Old Regime to 1848.* London: Cambridge University Press.
———. 1992. "A Theory of Structure: Duality, Agency, and Transformation." *American Journal of Sociology* 98:1–29.
———. 1993. "Toward a Post-Materialist Rhetoric for Labor History." In *Rethinking Labor History: Essays on Discourse and Class Analysis,* ed. Lenard R. Berlanstein. Urbana: University of Illinois Press. 15–38.
———. 1996. "Historical Events as Transformations of Structures: Inventing Revolution at the Bastille." *Theory and Society* 25:841–81.
Shaw, Barton C. 1984. *The Wool-Hat Boys: Georgia's Populist Party.* Baton Rouge: Louisiana State University Press.
Sheldon, William Du Bose. 1935. *Populism in the Old Dominion: Virginia Farm Politics, 1885–1900.* Princeton N.J.: Princeton University Press.
Simmel, Georg. 1971 [1908]. "Group Expansion and the Development of Individuality." In *On Individuality and Social Forms,* ed. Donald N. Levine. Chicago: University of Chicago Press. 251–93.
Sisco, John I. 1966. "Rhetoric in Failure: A Study of the Public Address of the Knights of Labor Movement." Ph.D. dissertation, University of Minnesota.
Snow, David A., and Robert D. Benford. 1992. "Master Frames and Cycles of Protest." In *Frontiers of Social Movement Theory,* ed. Aldon Morris and Carol Mueller. New Haven, Conn.: Yale University Press. 133–55.
Snow, David A., E. Burke Rochford Jr., Steven K. Worden, and Robert D. Benford. 1986. "Frame Alignment Processes, Micromobilization, and Movement Participation." *American Sociological Review* 51:464–81.
Sombart, Werner. 1976 [1906]. *Why Is There no Socialism in the United States?* White Plains, N.Y.: International Arts and Sciences Press.
Somers, Margaret R. 1992. "Narrativity, Narrative Identity, and Social Action." *Social Science History* 16:591–630.

———. 1994. "The Narrative Constitution of Identity: A Relational and Network Approach." *Theory and Society* 23:605–49.

Soule, Sarah A. 1992. "Populism and Black Lynching in Georgia, 1890–1900." *Social Forces* 71:431–49.

Steinberg, Marc W. 1991. "Talkin' Class: Discourse, Ideology, and Their Roles in Class Conflict." In *Bringing Class Back In,* ed. Scott G. McNall, Rhonda F. Levine, and Rick Fantasia. Boulder, Colo.: Westview Press. 261–83.

Steinfeld, Robert J. 1991. *The Invention of Free Labor: The Employment Relation in English and American Law and Civic Culture, 1350–1870.* Chapel Hill: University of North Carolina Press.

———. 2001. *Coercion, Contract, and Free Labor in the Nineteenth Century.* Cambridge: Cambridge University Press.

Steinmetz, George. 1992. "Reflections on the Role of Social Narratives in Working-Class Formation: Narrative Theory and the Social Sciences." *Social Science History* 16:489–516.

Stoller, Ann Laura. 1997. "Racial Histories and their Regimes of Truth." *Political Power and Social Theory* 11:183–206.

Stone, W.W., and Congressman Morrow. 1887. "The Chinese and the Labor Question." In *The Labor Movement: The Problem of To-day,* ed. George E. McNeill. Boston: A. M. Bridgman and Co.

Takaki, Ronald. 2000. *Iron Cages: Race and Culture in Nineteenth-Century America.* New York: Oxford University Press.

Taylor, Arthur Reed. 1973. "From the Ashes: Atlanta during Reconstruction, 1865–1876." Ph.D. dissertation, Emory University.

Thompson, E. P. 1966. *The Making of the English Working Class.* New York: Vintage Books.

———. 1967. "Time, Work-Discipline, and Industrial Capitalism." *Past and Present* 38:56–97.

Thornbery, Jerry John. 1977. "The Development of Black Atlanta, 1865–1885." Ph.D. dissertation, University of Maryland.

Tilly, Charles. 2003. *Stories, Identities and Social Change.* London: Rowman and Littlefield.

Tocqueville, Alexis de. 1994. *Democracy in America.* New York: Knopf.

Tolnay, Stewart E., and E. M. Beck. 1992. "Racial Violence and Black Migration in the American South, 1910 to 1930." *American Sociological Review* 57:103–16.

Tolnay, Stewart E., E. M. Beck, and James L. Massey. 1989. "Black Lynchings: The Power Threat Hypothesis Revisited." *Social Forces* 67:605–23.

Tomaskovic-Devey, Donald, and Vincent J. Roscigno. 1996. "Racial Economic Subordination and White Gain in the U.S. South." *American Sociological Review* 61:565–89.

Tracy, Harry. 1975 [1891]. "The Sub-Treasury Plan." In *The Farmers' Alliance History and Agricultural Digest,* ed. Nelson A. Dunning. New York: Arno Press. 336–54.

Turner, J. H. 1975 [1891]. "The Race Problem." In *The Farmers' Alliance History and Agricultural Digest,* ed. Nelson A. Dunning. New York: Arno Press. 272–79.

Tyler-McGraw, Marie. 1994. *At the Falls: Richmond, Virginia. and Its People.* Chapel Hill: University of North Carolina Press.

Tyler-McGraw, Marie, and Greg D. Kimball. 1988. *In Bondage and Freedom: Antebellum Black Life in Richmond, Virginia.* Richmond, Va.: Valentine Museum.

Voss, Kim. 1988. "Labor Organization and Class Alliance: Industries, Communities, and the Knights of Labor." *Theory and Society* 17:329–64.

——. 1993. *The Making of American Exceptionalism: The Knights of Labor and Class Formation in the Nineteenth Century.* Ithaca, N.Y: Cornell University Press.

Ward, Judson C., Jr. 1943. "The Republican Party in Bourbon Georgia, 1872–1890." *The Journal of Southern History* 9:196–209.

Ware, Norman. 1959. *The Labor Movement in the United States, 1860–1895: A Study in Democracy.* Gloucester, Mass.: Peter Smith.

Watson, Thomas E. 1967 [1892]. "The Negro Question in the South." In *Forgotten Voices: Dissenting Southerners in an Age of Conformity,* ed. Charles F. Wynes. Baton Rouge: Louisiana State University Press. 59–70.

Watts, Eugene J. 1974. "Black Political Progress in Atlanta: 1868–1895." *Journal of Negro History* 69:268–86.

——. 1978. *The Social Bases of City Politics: Atlanta, 1865–1903.* Westport, Conn.: Greenwood Press.

Weber, Max. 1947. *The Theory of Social and Economic Organization.* New York: Free Press.

Weinstein, Allen. 1970. *Prelude to Populism: Origins of the Silver Issue, 1867–1878.* New Haven, Conn.: Yale University Press.

Weir, Robert E. 1996. *Beyond Labor's Veil: The Culture of the Knights of Labor.* University Park, Pa.: Pennsylvania State University Press.

——. 2000. *Knights Unhorsed: Internal Conflict in a Gilded Age Social Movement.* Detroit: Wayne State University Press.

White, Harrison C. 1992. *Identity and Control: A Structural Theory of Social Action.* Princeton, N.J.: Princeton University Press.

Wilentz, Sean. 1984. *Chants Democratic: New York City and the Rise of the American Working Class, 1788–1850.* New York: Oxford University Press.

Wilhoit, Francis M. 1967. "An Interpretation of Populism's Impact on the Georgia Negro." *Journal of Negro History* 52:116–27.

Wilson, William Julius. 1980. *The Declining Significance of Race: Blacks and Changing American Institutions.* Chicago: University of Chicago Press.

Woodman, Harold D. 1990 [1968]. *King Cotton and His Retainers: Financing and Marketing the Cotton Crop of the South, 1800–1925.* Columbia: University of South Carolina Press.

Woods, Thomas A. 1991. *Knights of the Plow: Oliver H. Kelley and the Origins of the Grange in Republican Ideology.* Ames: Iowa State University Press.

Woodward, C. Vann. 1951. *Origins of the New South, 1877–1913.* Baton Rouge: Louisiana State University Press.
——. 1963. *Tom Watson: Agrarian Rebel.* New York: Oxford University Press.
——. 2000 [1955]. *The Strange Career of Jim Crow.* New York: Oxford University Press.
Wynes, Charles E. 1961. *Race Relations in Virginia, 1880–1902.* Charlottesville: University of Virginia Press.
Zolberg, Aristide R. 1986. "How Many Exceptionalisms?" In *Working-Class Formation: Nineteenth-Century Patterns in Western Europe and the United States,* ed. Ira Katznelson and Aristide R. Zolberg. Princeton, N.J.: Princeton University Press. 397–455.

# INDEX

Joseph Gerteis is an associate professor of sociology at the University of Minnesota.

Library of Congress Cataloging-in-Publication Data
Gerteis, Joseph, 1970–
Class and the color line : interracial class coalition in the Knights of Labor and the Populist movement / Joseph Gerteis.
p. cm.—(Politics, history, and culture)
Based on the author's Ph. D. thesis, University of North Carolina, 1999.
Includes bibliographical references and index.
ISBN-13: 978-0-8223-4210-6 (cloth : alk. paper)
ISBN-13: 978-0-8223-4224-3 (pbk. : alk. paper)
1. Knights of Labor—History. 2. Labor unions—Southern States—Political activity—History—19th century. 3. Coalitions—Southern States—History—19th century. 4. Southern States—Race relations—History—19th century. 5. Populism—Southern States—History—19th century. 6. Farmers—Southern States—Political activity—History—19th century. 7. Working class—Southern States—Political activity—History—19th century. I. Title. II. Title: Interracial class coalition in the Knights of Labor and the Populist movement.
HD8055.K7G47 2007
331.88089'00975—dc22 2007015033